Early Violence Prevention

Tools for Teachers of Young Children

Ronald G. Slaby,

Wendy C. Roedell,

Diana Arezzo,

and Kate Hendrix

National Association for the Education of Young Children, Washington, D.C.

Cover photos: Robert Kyle

National Association for the Education of Young Children
1509 16th Street, NW
Washington, DC 20036-1426
202-232-8777 or 800-424-2460

The National Association for the Education of Young Children (NAEYC) attempts through its publications program to provide a forum for discussion of major issues and ideas in our field. We hope to provoke thought and promote professional growth. The views expressed or implied are not necessarily those of the Association. NAEYC wishes to thank the authors, who donated much time and effort to develop this book as a contribution to our profession.

Library of Congress Catalog Card Number: 94-069779
ISBN Catalog Number: 0-935989-65-X
NAEYC #325

Editor: Carol Copple. *Design and production:* Danielle Hudson, Jack Zibulsky, and Penny Atkins. *Copyediting:* Millie Riley. *Editorial assistance:* Anika Trahan and Betty Nylund Barr.

Printed in the United States of America.

Contents

About the Authors

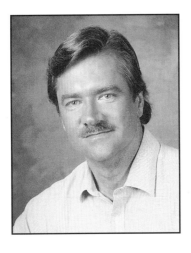

Ronald G. Slaby (Ph.D., University of Wisconsin) is Senior Scientist at the Education Development Center in Newton, Massachusetts, and lecturer on education and pediatrics at Harvard University. A research investigator in developmental psychology for more than 25 years, Dr. Slaby has published extensively on aggression, gender-role development, and television violence effects and has served as advisor for several award-winning children's television series. He has helped to shape a national agenda for preventing violence by coauthoring a violence prevention plan for the Centers for Disease Control and two reports on violence and youth for the American Psychological Association. He has presented testimony to the U.S. Congress on the prevention of youth violence and on television violence effects and remedies. Dr. Slaby has developed, field-tested, and published violence prevention programs for adult and juvenile offenders, athletes, middle school students, and preschool children.

Wendy C. Roedell (Ph.D., University of Washington) is a developmental psychologist who has worked in the field of early childhood education for 25 years, holding positions as preschool teacher, university instructor and researcher, and program administrator at state, local, and regional levels. She has coauthored three books and numerous articles on the education and development of young children and the special needs of gifted children. Dr. Roedell is currently the executive director of the Early Childhood Department at Puget Sound Educational Service District in Seattle, Washington, overseeing comprehensive early childhood programs serving children and families of low income.

Diana Arezzo (Ph.D., University of Wisconsin) is a clinical and developmental psychologist and the psychology coordinator for the Kennedy Day School, a special needs school at Franciscan Children's Hospital in Boston. She has taught in therapeutic and typical classrooms for young children, taught university courses, served as a treatment program administrator, and practiced child and family therapy for more than 20 years. Dr. Arezzo has developed treatment innovations and has lectured and consulted extensively in the areas of children's social skills, behavior management, and parent training. Her published works include articles and review chapters, and she has coauthored a book on helping children make friends.

Kate Hendrix (Sc.D., Harvard School of Public Health) is a behavioral scientist, specializing in public health education, research methodology, and child development. Her professional work has focused on school health education, children with special needs, and violence prevention—specifically domestic violence and media violence. She has presented workshops about media violence to educators and youth program coordinators and created programs to help children develop media literacy and critical viewing skills. Dr. Hendrix has also worked in a therapeutic child care program for preschool children who have been victims of violence and in several shelters for battered women and their children.

Acknowledgments

This book was developed through grants to Education Development Center, Inc. (EDC), from both the Florence V. Burden Foundation and the A.L. Mailman Family Foundation. Barbara Greenberg, former executive director of the Florence V. Burden Foundation, originally invited the development of a report that led to this book. Luba Lynch, executive director of the A.L. Mailman Family Foundation, recognized the urgent need for this report in the field of early childhood development. Gail Leavitt Gershon and Victoria Frelow provided valuable assistance as the respective project officers for these two foundations.

Project staff at EDC made substantial contributions to this project through their knowledge and wisdom. This book would not have been possible without the guidance of Cheryl Vince-Whitman, director of EDC's Health and Human Development Programs, the insightful monitoring of this project by Stu Cohen and Edward DeVos, the literature searches by Marc Posner, the administrative assistance of Yvonne Herring, and the research assistance of Beth Jacklin and Paula Szulc. Important and generous contributions were made to the conceptualization and content of this project by many members of EDC's Center for Family, School, and Community (CFSC), including Joanne P. Brady, director of the CFSC, Ingrid Chalufour, Shelia Skiffington, and Eleanor Lewis. Adele Eustis served as a video consultant from Corgi Productions, Inc., and produced informative video interviews with our reviewers.

A critical factor in the development of this project was the direct and experienced feedback we received from EDC's National Advisory Committee and our early childhood education reviewers. They generously offered their practical wisdom and their vision of what violence prevention for young children could be.

National Advisory Committee

Barbara Bowman, President, Erikson Institute

Sarah Greene, Executive Director, National Head Start Association

William J. Kreidler, Senior Conflict Resolution Associate, Educators for Social Responsibility

Mary Mindes, Professor of Education, Lesley College

Evelyn K. Moore, Executive Director, National Black Child Development Institute

Thomas Schultz, Director, Center on Education Services for Young Learners, National Association of State Boards of Education

Early childhood education reviewers

Patricia Delgado and Franklin Pierce, Early Childhood & Assistance Program, Washington

Mildred Downing, Child Development Associate Coordinator, ABCD Head Start, Massachusetts

Cindy Green, Resource Teacher, Cambridge Head Start, Massachusetts

Nancy Green, Teacher, Lynn Head Start, Massachusetts

Pamela M. Keenan, Clover Park School District, Early Childhood & Assistance Program, Washington

Allen Kesten, Educational Coordinator, Jamaica Plain Head Start, Massachusetts

Diane Kroll, Education Coordinator, Early Childhood & Assistance Program, Washington

Maggie S. Oldenburg, Peninsula School District, Early Childhood & Assistance Program, Washington

Linda Olsen, Renton School District, Early Childhood & Assistance Program, Washington

Cynthia A. Scott, Education Coordinator, Early Childhood & Assistance Program, Washington

The creation of this book out of the project report was made possible through the dedication and guidance of the National Association for the Education of Young Children. Carol Copple, the publications editor, guided the entire publication process with a remarkable balance of perseverance and compassion. She made major contributions to the conceptual clarity, practical utility, and scope of this book, and its relevance for the primary audience of early childhood educators. Millie Riley, the copyeditor, added to the clarity and cohesiveness of this book. We gratefully acknowledge the expert contributions of all of the NAEYC editorial staff in designing and producing the book.

We would like to thank the many children through whose experiences we have learned not only that violence produces devastating effects but also that violence is preventable. Finally, we would like to thank our families for their patience and for the support they gave us throughout the development of this book.

Foreword

"Children are different today than they were when I first started teaching." I have heard this over and over again from teachers across the country. They were the first to alert me to the devastating impact of violence on young children. Early childhood educators were struggling to understand and cope with an increasing number of children who exhibited aggressive behavior, high levels of stress, and limited social skills. Each year the problems were getting worse. Many of us were feeling helpless and hopeless; all of us wanted guidance and support.

In April 1989 NAEYC responded to these concerns by establishing the Violence in the Lives of Children Panel charged with the following: "to provide recommendations on how the NAEYC membership can be empowered—through educational activities and materials and through coalition building—to respond to manifestations of violence in the lives of children and to develop position state-

ments that (a) identify appropriate professional practice in a comprehensive education strategy to promote nonviolent conflict resolution and peaceful coexistence in our world and (b) identify appropriate guidelines for children's television programming and commercial advertising which relate to themes of violence." The panel's first position, a statement on media violence in children's lives, was approved by the NAEYC Governing Board in 1990, followed by its publication as a brochure for parents. Next, the "NAEYC Position Statement on Violence in the Lives of Children" was approved in 1993 and has inspired an increasing number of affiliate groups to focus local, state, and regional conferences on this topic.

During my two years of chairing the Violence Panel, I was outraged by the seriousness of the problem, but also encouraged by the increasing number of organizations, like NAEYC, actively working to stop the cycle of violence and offering guidance to practitioners.

The Centers for Disease Control and Prevention developed a national plan for preventing violence and injuries due to violence. Public television launched the largest media education and community outreach campaign in its history, designed to reduce youth violence. Zero to Three's Violence Study Group published papers and held conferences on the effects of violence on infants and toddlers. The American Psychological Association's Commission on Violence and Youth released two reports providing a comprehensive account of what we know and what we can do about youth violence. The Children's Defense Fund's "Cease Fire!" campaign focused the nation's attention on the seriousness of the problem. NAEYC collaborates with these groups and many others.

Early Violence Prevention: Tools for Teachers of Young Children answers the cry from practitioners for workable strategies to reduce violence and address the effects of exposure to violence in early childhood settings. The authors state in their first chapter, "Early childhood staff enter an arena in which the propensity for violence—promoted in so many areas of society—can be challenged and reduced through the developing hearts and minds of children. Teachers empower children by helping them develop the patterns of thought, feeling, and action that can effectively prevent violence." Many of the approaches described in this well-researched book will not be surprising to most readers, for they reflect those factors that define a quality program: positive interactions, a well-organized physical and programmatic environment, opportunities for children to make choices, carefully selected materials, and the teaching and modeling of prosocial skills. Social competence is an underlying goal of all early childhood programs—and the primary goal of Head Start and many other programs—and this book offers educators specific ways to actively work toward this goal.

Some of the strategies offered here may be new and surprising to readers. The authors show many instances of how our instinctive responses can work against our own goals. In seeking to promote sharing, for instance, we *direct* children to share—and unwittingly undermine the development of voluntary sharing. Or, without intending to do so, we give children attention at the worst time—when they are being aggressive. The authors provide us with a repertoire of proven approaches, such as teaching children how to stand up to aggressors in nonviolent but effective ways, controlling the effects of media violence, teaching social problem-solving skills, enhancing perspective taking and empathy, and many other proactive techniques. In this book teachers get help with one of the toughest challenges they face—children whose patterns of violent behavior are deeply rooted and not improved by the strategies that work with most children. The authors present a strong case for dealing quickly and firmly with any incidents of violent behavior and for systematically helping children change patterns of aggressive behavior. While some of the strategies offered for dealing with children who are frequently aggressive—developing a behavior-change plan, using time-out, offering concrete reminders and incentives—initially may make some early childhood educators, including me, uncomfortable, it is essential to consider applying some of these alternatives, which have proven worth for dealing with otherwise intractable problems.

Early Violence Prevention: Tools for Teachers of Young Children offers early childhood educators ways both to control and prevent violence. I am grateful to the authors for producing a very comprehensive and thoughtful resource that will advance our knowledge about the impact of violence on children and empower us to address it.

—Diane Trister Dodge
President, Teaching Strategies, Inc.;
former chair of NAEYC's Violence in
the Lives of Children Panel

To our children—

> *Lauren and Cara*
> *Lynn and David*
> *Chris and Jani*

And to all the children of the world—

> *Who deserve to live free from violence.*

1

Applying What Works

The old law of an eye for an eye leaves everybody blind. It is immoral because it seeks to humiliate the opponent rather than to win his understanding; it seeks to annihilate rather than to convert. Violence is immoral because it thrives on hatred rather than love. It destroys community and makes brotherhood impossible. It leaves society in monologue rather than dialogue. Violence ends by defeating itself. It creates bitterness in the survivors and brutality in the destroyers.

—Martin Luther King Jr.

Young children in America are growing up in a society currently experiencing extraordinary levels of violence, including lethal violence. Far from being protected from this violence, many young children are surrounded by it in their daily lives and are often direct observers or victims themselves. An increasing number of children live in conditions of chronic community violence that are often described as "inner-city war zones" (Garbarino, Kostelny, & Dubrow 1991). But children's experience with violence is by no means limited to the inner city. Throughout American cities, suburbs, and rural areas, young children often experience high levels of violence as victims of family violence and nonfamily assaults, witnesses of family and community violence, and viewers of media violence (APA 1993). Even those children who are not directly exposed are affected by this pervasive violence (NAEYC 1993).

Prevention and the early childhood educator

Each day the problem of violence in our society walks into the preschool classroom through the thoughts, feelings, and behaviors of young children. Although early childhood educators alone cannot be expected to remedy the problems children face with extreme violence in our society, they have a distinct opportunity to contribute to violence prevention through their interactions with the children, their parents, and their communities.

Early childhood staff enter an arena in which the propensity for violence—promoted in so many areas of society—can be challenged and reduced through the developing hearts and minds of children. Teachers empower children by helping them develop the patterns of thought, feeling, and action that can effectively prevent violence. Of the many factors that contribute to violence, none inevitably lead to violence. Violent behavior is learned, and it can be unlearned. Or we can change conditions so that violence is not learned in the first place. Young children are in the process of creating their social interaction habits and values that will guide the way they interact with others for years to come. Thus, it is easier for young children to make changes in the way they relate to others than it is for older children or adults who have had many years to establish patterns that lead to violence (Eron & Slaby 1994). Early childhood educators can indeed make a difference.

Teachers need to begin by establishing their *classrooms as safe havens from violence.* Any attempt to help young children cope with severe violence in their lives should include an effective program for preventing and stopping violent child behaviors in the center or classroom. If children are to believe that violence can be prevented or controlled, they need to see the principles of violence prevention realized in their classroom world. How are we to expect children to believe that violence can be stopped in the world outside if it is not effectively stopped in their own classrooms?

Patterns of violence develop early and last long

Violence does not simply appear mysteriously and full-blown in an adolescent. Rather, children acquire violent behavior patterns—or, alternatively, nonviolent, socially constructive behavior patterns—through specific and alterable processes of socialization and development. The patterns of violence-supporting behavior or nonviolent behavior that children learn in the early years often set them on a developmental pathway that guides them for years to come (APA 1993; Pepler & Slaby 1994).

When seemingly harmless patterns of aggression-related behavior are learned in the early years and practiced regularly, the behaviors often increase in their predictability, frequency, and severity, setting up a child for becoming involved in harmful violence in later years. Children and youth become involved in violence in several different ways: as *aggressors, victims,* and/or *bystanders,* who support violence through the instigation, active encouragement, or passive acceptance of violence (Slaby & Stringham 1994).

Aggressive behavior in early childhood, if not dealt with effectively, tends to persist throughout later childhood, adolescence, and even adulthood (e.g., Olweus 1979; Farrington 1993). Young children who act aggressively tend to show other difficult and maladaptive social behaviors, such as tantrums, defiance, and failure to cooperate. Persistent aggressive behavior directed toward peers often leaves the aggressively acting child with few or no positive, stable peer relationships. Thus, children with aggressive behaviors are at high risk for loneliness and lack of peer support to help them through difficult times (Hawkins, Von Cleve, & Catalano 1991). A high level of aggressive behavior in childhood is also predictive of a variety of serious problems in adulthood, including criminal violent behavior, other antisocial behavior, spouse abuse, and a tendency toward severe punishment of one's children (Huesmann et al. 1984).

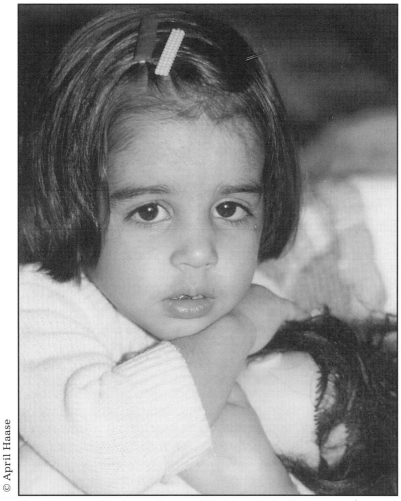

Teachers need to begin by establishing their classrooms as safe havens from violence.

Victims of aggression in early childhood, if not helped to respond effectively, are likely to be repeatedly victimized (Patterson, Littman, & Bricker 1967; Schwartz, Dodge, & Coie 1994). Victims of repeated bullying by peers often suffer long-term consequences of social rejection, depression, and impaired self-esteem (Olweus 1993b; Straus 1995b). Victims are also at risk for becoming aggressors, by their responding to the perceived threat with a preemptive aggressive attack, retaliating against their aggressor, or becoming a perpetrator of aggression against others (McCord 1983; Widom 1989; Straus 1991).

Bystanders (i.e., those who witness conflicts among others) often contribute to aggression among other children through direct instigation, active encouragement, or passive acceptance (e.g., Staub 1974, 1989; Slaby, Wilson-Brewer, & DeVos 1994). Even when bystanders play no direct role, their mere presence frequently serves as tacit social support and approval for an escalating conflict among their peers. Bystanders, if they are not taught how to respond effectively to aggression, are at risk for becoming accomplices, co-perpetrators, or victims of aggression. Alternatively, they can be taught to join with teachers, potential victims, and other peers in their classroom to provide active social support for constructive problem solving.

Violence is learned and can be changed

Children can learn to become *nonviolent problem solvers* who make flexible use of their skills and strategies to interact with others effectively. Children's early childhood experiences send them down a developmental pathway toward either destructive or constructive interactions with others. The earlier and more extensively children learn to use nonviolent behaviors, the better prepared they will be to apply these behaviors in later life and thereby lower their risk of becoming involved with violence. Thus, a key to prevention lies in early, systematic, and continuous intervention that reduces those social experiences contributing to violence and builds those internal resources protecting children against involvement with violence (APA 1993; Yoshikawa 1994).

The application of what works in the classroom

Teachers of young children have increasingly come to recognize both the opportunity and the critical need for helping young children build their social skills and preparing them to deal with the social issues that they must face in our society. There are early childhood education materials available to help teachers foster a variety of social skills for children, such as making friends, interacting noncompetitively, appreciating social equity and diversity, resisting peer pressure, and protecting themselves against abduction and sexual abuse. As we recognize the growing problem of youth violence in America, we increasingly see the need for early childhood educators to help young children prepare for the violent society in which they will grow up, while establishing and strengthening in children the behavior patterns needed to help change that reality.

How this book can help

Early Violence Prevention was designed to provide teachers and caregivers who work with children 2 to 6 years of age in preschool and kindergarten classrooms and centers the knowledge and practical strategies to manage, reduce, and help prevent aggressive behavior. We modeled this book after a National Institute of Education report for teachers (Roedell, Slaby, & Robinson 1976) and a subsequent book entitled *Social Development in Young Children* (Roedell, Slaby, & Robinson 1977). *Early Violence Prevention* presents teachers with research findings and teaching guidelines in six major areas:

1. **Preparing children to deal with the violence they face in the outside world.** Teachers can address violence in the real world by using a combination of strategies. Teachers can help children recognize violence and its consequences and provide them with a safe place to express their feelings and their fears. They can also talk about safety and self-protection topics with children and learn how to recognize and respond effectively to children's traumatic reactions to violence or abuse. Chapter 2—Addressing the Violence in Real Life presents suggestions for dealing with these and related issues.

2. Organizing the school environment to minimize violence. Teachers can structure the environment by arranging and reorganizing the physical space in their classrooms and the playground, their materials, and their activities, with the goal of minimizing aggression. Chapter 3—Designing the Physical and Programmatic Environment, Chapter 4—Selecting Materials, and Chapter 5—Structuring Cooperative Activities offer practical ways to address each of these aspects of the school environment.

3. Establishing sound procedures to respond to violence in the classroom. Teachers can respond effectively to routine incidents of conflict and aggression, as well as to those children who show repeated and severe problems with aggressive behavior. Specific procedures for responding to aggression in daily interactions with children are found in Chapter 6—Responding in Effective Ways. Teachers can use techniques for dealing with particular children who show severe or persistent problems with aggression, as discussed in Chapter 7—Helping Children with Aggressive Behavior Patterns.

4. Teaching children the skills they need to solve their conflicts constructively. Teachers can directly teach skills to children that the children need for solving social problems, shar-

ing, and interacting assertively and thoughtfully with others. Effective ways to help children develop these skills appear in Chapter 8—Fostering Social Problem-Solving Skills, Chapter 9—Encouraging Voluntary Sharing, Chapter 10—Teaching Assertiveness Skills, and Chapter 11—Enhancing Perspective Taking and Empathy.

5. Helping children learn from others. Teachers can help children see connections between themselves and others and learn constructive lessons from role models in the classroom and in the media. Teachers will find applications to guide children's learning by observation in Chapter 12—Providing Role Models and Chapter 13—Controlling Media Effects.

6. Taking the next steps in preventing violence in the classroom and the larger community. After reviewing the teaching tools presented throughout this book, teachers can implement a plan for reducing and preventing violence in their school and community. We discuss these steps in Chapter 14—Getting Started.

How to use this book

Early Violence Prevention was developed in several steps. First, we identified, gathered, and reviewed several hundred research studies. Second, a board of advisors reviewed the preliminary scope, organization, and strategy for developing the book and recommended additions and changes. Third, two panels of reviewers—each composed of preschool or Head Start teachers, education coordinators, and early childhood development specialists—reviewed, rated, and critically evaluated a preliminary draft of the book. Discussion of consistent and discrepant ratings of the strengths and weaknesses of each chapter was recorded, together with suggestions for improvements in the format and the presentation of the materials. Finally, a variety of expert researchers and practitioners in the field of early childhood education reviewed a second draft of the book, and we made final revisions. The goal of these procedures was to offer the most effective guidelines and present them in a format that would be most useful to teachers.

The chapters address distinct topics, but underlying issues are often interrelated. Where an issue raised in one chapter is discussed more extensively in another chapter, the reader is directed to this additional information. Each chapter follows the same format. Chapters begin with a *specific example* and *question* for teachers to ask themselves. The question also serves to stimulate a discussion among teachers about their own experiences and beliefs. The presentation of the chapter's topic begins with an *introduction,* followed by a brief review of *what research tells us* about the nature of the problem. A variety of *teaching guidelines,* drawn from research evidence on what works, are offered next. Finally, the chapter presents *points to remember* as a summary and review.

Program directors, education coordinators, and professional support staff may want to read directly through the entire book to obtain an overview of the range of tools available. Teachers may want to focus on one chapter at a time, taking time to digest each chapter thoroughly. They may find value in reading each chapter, discussing the recommended procedures with fellow teachers and staff, experimenting with the implementation of the procedures that fit best with their program, and practicing the new procedures until they feel comfortable.

*   *   *

There are two major types of knowledge—*evidence,* generated through objective and systematic use of the scientific method, and *wisdom,* derived through the subjective and changing practice of applying what seems to work. Either type of knowledge, alone, is limited. Scientific evidence uninformed by the wisdom of practitioners may be vacuous, and wisdom not grounded in scientific fact and held accountable to objective evaluation may be misdirected. This book envisions building a bridge between the scientist's evidence and the practitioner's wisdom, toward developing a sound set of tools for teachers of young children to use in the early prevention of violence.

2

Addressing the Violence in Real Life

The unrelenting violence in the life of a young African American boy living in a public housing project was chronicled in the *Wall Street Journal* (Kotlowitz 1987). Within a 15-day period young Lafeyette witnessed shoot-outs, gang recruiting and wars, grenade removal by a police bomb squad, assaults, drug dealing, family violence, and death—actual deaths, dreams of death, and constant fear of death. **How can teachers help young children who enter the classroom having witnessed or experienced severe and ongoing violence outside?**

Children respond in many ways to the pervasive violence in our society. They learn through TV, games, toys, stories, movies, newscasts, and adult conversations that violence is prevalent and disturbing. Many also directly witness or experience serious violence themselves. It should be no surprise that our society's young children display a wide variety of feelings toward violence, including curiosity, excitement, admiration, ambivalence, confusion, fear, sadness, and repulsion.

Each day young children bring their experiences and feelings regarding violence into the center or classroom. Although teachers cannot take the sole responsibility for dealing with all of the children's concerns regarding violence, they can contribute importantly by helping children deal with the violence they face in the outside world.

What research tells us

There is a growing awareness by researchers and those who work with children that the repeated eyewitnessing by young children of violent assaults against others is a problem of major proportions. Young children in high-violence neighborhoods observe extreme violence far more often than they directly experience it—two to four times more frequently, according to one study (Richters & Martinez 1993). In a Chicago housing development, each of the 10 mothers interviewed in one survey listed shootings as the most serious danger they faced. Nearly all reported that their children had by age 5 experienced a shooting firsthand, most often by witnessing someone being shot (Dubrow & Garbarino 1989). In a large-scale survey of elementary school children from

Chicago's south side, 26% reported that they had seen a shooting, and 30% reported witnessing a stabbing (Bell & Jenkins 1993).

The violence that children observe and experience most often involves family acquaintances or close family members, which greatly heightens the emotional impact. For example, 17% of a sample of murders occurring in Detroit in 1985 were observed by children, and in one quarter of these cases, the victim was a family member (Batchelow & Wicks 1985).

Some young children also experience violence directly in the form of physical abuse, battering, and weapons-related "accidents." It is also important to note that child sexual abuse is, first and foremost, a form of violence. Furthermore, many children whose direct experience with violence may not reach the level of the current legal definition of "abuse" do, nevertheless, suffer regular and sometimes severe physical punishment at the hand of caregivers (Finkelhor & Dziuba-Leatherman 1994).

The detrimental effects on children of repeatedly witnessing violence and living under conditions of constant danger are now recognized as a major and growing public health crisis. To compound this crisis, 25% of American children younger than age 6 live in poverty, which is the highest percentage for any age group (Children's Defense Fund 1992). This very large population of children who are disadvantaged often is the same body of children who face the most severe problems of violence. Yet their families and communities currently have very limited re-sources with which to deal with these problems. Some of the identified effects of exposure to violence include increased aggressive or disruptive behaviors, poor achievement, anxiety, fearfulness, social isolation, depression, and emotional distress (Bell & Jenkins 1991).

Parents often greatly underestimate the amount of violence and danger to which their children are exposed, relative to the children's own reports and other relevant facts (Richters & Martinez 1993). Parents also greatly underestimate the amount of emotional distress that violence causes their children, compared to the children's own reports (Martinez & Richters 1993). These findings suggest that young children traumatized by violence often lack adult support and understanding about their experiences and their feelings, in addition to lacking adequate protection.

Of course, early childhood educators alone cannot be expected to remedy the problems that violence poses for our children. Nevertheless, they do play a number of helpful roles through their interactions with the children, their families, and their communities. Early childhood educators can

• help children to identify violence and its consequences,

• recognize and talk with children about real-world violence,

• recognize and respond to children's traumatic reactions to violence,

• train children in basic violence-related safety and self-protection,

• help reduce "disciplinary" violence toward children, and

• support families in their helping children to cope with violence.

These strategies for dealing with real-life violence are particularly important to use in high-violence communities; however, they are also important and relevant for all young children growing up in our society.

Each teacher needs to adapt these suggestions to the particular circumstances of the children in her class. Another way for teachers to respond to the violence problem is to make their classrooms "safe havens" from violence by preventing and stopping violence by children within the classroom (see chapter 7).

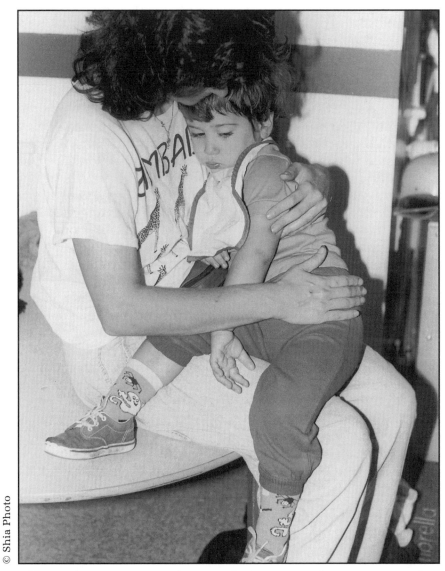

© Shia Photo

Effects of exposure to violence include increased aggressive or disruptive behaviors, poor achievement, anxiety, fearfulness, social isolation, depression, and emotional distress.

Teaching guidelines

In responding to the violence in children's lives, teachers will find these research-based guidelines useful.

Help children identify violent and nonviolent behaviors

When urban primary school children were asked to think about how they express their strong feelings, they gave a list of highly violent responses, such as breaking windows, beating up little kids, and destroying objects or their own artwork (Parry 1993). Several years ago some children identified with and imitated TV's *Incredible Hulk*, who turned into a ferocious and destructive monster whenever he became sufficiently angry. Many children have learned from adults and from portrayals of violence in the media to use violent acts in response to strong emotions, problems, or threats. For this reason, it is important to teach and demonstrate to children that violence is not inevitable but, rather, a harmful choice that people sometimes make. People have the power to make choices and to control how they will act and how they will solve problems. In order for children to be able to avoid the harmful choice of violence, they need to be taught viable nonviolent alternatives for expressing strong feelings, solving problems, or defending themselves (APA 1993). Much of this book is devoted to suggesting ways to do just that.

One approach to violence prevention begins with helping children to identify violence in the world, on TV, and in their own experiences, and to understand the hurtful and destructive nature of violence in all its forms (Parry 1993). Children can learn to identify and name violence through discussions of real-life incidents of severe violence, either as directly observed in the community or as reported in the news media. But it also involves teaching children to identify violent actions between playmates, toys that invite violence, and entertainment portrayals of violence on TV (see chapter 13). Children will learn not only that an adult shooting someone or setting a fire is violence but also that a 4-year-old kicking a classmate or smashing a toy is violence. They need to see that in both cases, and in all cases, violence hurts or destroys people, places, or things.

Teachers can help children identify "nonviolent" actions they observe in the world around them and distinguish these from "violent" actions (or, in the case of younger children, know "helpful" actions from "hurtful" actions). For example, when going on a walk, teachers might prepare children to look for examples of people helping each other, such as giving directions or helping someone to cross the street. Workers coordinating their efforts or sharing a heavy load are also good examples of mutually helpful behaviors that children can observe and discuss. At the same time, if children observe hurtful acts (e.g., people shouting angrily at each other or treating each other roughly), these acts and their consequences might also be discussed later.

Teachers need to talk about their own feelings and demonstrate in their own behaviors the helpful choices they make, as well as the consequences of those choices. Most importantly, teachers influence children's behavior by identifying and commenting upon the children's spontaneous helpful verbalizations and behaviors. Children more easily learn the natural rewards of nonviolent choices when teachers specifically refer to these consequences in their comments (e.g., "First you helped her build that one, so now *she's* helping *you!* You two are learning how to help each other"). Children thereby learn within the context of their own experiences and observations to recognize violent and nonviolent choices and to identify the consequences of each.

Recognize and talk about real-life violence

It may be tempting in the relatively sheltered and controlled environment of a preschool or kindergarten classroom to ignore the disturbing realities of the outside world; however, for those who teach in communities with high rates of violence, avoiding the topic is not realistic or in the best interest of children. Instead, an honest approach aimed at helping even young children recognize, understand, and deal with violence at all levels is a cornerstone of violence prevention and treatment.

Because violence is a personal, volatile, and disturbing issue for teachers, as well as for children, a first step is for teachers to address their own experiences and feelings toward violence. An important beginning for teachers planning a violence-prevention curriculum is to discuss and analyze among themselves the violence that they have experienced in their own lives and witnessed in the lives of children and families. Specially designed inservice training has been used to help teachers explore their

own strong beliefs, feelings, and strategies toward violence (Parry 1993).

The National Association for the Education of Young Children (NAEYC) recognizes that teachers need to receive support in dealing with the issues of violence. NAEYC's Position Statement on Violence in the Lives of Children calls for the development of ongoing consultation services for teachers to "support teachers' mental health, address their fears and trauma, and provide assistance as they work with children who have multiple needs" (NAEYC 1993, 84). These services are needed by all teachers and especially by those who work in communities with high rates of violence. Teachers may want to add their voices to those already expressing the need for such staff support services. Meanwhile, informal networks formed by teachers can offer them ongoing support about violence and its prevention.

There are several forms of severe violence to which young children are exposed. Each form calls for a different type of teacher response. Teachers may decide to use discussions of real-life incidents to support the violence-prevention strategies described in this chapter (e.g., to illustrate the point that violence can hurt or destroy). In doing so, however, teachers need to take care not to unnecessarily increase children's alarm or fear. Individual children are likely to have very different experiences, needs, and vulnerabilities with regard to violence. Issues of privacy and confidentiality must also be considered. These multiple considerations result in a difficult balancing act for the teacher, calling upon his or her best judgment, as well as support from peers and professional consultants.

Young children are less likely than are older children to be aware of real incidents of severe violence reported and shown on TV news but not directly observed by them. In most cases, teachers need not raise these incidents for discussion and thereby risk increasing children's fearfulness. If children themselves ask about a violent incident in the news, teachers can help by discussing it honestly, labeling it as "violent," but refraining from describing graphic details that may be disturbing to young children.

Violent events that occur sporadically or chronically within children's own neighborhoods and violent events that many children simultaneously experience are generally more important to discuss. These events include witnessing assaults, stabbings, and shootings; and hearing gunshots, the cries of victims in distress, and emergency-vehicle sirens. Because parents often underestimate their children's exposure to and distress from such events, the teacher can play an important role by inviting children to discuss concerns and by offering support in the form of listening and providing guidance. Older preschool and kindergarten children may benefit from learning that their peers are also frightened and from having an opportunity to talk with their peers and teachers about their experiences, feelings, and concerns.

The situation may be even more complex and potentially frightening for those children who are aware that their own family members have been involved in community violence (e.g., gang fights, assaults in the street, violent mob actions). These children are often reluctant to talk about their own feelings for fear of getting family members and friends into trouble. They may also be vulnerable to the influences of the violent examples around them. It is important for such children to have someone in whom to confide. Direct and honest talks with a trusted adult outside of the family help children realize that, regardless of their family situation, they can personally choose a nonviolent path as they grow up. For example, they won't need to join a violent gang because their big brother or sister is in a gang. For children to be willing to talk openly, they need to trust that the adult will not bring harm to their family because of what they say. In certain cases, attempting to maintain confidentiality presents ethical or legal dilemmas for teachers or administrators if they become aware of information about a situation that poses a serious risk to the child or to others. If the teacher chooses to make himself available as a resource to the child, despite these potential complications, he would not act as an interrogator seeking information but as someone the child could turn to in an attempt to cope with the baffling issues of fear, family loyalty, and personal concern about the future.

Recognize and respond to children's traumatic reactions to violence

The National Center on Child Abuse and Neglect of the U.S. Department of Health and Human Services has produced several documents as part of its user manual series, designed to help caregivers and early childhood educators deal responsibly with the prevention and treatment of child maltreatment.

Two such documents are *Caregivers of Young Children: Preventing and Responding to Child Maltreatment* (Koralek 1992) and *The Role of Educators in the Prevention and Treatment of Child Abuse and Neglect* (Tower 1992). Early childhood programs would do well to obtain such materials, develop their own policies and procedures, and train staff members in the specific applications of these policies. In addition, all teachers, and particularly those who work in communities with high rates of violence and substance abuse, will often benefit from inservice training concerning child abuse. Teachers might also consider working to develop greater professional support and access to resources.

There are several levels at which teachers can be responsive. At the first level, teachers alert themselves to more severe, individual child reactions to violence witnessed or experienced directly. They can look to children's play and other expressive activities, as well as to their comments and general behavior, for signs of severe stress reactions. Of course, many children include violent actions in their play at times, so no single observation is definitive; but the teacher might be sensitized to watch for a pattern of signs. Symptoms of post-traumatic stress disorder (PTSD) in children include the following: reexperiencing the event in play, dreams, or intrusive memories; subdued behavior and inactivity; limited display of emotions and reduced interest in activities; sleep disorders, avoidance behaviors, and startle reactions (Bell & Jenkins 1991). Preschool children are more likely than are older children to show passive PTSD symptoms, including bed-wetting and other regressive behaviors, reduced talking, and clinging behavior. Nevertheless, it is not uncommon for preschool and kindergarten children to display a frequently noted characteristic of older children who are exposed to violence—difficulty controlling aggressive impulses, combined with emotional withdrawal and passivity (George & Main 1979; Bell & Jenkins 1991). Domestic violence is likely to lead to disruptions in the child's care at home. Indications of such domestic disruptions might include increased sleepiness, changes in appetite, or inadequate grooming.

At the next level of responsiveness, if a child shows symptoms of PTSD or other severe stress reactions to violence, the teacher or other program staff can make an effort to work with the family. In addition, the staff may consider making a referral and assisting the child and family in getting specialized treatment services. If a child appears to be traumatized by physical punishment he is experiencing at home, the family is clearly in need of counseling, including training in effective nonviolent parenting methods. If the violence in the home is primarily between other family members or related to substance abuse, then the family could benefit from other support and treatment services as well.

Finally, teachers may have reason to suspect that child maltreatment has reached the level of "child abuse" or "neglect." Every teacher, of course, needs to be familiar with the legal definitions and procedures concerning abuse and neglect in his or her state. Teachers must also know when they are legally mandated or ethically obligated to file a formal statement of suspected child abuse or neglect with the local child welfare agency. If a teacher has

Early Violence Prevention

concerns and believes she might need to file a claim of suspected child abuse, she would take the following initial steps: (1) keep dated and specific notes about all related observations and (2) inform her supervisor and other professional staff (e.g., nurse, social worker, psychologist, or counselor).

Each program or school should have a written procedure for establishing a "case manager" to coordinate information and make decisions in potential child abuse cases. In certain cases the teacher might be appointed to act as the case manager; in other circumstances a counseling, medical, or administrative staff person might be designated. Relevant information might include documented observations by the teacher or other staff members of the child's behavior or verbal comments; evaluations by school medical staff of atypical physical conditions; and current or past family information available in the child's records, obtained from family members, or collected from other sources. This body of information needs to be considered as a whole because information from any one source alone could be misleading. For example, a child's suspicious verbal statements or marks on a child's body may be understandable in the context of family or medical information. Thoughtful weighing of information is necessary, because decisions about filing a formal claim of suspected child maltreatment are often not clear-cut.

Regardless of the source or the strength of a teacher's suspicions about child abuse, it is important that neither the teacher nor any other person untrained in abuse evaluation asks the child repeated or leading questions about physical or sexual abuse. Leading questions reveal the adult's suspicions to the child (e.g., "Did a grownup hurt you?"); open-ended questions (e.g., "What happened?") avoid putting ideas in the child's mind. Inappropriate questioning prior to a formal, professional evaluation can invalidate the evaluation. Young children can be extremely suggestible. Research has demonstrated that young children may be convinced that a contrived event actually happened to them if they are told that it happened, if they are asked leading questions about it, or even if they are simply, repeatedly asked about it in a nonleading way (Ceci & Bruck 1993).

In regard to sexual abuse, the issue of children's suggestibility, combined with possible adult bias, is of particular concern. Only someone specially trained in making sexual-abuse evaluations should do the actual assessment, and the specific content of the evaluation should not be discussed with the child beforehand. If the child spontaneously makes statements or displays behaviors (e.g., sexualized behaviors that are unusually precocious), the teacher should keep an objective written record of these events but not directly question the child about sexual abuse. A teacher might privately say to a child, "You seem upset. Is something bothering you?" But it would be inappropriate to ask, "Did someone touch your private parts?"

In cases of suspected physical abuse, all observations of physical injuries or abnormalities need to be carefully recorded and brought to the attention of school medical personnel if available. One staff member is designated to ask the child about the physical injury. This needs to be done in private and without leading questions.

For example, the school nurse might say to a child in her office, "I see you have a bruise here. Can you tell me what happened?" It would be inappropriate for her to ask, "Did someone hit you?" The child's nonverbal reaction is noted, as well as his answer. For example, an abused child might answer, "Nothing happened," while looking scared and starting to cry.

In accordance with program or school policy, the designated case manager with input from others determines whether and when to file a formal claim of suspected maltreatment. The teacher's written observations help in making this determination, and they could be useful to an abuse investigator and of critical importance if legal issues arise. Although it is normally preferable for a program to utilize a coordinated effort and case manager in potential child maltreatment cases, each caregiver or teacher bears the *individual* legal responsibility to file a claim of suspected child maltreatment under certain specified circumstances. (Teachers should study their local legislation.) Therefore, in some cases, if program or school administrators put up barriers against the filing of a necessary claim, the teacher may have to act individually to meet the requirements of the law and to protect the safety of a child.

An immediate claim is called for if there is reason to suspect that the child has been seriously injured or may be in imminent danger. If there is no indication of imminent danger, taking alternative actions first is often preferable. For example, a staff member might express concerns to the family; hear what the family has to say; and offer support, assistance, or referrals. In some cases such intervention clarifies an ambiguous situation or leads to substantial improvements in the child's care at home. If the concerns of a teacher or case manager persist, the situation then requires the filing of a claim of maltreatment. The criterion for filing is never proof of maltreatment, but only reasonable suspicion. Although most states allow claims to be filed anonymously, it is usually recommended that program staff directly inform the family before the family is contacted by the investigating agency (Koralek 1992; Tower 1992). Having a case manager ensures that one person represents the program and communicates with the family about these very sensitive issues. If program staff have reason to believe that the child may be at increased immediate risk because of the filing of a claim, they should inform the investigating child welfare agency of this at the time of the filing.

If a suspicion-of-abuse claim is filed, the state's designated child welfare agency carries out a mandatory investigation within a short period of time. In most cases this would be the beginning of the process of trying to provide family support, assistance, and treatment to improve conditions for the child and family. In extreme cases the agency could take immediate steps to protect the child from potential dire or life-threatening dangers.

The filing and the investigation of an abuse claim do not solve the problem. In suspected abuse cases, teachers and other school or center personnel play two important continuing roles: (1) serving as a resource for the family and (2) monitoring the situation in order to detect any renewed threat to the child's welfare. These sometimes conflicting roles are enacted simultaneously or at different times for a given family. Managing these role responsibilities often becomes a difficult and highly stressful balancing act for staff, while having critical consequences for the child. When schools clearly spell out a policy and carefully follow it and staff work together in a supportive manner, they minimize difficulties and best serve the child.

In summary, it is important for teachers to let young children know that they can talk with them about their personal fears and unsafe experiences. Teachers need to assure children that they may talk to them privately and in confidence about such matters. The teacher serves as a supportive and sensitive listener, taking care to avoid questions or comments that may reflect personal bias or suspicions. If a teacher is concerned about conditions in the home, he might offer assistance to the family directly or through referral. If he has reason to suspect physical or sexual abuse, then he needs to consult with other staff members and follow the school's policy with regard to filing a claim of suspicion of child abuse. In any case, teachers provide support for both the child and the family and contribute to the ultimate goal of ensuring the child's safety and well-being.

Provide safety and self-protection training

Young children surrounded by violence benefit from learning about personal safety and self-protection against violence. One basic message to give children is to leave a violent scene quickly or to seek shelter but definitely *not* to try intervening. In the commu-nity, children need to know that if they hear gunshots or see fighting, they should go to the nearest indoor shelter and seek adult help. Once they are inside a building, children should move to interior rooms, away from windows that face the outside, and seek help from adults or older youth. Young children who try to intervene in domestic violence too easily become victims themselves. Therefore, children need to know that if they see serious violence between adults, their only job is to protect themselves and to get out of the room. It is not the child's job to try to help individuals or stop the violence.

As they are developmentally ready, children can be systematically taught when it is appropriate to call for help (local emergency response, usually 911), how to dial, and how to state their problem and exact location. When teaching such skills to children, care should be taken not to frighten the children unnecessarily about hypothetical situations. It can also be beneficial to assist families in instituting household and neighborhood safety procedures. A child can learn to identify one or two trusted neighbors and how to find their residences or to call them in an emergency (using automatic dialing buttons on phones, if available). If children "overlearn" these responses (i.e., engage in repeated practice to the point that they can perform them reliably and confidently), they will be more likely to respond appropriately and effectively in a crisis situation. A young child may find himself alone with an injured or unconscious victim; there have been numerous cases of young children successfully obtaining emergency response.

It is never too early to teach children the potential danger of all weapons and particularly of guns of all kinds. Young children in all neighborhoods, and particularly those in high-violence neighborhoods, need to be able to recognize and take precautions against the danger of guns. They need to know that if they see people carrying guns, and particularly if people are pointing guns at others, they should immediately seek shelter and adult help. Children need to be specifically taught that if they see or find a gun, they must (1) not touch it or even get close to it and (2) immediately tell an adult where the gun is. Young children sometimes think they can tell if a gun is loaded by looking at it or picking it up. They need to be taught that *any* gun could be loaded, that they cannot tell whether it is loaded or not, and that it is very easy for guns to go off by accident and hurt or kill people.

Teachers must point out that some real guns look like toy guns. Children should never pick up a gun to see if it is a toy. Even if they think it is a toy, they should ask an adult for help. Because children's play with toy guns often involves imitation of real violence and is tantamount to rehearsing the use of real guns, teachers would do well to restrict the use of toy guns in the classroom (see chapter 4).

Gun safety is an issue that obviously involves the family. School staff can help to educate all parents about gun safety and about the greatly increased risks to everyone in the family of having a gun in the home. Up-to-date educational resources about gun violence and its prevention are available to schools for this purpose (e.g., Children's Safety Network 1994). Hand-guns and guns that are accessible and loaded present especially high risks.

Contrary to the myth that guns generally offer protection to a family, a gun in the home is far more likely to be used to kill a family member than to protect against an intruder—*43 times* more likely, according to one study (Kellerman & Reay 1986). Gun violence in the home usually occurs in an impulsive moment of anger, desperation (in the case of suicide), or by accident. Many tragic accidents involve curious young children. By far, the most effective action a family can take to reduce the risk of violent injury or death to family members is to eliminate all firearms from their home. At the very least, any gun in the home needs to be stored unloaded, out of sight, and locked up, with bullets stored and locked in a separate location. Parents might also be advised to ask about gun safety in the homes of friends or relatives whom their children regularly visit. A child may reveal to school staff a particular fear of or fascination with guns in his home. In such cases the teacher may want to discuss with the family the child's specific responses, within the context of general gun-safety issues. In doing so, the teacher would focus on the family's desire to protect the child from emotional or physical harm, while making every attempt to respect the family's personal sense of privacy. School staff may also want to work with the community on gun awareness and safety issues or toward major policy changes that would restrict the availability of firearms, especially to children and youth (Dolins & Christoffel 1994).

Finally, young children can benefit from training programs in sex-abuse

© Nancy P. Alexander

Teachers should discuss their disciplinary and educational approaches with parents so that parents can work with the child in ways that are consistent and supportive of school efforts.

prevention that are specially designed for their developmental level (e.g., Beland 1986). Children can learn to distinguish between "good" and "bad" touches and to understand their rights to be "the boss" of their own bodies. They can also learn to say, "No," loudly, to leave the scene, and to tell a trusted adult. If the sexual or physical abuse is committed by a parent or other adult in the home, as is usually the case, the child is in a far more difficult and traumatic situation than if the perpetrator is a stranger or mere acquaintance. Many abuse-prevention programs appear to evade this issue.

Children may be realistically fearful of getting loved ones into trouble or of suffering reprisals themselves for reporting abuse. Teachers need to let children know that *no one*, not even a parent or relative, has the right to use violence or sexual touching against them. A teacher often is the most trusted adult the child can turn to in such cases, particularly if she makes herself available in this role. Each case must be treated individually, with sensitivity, and with a realistic understanding of the dangers and fears the child may face. Professional therapeutic consultation or intervention may be called for.

Reduce "disciplinary" violence toward children

The United States, unlike most other industrialized countries, permits corporal punishment (i.e., physical punishment) in schools; it is currently permitted in 30 states and has been supported by U.S. Supreme Court rulings in 1977 and 1989 (Parry, Walker, & Heim 1990). The widespread practice of hitting, spanking, paddling, or beating children in schools continues. U.S. Department of Education research indicates that about 30,000 children each year require medical treatment for injuries sustained through corporal punishment in school (Parry, Walker, & Heim 1990). These facts are nothing short of a national disgrace.

Determining the level of disciplinary violence in child care centers, family child care settings, and other early childhood programs outside the schools is more difficult, but incidents are reported across all these settings; unreported incidents are undoubtedly far more numerous. When adults who teach and care for children use corporal punishment, they teach children that hurting others is an acceptable way to control the behavior of others (NAEYC 1993). The use of corporal punishment in a school or child care center, or even the threat of such punishment, would undermine the key premise of any violence-prevention program. A program or profession that preaches nonviolence for students while using corporal punishment against them demonstrates hypocrisy of the worst kind. Teachers committed to preventing violence may wish to support public policy changes that would prohibit corporal punishment in all schools and child care programs, as is proposed by the National Association for the Education of Young Children (NAEYC 1993).

The use of physical punishment by parents is even more widespread and socially accepted than is corporal punishment in schools and child care settings. Such punishment provides the same proviolence messages and models to children. The use of corporal punishment at home has been repeatedly shown to contribute to aggressive behavior in children (Slaby & Roedell 1982; Greven 1990; Straus 1995a).

The child who is physically punished by family members learns that it is legitimate to control the behavior of loved ones by using physical force and by inflicting pain. In addition, corporal punishment in the home easily escalates to physical abuse, particularly when family stress is high (Patterson 1982). Early childhood educators can participate in educating parents in general about the harmful consequences of physical punishment and the advantages of alternative parenting methods. Useful materials for parents and teachers are available regarding "myths" about spanking and the harmful effects of corporal punishment (Straus 1995a).

Some parents who rely on physical punishment benefit from parent training offered at local clinics or continuing education programs. When school staff suspect that physical discipline is escalating to potentially harmful levels, it is important to inform families frankly of the unacceptability of such discipline and of the legal mandates that may be involved, while offering them support and assistance in finding safe disciplinary alternatives and relief from other family stressors.

Some families have well-established patterns of advocating and using harsh physical punishment. Some of these patterns are rooted in religious interpretation, others in long-standing cultural practices or in parents' personal experiences (Greven 1990). Attempting to change these beliefs and behaviors in any significant way is no easy matter, even for professionals who specialize in parent training. Various disciplinary methods might be discussed with parents, as a group or individually, in the context of the program's overall violence-prevention efforts. For example, if children are to receive training in self-protection against child abuse, then parents need to know beforehand what their children will be taught and the reasons for it. Although the subject is sensitive, it is also important. Children need to be taught that they have a right *not* to be physically harmed by anyone, even a family member. Teachers who choose to address the use of physical punishment that falls short of causing physical harm need to discuss the issue with parents rather than children. If, however, a child raises questions about home discipline, then the teacher will want to honestly express his position, while showing respect for the child's parents.

Teachers may also choose to support educational and regulatory efforts to change the widespread societal acceptance and legal prerogative of parents' use of physical force with impunity to control their children. Forcefully striking a stranger is considered "physical assault" and carries stiff legal penalties. The same forceful strike against one's own young child is often considered acceptable discipline, a parent's right, and even a parent's responsibility. A sub-stantive change in our society's tolerance for the physical punishment of children would contribute greatly to other violence-prevention efforts.

Support families

The combination of early provision of family services together with quality early childhood education has been demonstrated, through a large body of evidence, to be especially effective in countering the impact of violence (Yoshikawa 1994). These family services include pragmatic assistance, education and job training, parent effectiveness training, and mental health or substance abuse treatment. Such services can reduce the amount of violence within the home, and they have been found to substantially reduce the likelihood of the child developing chronic violent behaviors in later childhood and adulthood.

The National Association for the Education of Young Children proposes that early childhood professionals foster partnerships with parents to "help families deal with stress and enhance their ability to help children cope with violence" (NAEYC 1993, 83). NAEYC offers a number of suggestions:

• Support the critical role that parents play in promoting the development of behavior.

• Collaborate with parents to bring about changes needed in local communities to prevent violence.

• Support the importance of the parental role in the lives of children by providing education for parenthood, helping parents develop positive parenting skills, and supporting proven programs that prevent child abuse and neglect.

• Increase the ability of families to find and use community resources to support and protect children and families.

It is mutually beneficial for program staff and families to be in close and regular contact regarding individual children. Teachers can learn a great deal from parents and thereby better understand and respond to the chil-dren. They should discuss with parents the approaches being used in the school so that family members can work with the child in ways that are consistent and supportive of school efforts. Parents may particularly benefit from consultation and advice about using nonviolent discipline approaches at home, as well as other violence-prevention strategies that will be discussed throughout this book.

Points to Remember

Discuss and analyze your own experiences, feelings, and values related to violence. Seek support from other teachers and supervisors, if needed.

Help children to identify violence and its consequences. Discuss children's feelings about violence in their communities, in the media, and in their own relationships.

Talk with children about the violence they may face. Be realistic and be available.

Recognize and respond to children's traumatic reactions to violence. In such cases, seek professional consultation and consider making referrals.

Be alert to signs of physical or sexual abuse. Note suspicious events, but do not ask leading questions.

Follow ethical and legal guidelines for reporting suspicions of child abuse and neglect. Familiarize yourself with your state's definitions, legal obligations, procedures, and services.

Seek inservice training about children who witness or become victims of violence.

Teach children safety responses to extreme violence. Teach children *not* to intervene and when and how to seek shelter and help.

Teach children and families about the dangers of guns and about gun safety.

Teach children sex-abuse prevention and safety responses to strangers. Use materials designed for the children's developmental level.

Reduce "disciplinary" violence toward children. Work toward the elimination of corporal punishment of children by teachers and parents.

Support families to help them reduce and cope with violence. Communicate with families to facilitate mutual understanding, cooperation, and assistance.

3

Designing the Physical and Programmatic Environment

Three children run across the open expanse in the middle of the classroom, gleefully knocking down block structures built in their pathway. In one corner of the room, five children push and shove each other as they try to play with the popular Legos at a table equipped with only one chair. Four children waiting in line to use the easel grow bored and begin to kick each other in frustration. **How could a teacher prevent these problems with some simple changes in the classroom environment?**

One of the early childhood teacher's most important tasks is to design an environment that nurtures and supports children's cognitive, physical, social, and emotional development. The *physical environment* has a strong effect on children's social behavior. A well-designed environment decreases the chances of aggressive behavior occurring and increases the opportunities for prosocial interactions (cooperating, sharing, helping) (Goldstein 1994).

When teachers design a classroom space, immediate questions arise. What activity/learning centers should be established? How large should various spaces be? What kind of layout will work best? In addition to the physical environment, the *programmatic environment* also has an impact on behavior. What size groupings

work best? What are the effects of teacher-structured versus child-structured activities? What type of schedule will work well? By understanding the environmental factors that influence the occurrence of both aggressive behavior and prosocial behavior, teachers can develop settings in which children are most likely to learn to help, cooperate, share, and resolve their conflicts nonaggressively, through the use of assertive skills and prosocial behaviors.

What research tells us

Much useful information for early childhood educators is available from research on children's aggression in relation to various dimensions of the physical environment and the program structure (e.g., schedule, group size).

Physical environment

The amount and type of social behavior in each classroom differ, depending on how the room is arranged and the types of activities that the materials invite in each area of the room. Each classroom arrangement stimulates its own unique patterns of social interaction within and between the various activity centers. Observational studies indicate that the most complex social behavior usually occurs in the dramatic play area (Parten 1933; Rubin 1977; Quay, Weaver, & Neel 1986). Other centers that encourage cooperative play include those involving games, woodworking, sand, and manipulatives. Reading and language centers promote social activity when teachers encourage conversation about what is being read, but the setting can also lead to solitary play if equipped for highly structured activities, such as the use of tape recorders with earphones. Nonsocial, solitary play often takes place in areas where children use paints, crayons, playdough, or puzzles (Rubin 1977; Quay, Weaver, & Neel 1986) unless social interaction is stimulated by encouraging children to share materials or work together on group projects.

The balance between prosocial behavior and aggressive behavior also depends upon activity center content. A higher percentage of aggressive behavior has been observed in the block area, the dramatic play area, and the woodworking area than in other classroom centers, possibly because of the high levels of interaction elicited by these activities (Shapiro 1975; Rubin 1977; Quay, Weaver, & Neel 1986). Teachers should be alert to the possibilities for aggression arising in these areas of the classroom. They can use these potential conflict situations as an opportunity to teach essential conflict-resolution skills.

In addition to the nature of the activities available in an activity center, the degree of crowding and the size of the group influence the frequency of aggression. It is not surprising that crowding large groups of children into small spaces can result in an increased level of aggression (McGrew 1972; Ginsburg 1975). Not only are accidental physical encounters more likely to occur and to be misunderstood under such conditions, but children's ongoing play activities are more likely to be accidentally interrupted or their constructions destroyed. Young children often misinterpret accidental pushing and shoving as intentional attacks and frequently retaliate, escalating unintentional incidents into intentional aggression (Shantz & Voydanoff 1973; Gump 1975).

Putting a small group of children in a large open space, however, can also result in an increase in aggression (Loo 1972). The running-and-chasing games that often occur in large spaces can escalate into aggressive incidents. Aggression is likely to occur, for example, during rough-and-tumble play (Dodge et al. 1990). The least aggression occurs when small- to moderate-size groups of children are given a space large enough to avoid crowding but not so large and open as to encourage wild running.

Finally, children are more likely to help and cooperate with one another if they are relaxed, happy, and engaged rather than bored (Eisenberg & Mussen 1989). Classroom arrangements that create pleasant surroundings through neat storage, attractive room decorations placed at a child's eye level, and easily available materials promote positive rather than negative social behavior.

Programmatic environment

The degree of structure in the program also has a profound effect on children's social behavior. Under conditions of high structure, the variation in children's potential activity is limited. The teacher or types of materials that can be used in only one way may define structured limitations. Under these conditions children tend to show high conformity to adult expectations, less independent task behavior, and more teacher-directed task behavior (that is, they continue the activity only while under the teacher's supervision). They also show low amounts of social interaction and low levels of aggression. Because their behavior is controlled by the teacher, they are more likely to wait patiently during structured transitions and to pay attention to the teacher during group time than are children in less-structured settings. But because their behavior is externally controlled, children have little opportunity to develop internally controlled social skills under these conditions. In highly structured situations children learn little about independent decisionmaking, self-control, or spontaneous cooperative behavior.

During conditions of low structure, teachers provide a variety of open-ended materials and allow children great latitude in using them. Under these conditions, children show more imaginative play and creativity, more social interaction, more prosocial behavior, and higher levels of both assertiveness and aggression (Huston-Stein, Friedrich-Cofer, & Susman 1977). Clearly, during less-structured times of the day, teachers should be alert to the potential for aggression, as well as for opportunities to guide children toward nonaggressive solutions to their conflicts. If the aggressive behavior is not effectively controlled, it is very likely to increase. Children's aggressive behavior often increases because it is rewarded when a victimized child submits to the aggressor. Other children who observe that aggressive behavior is permitted and rewarded in this way may then begin, for the first time, to engage in aggressive behavior (Patterson, Littman, & Bricker 1967). Teachers can use unstructured time as an opportunity to guide children in nonviolent problem solving when conflicts arise, using the strategies described more fully in other chapters, especially chapter 8.

Substantial time during which children engage in activities of their choice, supported by teacher guidance, is important for social development. For example, children who have participated in high-quality infant care, characterized by an unstructured, nurturing environment, are likely to show less aggression and more prosocial behavior later on in both preschool and elementary school (Field 1991). Low-structure activity time fosters self-regulating behavior (Huston-Stein, Friedrich-Cofer, & Susman 1977). Under these conditions children can choose whether to behave aggressively or cooperatively, developing their own internal social motivation and experiencing for themselves the natural social consequences of various behaviors.

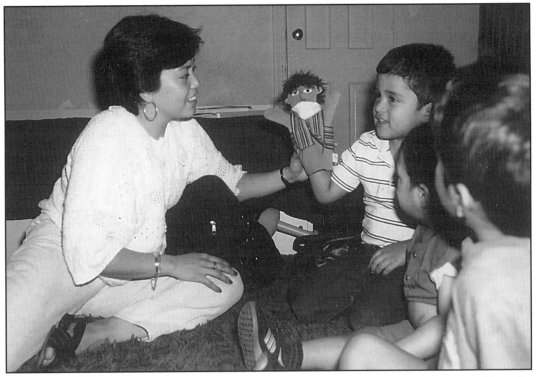

The types of activities that teachers plan and direct during group times affect the levels of prosocial behavior that children exhibit during free play.

The types of activities that teachers plan and direct during group times affect the levels of prosocial behavior and aggression that children exhibit during free play. Children who are encouraged to play aggressive, highly competitive games, for example, are likely to behave more aggressively during unstructured free play (Davitz 1952). On the other hand, children engaged in structured activities involving cooperative behavior (such as working together on a mural) or in structured practice of social skills are more likely to behave in prosocial, nonaggressive ways during unstructured free play (Chittenden 1942; Davitz 1952; Spivack & Shure 1974). The more frequently children voluntarily practice positive social skills in a structured setting, the more likely they are to use these skills in less-structured situations (Staub 1971; Rosenhan 1972; Bryan 1975). Teachers enhance the quality of social interactions during free-play time by developing group-time activities that teach cooperation skills. Reading a story in which characters help each other or engaging children in a social, problem-solving activity using puppets increases the chances that helpfulness and problem solving will take place later during free time.

In planning a program, teachers need to allow a balance of structured and unstructured time, with variations in group size and levels of teacher involvement and child-initiated choice. Children are introduced to important skills and concepts during structured, teacher-led circle times or small-group activities. How-ever, open-ended activities with supporting teacher guidance provide important opportunities for young children to regulate their own activities and to internalize their own code of behavior toward others. When the classroom activities allow children freedom of choice and decisionmaking, teachers can use their attention and other guidance techniques to encourage prosocial behavior and discourage aggressive actions. Adult guidance and intervention in social play are reduced as the children increasingly learn and use social skills independently and experience the natural rewards of cooperative social interactions. As children practice making choices, try out social skills, and experience different patterns of social interaction, they internalize their own codes of behavior toward others.

Teaching guidelines

From the research summarized here emerge guidelines for the design of the physical environment and program structure.

Designing the physical space

Minimize crowding. Classroom space should be set up to minimize unnecessary crowding and accidental physical contact with both people and play equipment. Although it is not always possible to do so, limiting group size is another method for controlling aggression. Some teachers choose to post and maintain limits on the number of children who can use a particular activity area to prevent overcrowding. In this way children can self-manage group size. Limits can result in conflict when too many children want to choose a particular area. Teacher assistance in establishing waiting lists and other turn-taking habits help prevent such conflicts.

Clearly define activity areas and pathways. When designing a space, it is important to consider the travel pathways in the classroom and the access to the different areas. The block area, for example, should be shielded from normal pathways to prevent children from walking through and accidentally upsetting other children's block buildings. Large, open pathways can result in uncontrolled running and chasing that can easily escalate into aggression. Using barriers, such as low bookcases, to break up the areas where children walk through the room will automatically reduce this behavior.

Effective classrooms have clearly defined activity areas set apart by low shelves or other furniture. Teachers need to plan a variety of spaces to meet the varying needs of the class. On a given day, one or two children may appreciate a private space for looking at books, equipped with soft pillows and set off from the classroom bustle. Others may need a place to be messy with paint or clay, as they express their emotions through art. Still others may need a substantial space to accommodate a large block-building project, an area where they can dress up and create new roles for themselves, or a table at which they can work quietly on a puzzle. Creating enough space for several children to play in areas that encourage social interaction reduces the chances of conflict. When the block area is large enough and equipped with sufficient numbers of blocks, for example, several children can choose to play either cooperatively or independently, and they have room to build without fear of disruption. Careful room arrangement with a variety of choices for children's activities will reduce conflicts over space and equipment.

Provide open access. Providing more than one point of access to some areas helps prevent children from becoming exclusive about a space. For example, children may quarrel over who enters a loft with one entrance, while they may accept many visitors when there are two ways in (Ramsey 1980).

Extend play opportunities. Easy access between potentially linked areas, such as areas for housekeeping and blocks, facilitates increased cooperative play among children in each center (Doescher & Sugawara 1986). In one classroom a post office was set up next to the housekeeping area, resulting in complex social interactions. Some children staffed the post office; others dressed up in the house area, wrote letters, and took them to the post office; still others were involved in delivering mail. The unstructured setting, with inviting, open-ended realistic props that suggested cooperative activities, encouraged positive social interactions (Roedell 1992).

Monitor for potential conflicts. Knowing that some activity areas are more likely than others to result in aggressive interactions, teachers may, at least part of the time, want to guide children who are habitually aggressive to the areas that encourage prosocial be-

havior. Teachers may also choose to work more closely with children in the areas where aggression is likely to occur, guiding them to use assertive, nonaggressive strategies to solve their conflicts before violence occurs (see chapter 10).

Empower children's independent behavior. When an environment is designed so that children help themselves and each other in preparing, obtaining, and replacing materials, teachers are more free to provide guidance and prosocial modeling because they are less involved with materials. In addition, teachers can refer children to each other for help in such an environment, allowing children the opportunity to practice helping and sharing skills. These skills include learning to ask for or offer objects to each other and responding appropriately. When teachers refer children to each other for help rather than attempting to provide everything themselves, they create an ethic of helpfulness and group spirit in the classroom. Low shelves with easily accessible props and materials that allow a child to choose independent or cooperative activities will contribute to the development of positive social behavior.

Create pleasant surroundings. Because children are less likely to behave aggressively when they are in a positive mood, the environment should be designed to enhance a feeling of well-being. Attractive materials, calm voices, and positive interactions contribute to mood, as do soft music and cheerful colors. Decorations should be neat and placed at children's eye level.

Conditions that can result in stress or overstimulation should be avoided. For example, playing loud music during free-play time makes it more difficult for children to talk quietly with one another and resolve problems before they become conflicts. Crowded open storage of materials not available for children's use can cause visual over-stimulation and conflict over use of prohibited materials. A cluttered room with no clearly defined use areas can create confusion and frustration that, in turn, can increase the likelihood of aggression.

Planning the programmatic environment

Provide blocks of time for free play. Because children are more likely to participate in complex social interactions in unstructured environments, providing large blocks of choice time gives children the opportunity to practice their social skills. This less-structured time will be particularly beneficial if it has been preceded by teacher-led activities that focus on cooperation, helping, and building skills in solving problems assertively and

© Judy Burr

Children working on group projects say, "Look what we did!" rather than, "Look what I did!" Having experienced the natural pleasure of such joint efforts, they are more likely to cooperate by choice in the course of their play.

constructively. Group projects, such as painting murals, creating a class collage, or engaging in cooperative cooking or building projects, create learning opportunities for prosocial behavior. When children can say, "Look what we did!" rather than, "Look what I did!" they experience the natural pleasure of working together and are more likely to continue cooperating by choice during less structured times.

Promote helping roles. Family-style settings for meals or snacks, where children pass food to one another and help the entire class by setting up and clearing the table, provide wonderful opportunities for cooperative social interaction. Children who participate in structured activities involving helping or sharing are more likely to help others later on their own (Rosenhan & White 1967; Staub 1971; Rosenhan 1972). Assigning personal responsibility for helping roles in the classroom gives children practice in using helping skills and encourages them to be helpful on their own initiative (Staub 1971; Bryan 1975; Mischel & Mischel 1976). For example, children can share rotating assignments for watering the plants, feeding the class pet, helping the teacher bring in the snack, and handling other daily classroom jobs. They are then more likely to be helpful during the ongoing classroom routine because they have practiced these tasks and received recognition for their help in the past.

Maintain a calm manner. Adults create a comfortable, warm atmosphere by speaking in calm, pleasant tones, smiling in a friendly way, and moving in an unhurried manner. It is important, for example, to avoid shouting across the room to gain a child's attention, because loud noises can create a tense mood for the entire group. When a teacher moves to the area where the child is playing, gets down to the child's level, and speaks in a soothing tone, an atmosphere of peace and harmony is created.

Plan a consistent routine with smooth transitions. Teachers also reduce the chances of aggression simply by having materials prepared ahead of time and planning smooth transitions between activities. Children may jostle and push and begin hitting and kicking each other if asked to wait for long periods of time with nothing to do. When children are engaged and interested in activities, they are less likely to behave aggressively.

A program schedule that balances active with quiet activities and minimizes unnecessary waiting with nothing to do will reduce children's frustration and create a better atmosphere. A smoothly flowing program in which children are busy with interesting cooperative activities provides a setting where prosocial behaviors are learned and practiced and aggressive behavior is less likely to occur. A consistent routine for the day with regular, smooth transitions helps to establish a positive climate. Children need to know what to expect and to have plenty of time to move between activities. Giving a warning before ending the free-play period allows children to complete their activities, put away their materials, and move on to the next activity in a calm, unhurried manner. For example, teachers in one preschool make a practice of signaling a forthcoming group activity by ringing a chime and singing, "Five more minutes 'til meeting time" (Slaby 1994b). This gentle cue not only generates a positive atmosphere during transition to the next activity, but it also indicates teachers' respect for children's projects and their need to plan ahead.

Points to Remember

Create classrooms with sufficient space in those activity centers that are likely to encourage social interaction. Crowding can result in an increase in aggression.

Design classrooms with distinct walkways and play spaces to eliminate accidental physical contact with people and objects. Young children often interpret accidental contact as aggression and are likely to retaliate.

Design an environment where children can help themselves and others with material preparation and activities, freeing teachers for positive guidance roles. Referring children to one another for help creates an ethic of helpfulness and group spirit in the classroom.

Provide extra guidance during unstructured times and when children are playing in activity areas where aggression is likely. Teacher guidance helps children learn the skills they need to solve problems nonviolently.

Plan activities in which children can practice cooperating, sharing, and helping, including assigning classroom helper roles. Children who practice positive social behaviors in a structured setting are more likely to engage in positive social interaction during free time.

Support a positive classroom atmosphere through pleasant interactions, neat storage, and attractive decorations. Children are less likely to behave aggressively when they are in a positive mood.

Eliminate the frustration of abrupt transitions, excessive waiting, or sitting for long time periods. By planning a balanced set of activities with smooth transitions, teachers can eliminate many routine sources of frustration for children.

4

Selecting Materials

The teacher reads the story "The Three Billy Goats Gruff" to a group of 4-year-old children. Later, during free play, she notices several children pouncing on each other, saying, "I'm the troll and I'm going to eat you up!" This confrontational play escalates. Pretty soon blows have been struck and several children are in tears. **What strategies or actions could the teacher have used to prevent this fight?**

As teachers set up the classroom environment, they have many choices regarding which materials to choose and how many materials to set out for the group. The choices teachers make regarding materials have an influence on children's social behavior. The characteristics of the materials themselves can limit or expand possibilities for cooperative social interaction. Some materials tend to evoke aggressive behavior, while others facilitate cooperation and sharing. Eliminating materials that foster aggression can reduce children's aggressive classroom behavior. Because cooperation is incompatible with aggression, choosing materials that support cooperative interactions encourages children to engage in cooperative behavior rather than aggression.

What research tells us

The number and type of toys and materials available affect the likelihood that children will either share or compete. In some instances children are more likely to engage in conflict over materials when the number of toys available is reduced, particularly if there are sufficient resources one day and fewer the next (Smith 1974; Caplan et al. 1991). Aggression is also likely to increase when one or two new and desirable toys are added to the classroom collection, particularly when these toys can only be played with by one or two children at a time (Smith 1974). Teachers can anticipate this problem and create a system for sharing, using a timer and a waiting list to help children avoid conflict and feel that they will get a turn. If there are adequate resources for every child to find something interesting to do, or if there is a clear system for sharing the use of materials, conflict over materials will usually diminish (Gump 1975). Providing duplicate toys may decrease conflict, particularly for younger children.

Although scarcity of resources generally creates greater potential for conflict, it also provides opportunities for children to share or take turns (Smith 1974; Caplan et al. 1991). Whether children respond to scarce resources by sharing or by quarreling depends on such factors as their developmental level, the level of teacher guidance, the type of materials in question, and children's current feelings of frustration and stress (see chapter 9).

Children's developmental levels also influence how they interact with materials. Very young children tend to play alone or side by side with peers who are engaged in similar activities but carry them out independently (Parten 1933; Whiteside, Busch, & Horner 1976). Children at these levels of play are more likely to need duplicate materials for conflict-free interactions. As children gain social experience, they become better able to play together, sharing materials that focus on a common theme and relating to the materials in a variety of ways. For example, a child might deliver blocks in a truck to another child engaged in building a structure. Rather than providing duplicate materials for children capable of complex cooperative play, offering a variety of materials that complement each other or elaborate a play theme is more effective and encourages cooperative and creative interactions.

Materialism in the early childhood setting

Most of the quarrels that take place among young children involve disputes over possession of an object (Hay & Ross 1982). Such interactions are more likely than other kinds to lead to aggression. The types of disputes vary with the developmental play level of the children involved. Very young children who have fewer negotiating skills are more likely to grab a toy from another child, while older children may make verbal demands. Two-year-old children are likely to want the same toy that a peer is playing with, even if a duplicate toy is available. Seeing another child with a toy makes the toy more desirable (Hay & Ross 1982; Caplan et al. 1991). As older children learn to share and take turns with toys and equipment, they sometimes become as possessive about their turn as they are about the actual object in question (Ramsey 1980).

Having control or possession of things is a key concept in our society, and frequently teachers, without thinking about it, focus children's attention on ownership and on material possessions. When teachers ask children what they want for their birthday or suggest that they bring a favorite possession to school for "sharing time," children's attention is focused on material goods. Minimizing such comments and practices may help to create an atmosphere in which fewer conflicts erupt over toys and other prized items.

Another important reason to de-emphasize material possessions is the large economic inequality between people and groups in our society, as well as the painful discrepancy between the deprivation faced by so many children and the lavish material consumption that is the focus of our popular culture. In the context of violence prevention, researchers have pointed out that high levels of violence are not so much related to poverty per se but rather to the degree of economic disparity between groups in a given society—to socioeconomic inequality (Messner 1990; Hawkins 1993). Of course the early childhood teacher cannot solve this fundamental problem of social justice. However, deemphasizing the importance of possessions serves as a small step toward counteracting a materialistic societal preoccupation that serves to divide people and invite conflict.

Teachers can make an effort to anticipate classroom conflicts over possessions and be ready to help children negotiate disputes that are likely to occur around certain types of materials. For example, small objects, such as beads, pegs, puzzles, Lego blocks, and sand toys, are more likely than big objects to generate ownership/control

© Hildegard Adler

Children tend to argue over individual swings but become cooperative around tire swings that can hold several children, even calling out to others to join them.

disputes in the classroom. These toys are easily clutched and more difficult to find cooperative uses for, without teacher guidance (Ramsey 1980). Fewer ownership disputes occur over large and nonportable equipment, such as climbing bars. Children tend to argue over individual swings but become cooperative around tire swings that can hold several children, even calling out to others to join them (Ramsey 1980). In fact, equipment that is best used by two or more children invites cooperative behavior. Tire swings, seesaws, rocking boats, wagons pulled by tricycles, all require that children work together for maximum enjoyment and automatically encourage and reward cooperative behavior with natural consequences (Cooper & LeBlanc 1973). Providing such equipment in the physical environment presents naturally occurring opportunities for children to practice cooperative skills during their ongoing activities. Single-user items, such as individual swings, also have their place because cooperative turn taking is a valuable social skill that teachers can foster as children use these items.

Materials to invite positive social interaction

Certain toys lend themselves to role playing in dramatic play or social skills-building activities. Dramatic play props invite children to engage in complex social interactions. In addition, puppets, dolls, and small animals are useful to model, instruct, and provide opportunities for children to practice during structured social skills activities (Spivack & Shure 1974, 1982; Shure

& Spivack 1988; Mize & Ladd 1990). If these materials are left in the classroom during free-play time, children are likely to reenact the scenes they practiced during the teacher-led activities. In addition, children will use their imaginations to create other dramatic play scenarios that are more likely to be prosocial in content if the mood has been established during group learning times. Children who are shy or not very verbal may be more comfortable using puppets or dolls to express their feelings and ideas to teachers and peers. These materials can provide an important outlet for such children.

Children are more likely to empathize with and want to help individuals they perceive to be like themselves (see chapter 11). Classroom materials that portray individuals with disabilities and members of different ethnic/cultural groups involved together in common activities help children view as similar to themselves people who may look different.

Use of play materials that suggest aggressive themes will often result in increased aggression, both related and unrelated to the theme of the play, while materials that focus on prosocial themes of helping and cooperating tend to encourage positive social behavior (Feshbach 1956; Mallick & McCandless 1966; Turner & Goldsmith 1976). For example, children who select and play with materials related to aggressive themes (such as soldiers or superheroes) will behave differently than children who play with materials related to nonaggressive themes (such as trains, farms, and stores). The former are likely not only to play more aggressively with the aggression-related toys but also to instigate aggressive interactions with other children outside the theme of the play. In particular, the presence of toy guns in the environment can elicit aggressive responses in children's play (Turner & Goldsmith 1976). The physical presence of a toy gun results in more aggression than occurs when children simply create guns, using their fingers or other objects. A toy gun has only one use, whereas fingers or open-ended materials, such as bristle blocks or playdough, can more readily be adapted to other uses (Carlsson-Paige & Levin 1987, 1990).

Even folktales that portray aggression, such as "The Three Billy Goats Gruff," can result in increased aggressive behavior in the classroom. Acting out such stories is tantamount to rehearsing aggressive behavior (Slaby & Roedell 1982) and often results in increased aggression during the free play that follows.

Introducing folktales and fairy tales may be a valuable way of connecting children to the universal themes portrayed in this literature. But for stories that involve themes of aggression and violence, such benefits must be weighed against the substantial evidence of negative effects, particularly for young children in a group setting who are just learning prosocial skills. Specifically, reading children stories with aggressive themes or involving them in acting out such stories increases the chances that they will behave aggressively in their ongoing interactions. When a group of children show high levels of aggression and rough play, the teacher may want to give careful thought to the stories she reads during other times of the day. Perhaps

folktales with aggressive themes could be introduced during individual or small-group reading sessions to minimize the potential influence on the larger group's social behavior and to allow for constructive discussion about the aggressive themes. In these discussions teachers can help children analyze and even reinterpret messages found in the traditional stories of many cultures, with themes of cooperation, nonviolence, and assertiveness in mind (as described more fully later in this chapter). Some teachers may decide to leave such stories for parents to read at home and choose to use class time in reading materials that will enhance rather than impede children's development of positive social skills.

Rehearsing aggressive behavior in any type of structured setting tends to increase children's levels of aggression later on (Berkowitz 1993). Contrary to popular opinion, providing materials such as rubber punching dolls or "hitting pillows" and suggesting that a presumably angry child punch the doll or hit the pillow does *not* decrease the probability that the child will behave aggressively toward peers; in fact, quite the opposite is true. Research evidence is clear on the inadvisability of this practice (Mallick & McCandless 1966; Bandura 1973; Berkowitz 1993) (for further discussion, see chapter 6). Therefore, having special materials available as substitute targets for aggression is not recommended.

Teaching guidelines

The research on the impact that materials have in creating positive social interaction suggests the following guidelines.

Provide enough materials to elicit sharing and cooperation

Teachers need to judge the quantity of materials best suited to promoting sharing without eliciting conflict over resources. A careful balance must be reached between providing so many materials that there is no need to share and providing so few that children must either compete with each other or wait with nothing to do (Doescher & Sugawara 1986). For example, children working together on a mural can share a set of marking pens. It would be asking for trouble, however, to call upon five children to share three pens.

For very young children, teachers can provide sets of duplicate materials to support the solitary and parallel play characteristic of this group. Teachers might consider changing the number and selection of materials during the course of a year as children's play levels become more complex. At the beginning of the year, more duplicate sets might be needed, while later in the year a diversity of materials supporting common themes that can be used together help facilitate cooperative, interactive play.

Providing enough play choices in a room prevents needless conflict. If children in a class are often arguing over materials, the teacher may want to count the number of play opportunities in the room, with the goal of allowing for three or four choices per child. If too few play opportunities are available, teachers might provide additional sets of materials or enlarge the play space in popular areas to permit more children to use these at any given time.

Suggest complementary roles to facilitate cooperation

In guiding children toward sharing materials, teachers can stress the cooperative or complementary use of equipment rather than focusing on the possessiveness inherent in turn taking. For example, rather than focusing on whose turn it is to ride the tricycles, teachers might suggest that waiting children start a car wash, open a repair garage, or create a cargo-loading zone for piling blocks into wagons that can be hauled by the tricycles. Rather than providing a piece of identical equipment for each child, or even lining up children to wait their turns, teachers can help children create complimentary roles that would permit all children to participate.

Deemphasize children's possessions

A focus on material possessions often results in rivalry and conflict. In addition, children in our society have vastly different access to personal possessions, and this socioeconomic inequality is often a major source of tension. For these reasons teachers should consider deemphasizing the importance of possessions and commercial products (Ramsey 1980). They might talk instead about how the materials are used by saying, "We have some new colors in the paint area— I'll be interested to see how they look in your picture" rather than "Look how many crayons you have." This focus will help to direct the child's attention to the use of the materials rather than to the accumulation and possession of a large quantity.

The emphasis on ownership of material goods that often accompanies show-and-tell can be avoided by asking children to tell about an unusual experience; a new skill; a friend; a favorite food, animal, or song; or a feeling they had when they helped someone. Having children bring related photos or drawings (e.g., a photo of their dog), or audiotapes (e.g., music to dance to), or natural objects found outdoors may make their presentation more concrete. Parents can be brought into discussions about the goal of deemphasizing possessions and encouraged to cooperate with these goals. Around holiday times children can be encouraged to talk about family, friends, and special activities rather than to focus on gifts. In commenting on everyday occurrences or themes raised by books and stories, teachers can emphasize the value of experiences, relationships, and aspects of the natural world rather than goods and possessions. Teachers need to be aware of how comments about children's clothing can draw unwanted attention to who has new clothes and who does not. Comments such as "What a pretty dress!" or "You have new sneakers—they're really fancy!" emphasize the desirability of material possessions and appearance instead of the child's own inner strength and developing capabilities. When a child proudly shows off a new item, his excitement can be acknowledged by commenting on the clothing's usefulness or warmth rather than its "newness" (Ramsey 1980).

It may also be helpful, whenever feasible, to make use of simpler handmade toys and equipment for the classroom in place of expensive store-bought items. The children can participate individually or together in creating some of their own classroom resources (e.g., simple musical instruments, toys, games, and decorations), using natural or recycled materials where appropriate. Such cooperative effort toward a functional common goal is educationally valuable in itself. These practices also show children that creating useful things can be fun and that resourcefulness and shared effort can more than compensate for not having much money to spend on commercial products. Such experiences may be particularly important when children are economically disadvantaged or when large discrepancies in economic resources exist among children in the class. Many activity books include suggestions for making toys and equipment; for instance, *Toy Book* by Steven Caney (1972) gives directions for making more than 50 creative and functional toys by using simple materials.

Eliminate materials that suggest aggression

Eliminating materials that suggest aggressive themes can also help reduce conflict and aggression. Batman, Power Rangers, or Ninja Turtle outfits; stories glorifying aggressive themes; ferocious puppets with large teeth; or toy weapons frequently lead to pretend aggression that often escalates into real aggression against classmates. Teachers may choose to discuss with parents the influence of these toys on aggressive behavior and request that parents not send such items to school. When children do engage in spontaneous play around aggressive

Reading or telling stories to children invites questions and comments about the social values, behaviors, and feelings portrayed.

themes, teachers can redirect the topic of the play while still using the children's ideas. For example, when a group of children became Ninja Turtles in her classroom, one teacher convinced the group to become champion problem solvers who didn't use weapons. She guided them into team activities and story lines that focused on overcoming natural catastrophes (Carlsson-Paige & Levin 1991).

Include materials that celebrate diversity

Materials that perpetuate culture or gender bias perpetuate the belief that some individuals are "different" and are appropriate targets for aggression. For example, books that show girls only in passive, helpless roles or that reinforce cultural stereotypes by showing Native Americans in war paint and wielding tomahawks have the potential for influencing long-term attitudes far beyond the immediate context of the classroom. Including multicultural materials that show how all individuals are different in some ways but similar in others helps promote empathy toward people who may appear different (Aboud 1988). Materials from different cultures should be integrated into classroom life rather than being brought out for the special ethnic celebration activities that have been labeled as *tourist curriculum* (Derman-Sparks & the A.B.C. Task Force 1989). For example, the dramatic play area might include chopsticks and a wok; the music corner could include music and instruments from different cultures; and the everyday snacks might include food and recipes from different cultural menus. Food packages and cans from ethnic grocery stores help enliven a housekeeping corner. The art area might also include collage materials with images, symbols, and patterns from a variety of cultures. The room's library should include books showing children of different ethnic groups engaged in ordinary, rather than exotic, activities.

Classroom decorations can include pictures of families from different cultures and families that include family members with disabilities playing, working, laughing, and showing affection with one another, as all families do. Whole sets of "people color" crayons are now available, permitting children to portray people with a variety of skin tones. Manipulative materials can include coins, grains, and beads from other countries, as well as puzzles representing a wide range of people, animals, places, customs, and occupations. Photographs of diverse dwellings (e.g., hogans, igloos, chalets, mobile homes, apartments) near the block area help stimulate creative block play. Making class books or posting pictures of children from the class and their families, using the classroom camera or photos from home, is one way of indicating that all the children in the class are important and have a family life (Ramsey 1987; Derman-Sparks & the A.B.C. Task Force 1989).

Teachers can also use a structured planning approach for including cultural materials in various areas of their classroom by creating a planning chart. Areas of the room are listed down one side (e.g., dramatic play, blocks, books, table toys) and specific cultural backgrounds of children in the class across the top. After the teacher fills the chart with items to be included in various areas of the room that reflect specific cultures of the children in the class, items can then be added from other cultures represented in the neighborhood or broader community. If all the children in the class share similar cultural backgrounds, adding materials from other cultural groups will increase children's appreciation of diversity. One effective way to gain a new perspective on which cultural materials to include is to talk with the parents of children in the class, as well as with leaders in local ethnic communities. It is important to include materials in a way that respects their cultural origin. For example, many types of Native American dress have particular cultural or religious significance. It would be inappropriate to include these items in a dramatic play area.

Include role-playing materials

Cooperative interactions are often elicited by introducing materials that suggest prosocial themes or materials that invite a variety of roles for children to enact. For example, thematic prop boxes with dressup accessories and related items that suggest a theme generate many possibilities for children to engage in complex interactions without conflict. A doctor/hospital prop box focused on a helping theme might include white lab coats, toy stethoscopes, bandages, and even a small wheelchair and crutches. A post office prop box might include paper, envelopes, stamps, stamp pads, pens, staplers, large delivery envelopes, mailbags, scales for weighing, and mailboxes. Puzzles and books that support the theme and show individuals of different ethnic groups and genders actively engaged in the thematic activities enhance the activity. Varying the materials and themes in the dramatic play area can result in an increase in cooperative group interaction as children discuss the new materials and new roles that can be assumed (Howe et al. 1993; Myhre 1993).

Provide materials with prosocial themes

Teachers can choose books and stories that support prosocial and nonviolent themes and principles of justice (Carlsson-Paige & Levin 1987). Specially selected books, stories, and dramatic play materials can help children understand and respond to the needs and the rights of others. Annotated lists of such books offer guidance in selecting materials (e.g., Fassler & Janis 1983).

The teacher can provide specific and concrete examples of otherwise abstract concepts and present pro-social role models for children to emulate. For example, the familiar fable of "The Lion and the Mouse" provides an engaging example of problem solving in a tight spot to prevent violence, keeping a promise, and helping another. Despite his tiny size, the mouse is able to save the powerful lion by using resourcefulness, persistence, and courage. Most versions end with the lion expressing appreciation and the two becoming friends despite their differences.

Reading or telling stories to children in an interactive format invites questions and comments about the social values, behaviors, and feelings portrayed. Teachers can talk with children about the messages presented in stories and how aspects of the stories relate to their own experiences. As mentioned previously, in discussing traditional stories with children, teachers can help them analyze and even reinterpret messages found in the stories, keeping in mind cooperation, nonviolence, and assertiveness. The children might use dolls, puppets, or costumes for acting out scenes from the stories, as well as possible alternative scenes related to the stories. How did Cinderella feel when she was spoken to and treated abusively (Parry 1993)? What could she have done if the fairy godmother had not shown up? Why were the three bears so mad at Goldilocks? What could she have done instead if she wanted to visit the bears? What could she do to make up for her mistake? Teachers can guide children to create and dramatize nonviolent alternative situations portrayed in the story.

Materials that encourage discussion of feelings or role-playing experiences also support social skills-development activities. Pictures showing children of diverse ethnicity, with and without disabilities, and experiencing a variety of emotions and stories that depict emotional events can generate discussions that encourage empathy and perspective taking. Puppets, dolls, and stuffed animals can help children act out scenes, using appropriate social skills. Books that show children coping with feelings and solving problems cooperatively also promote positive social behavior. With these materials at hand, teachers can readily guide structured presentations and discussions that will enhance children's abilities to negotiate conflicts and solve them nonaggressively while, at the same time, learning the skills of sharing, helping, and cooperating.

Provide equipment and materials that invite cooperation

Equipment that can be used by several children at once and materials that encourage children to help each other will also promote prosocial behavior. For example, children can help each other fasten paint smocks with Velcro closures. Group play with a parachute or large bedsheet demonstrates how everyone working together can make something wonderful happen. Tire swings and rocking boats elicit cooperation because they are best used by more than one child.

Provide materials to extend group play

Teachers may want to acquire complementary materials that can be brought out to support ongoing cooperative play. For example, children building together in the block area might participate longer if the teacher facilitates play by bringing out a set of play people, vehicles, or new building materials and by commenting, "Look how well you are working together!"

Points to Remember

Provide adequate resources to reduce conflict but not so many materials that children have no need to share. Providing materials that complement each other, such as small cars and trucks to use in the block area, can enhance play and reduce conflict.

Reduce the emphasis on possessions and focus instead on how children can take different roles to play together. Help children find roles that will lead them into the joint activity. For example, a child might use the phone to call the firefighters who are ready with hose and rubber boots.

Eliminate materials with violent themes or cultural or gender bias. Violence-related materials, such as toy weapons, encourage aggression that often carries over into all areas of the classroom.

Choose materials that celebrate diversity and show people of different cultures and genders, both with and without disabilities, engaged in everyday activities. Integrate materials from a variety of cultures into all areas of the room.

Create "thematic prop boxes" that suggest helping, cooperative roles for children to enhance cooperative play. Props designed around themes that encourage helping behavior, such as doctor, zookeeper, or garage mechanic, encourage children to act out positive roles, interact positively with one another, and be more likely to help each other during subsequent activities.

Choose books and stories that support prosocial and nonviolent themes. Help children to talk about these stories, to act out alternative endings, and to make connections to their own lives.

Provide materials that promote discussion and role playing to engage children's skills in perspective taking and prosocial problem solving. Puppets and dolls acting out stories with social conflicts to be solved help children increase their repertoire of nonviolent problem-solving skills and encourage less-verbal children to express their feelings in a nonviolent way.

5

Structuring Cooperative Activities

"Let's see who can make the best picture," says the teacher. "I'm going to hang the best ones on the wall." Five minutes later three children are hitting each other, fighting over the colored pens, insisting they each need all the pens to make their picture the best. **How could this activity be structured to prevent the fighting and to increase children's willingness to cooperate?**

Cooperation refers to an activity in which two or more people work together toward a common, mutually desirable goal. Truly cooperative activities involve interdependent behaviors among children, and they must permit children to negotiate, add their own ideas, coordinate their efforts, and "contribute to the structure and direction of the activity" (Goffin 1987, 78). In a cooperative activity the benefits for the group take precedence over the benefits for the individuals within the group. Besides their group focus, cooperative activities can be distinguished from competitive activities in that no individual or group attempts to "win" by beating out or defeating other individuals or groups, and consequently there are no "losers." Although it may be possible for group or team members to work together cooperatively while competing against another group, the goal of beating an opponent group sometimes renders the overall activity less than truly cooperative. The cooperative spirit encompasses mutual acceptance, encouragement, sharing, and constructive problem solving by all, and it excludes hostility, hurtfulness, putdowns, and rejection.

Increasing children's cooperative interaction skills is an important part of any approach to reducing violence. Violence is best dealt with as one of several interrelated types of social behavior. It is both a means of responding to interpersonal conflict and a powerful way of getting a reaction from others. When children learn a variety of social skills that allow them increased options, they are less likely to resort to violence. Cooperative activities, as compared to either individual or competitive activities, have been found to encourage perspective taking, peer support, more complex forms of social interaction, effective communication, and positive self-concepts (Goffin 1987). When teachers structure classroom activities that encourage children to practice cooperation skills, children usually show increased cooperation and decreased aggression during less-structured times as well (Davitz 1952; Shure & Spivack 1982). When teachers make a point of attending to preschool children's use of cooperative verbalizations, not only do such verbalizations increase, but at the same time cooperative behaviors increase while aggressive verbalizations and behaviors decrease (Slaby & Crowley 1977). The conclusion is that cooperative behavior is generally incompatible with violence. Increasing one usually decreases the other.

What research tells us

Relative to many other cultures, we in the United States have placed a strong emphasis on individual expression, individual achievements, and individual rights, rather than on group goals, social cooperation, and the common good. These cultural values are reflected in early childrearing styles and expectations, including the emphasis on individualized adult attention for infants and toddlers rather than on social experience with peers. We have come to accept as developmentally typical that toddlers and young preschool children will be highly egocentric and possessive of objects in their play, as well as negative toward authority. Popular culture has referred to this developmental period around 2 years of age as the "terrible twos." Some cultural groups routinely provide children with group care and cooperation training from infancy while placing strong value on group rather than on individual goals (e.g., in the former U.S.S.R. and on Israeli kibbutzim). It is noteworthy that even very young children in these cultures are observed to be strikingly less egocentric and more cooperative with adults and peers than are American children (e.g., Bronfenbrenner 1970). Such observations suggest that early cooperative behaviors may be more susceptible to cultural and educational influences than one might infer from descriptive American developmental studies.

It has been widely believed that preschool and kindergarten children have only limited ability to see another's point of view. It has been assumed, therefore, that truly cooperative activities, which require such perspective taking, are too difficult for them. However, research suggests that young children may not be as limited in perspective-taking ability as was originally thought (e.g., Rubin & Everett 1982) (see chapter 11). Furthermore, there is reason to think that perspective taking and social problem solving in young children vary with the situation and can improve when children have more opportunities to consider the views of others (Damon 1983). These findings suggest that it may be developmentally appropriate and potentially valuable to promote joint-venture cooperative activities among young children (Goffin 1987).

In our society we are becoming increasingly aware of the importance and the utility of cooperative effort for people of all ages. Increased expecta-

© BmPorter/Don Franklin

In true cooperative play, children plan the activity together and modify their own ideas in response to the ideas of others.

tions about how much cooperation is possible for young children and increased efforts to specifically teach cooperation to young children are consistent with the recent resurgence of interest in "cooperative learning" in elementary education, as well as in efforts to foster adult collaborative work skills in industry and technology. The early childhood educator has the opportunity and the challenge of helping to build a strong foundation of cooperative values and practices. For many years early childhood educators working with preschool children have tended to emphasize the development of cooperative values and skills to a greater extent than either the K–12 schools or parents and other caregivers of infants and toddlers. The years between ages 3 and 5 were for most children the first social experience with peers, and this time was regarded as appropriate for learning to cooper-

ate. Even so, early childhood programs for children 3 to 5 years of age in this country reflect the societal emphasis on the individual, and most do not stress cooperation to the extent that preschools in many other countries do.

Development of cooperative play

In addition to the cultural influences referred to above, children's capacity for learning cooperative behavior is related to developmental levels and personal experience. For example, children's ability to cooperate with others depends, in part, on the development of their ability to take the perspective of another person (see chapter 11). Both abilities increase with age and with guided social experience. Very young children tend to spend most of their playtime in solitary activities, although they may watch other children extensively and closely (Eckerman

& Rheingold 1974; Whiteside, Busch, & Horner 1976).

Near the end of their second year, children begin to spend increasing amounts of time in *parallel play*, in which two or more children work next to each other carrying out similar activities independently (Parten 1933; Whiteside, Busch, & Horner 1976). For example, two children might sit side by side, each using playdough independently. One might be making a ball, while the other might be using a rolling pin and cookie cutters.

Three- and four-year-old children engage in *associative play*, in which two or more children interact around a common theme, although each child still tends to pursue his own interests without being much influenced by the other child. These children might all choose to be making cookies at the playdough table, but each child still works independently.

As children approach 5 years of age (or earlier, depending on their levels of cognitive and social development and their experience), they sometimes engage in true *cooperative play*, which involves a mutually agreed-upon sharing of roles and activities. Children plan the activity together and modify their own ideas in response to the ideas of others. Conversations are reciprocal and meaningful, and rules of operation (either for games or for carrying out fantasy plots) are mutually accepted and important to the interaction (Parten 1933; Whiteside, Busch, & Horner 1976). As children become more adept at cooperative play, their skills increase in negotiating conflicts and assertively expressing their needs and rights without offending others. Effective conflict resolution skills require children to coordinate their activities with one another, take into account what their partner says, and see that their own needs and wants are understood (Eisenberg & Garvey 1981; Garvey 1984). Children engaged in cooperative play might create a meal using playdough and assign roles to each other. One child might make the cookies, while another cooks the stew, and a third child gets plates and silverware from the housekeeping area to serve the food.

Teachers' expectations regarding children's abilities to engage in complex social interactions and to cooperate effectively should be guided by an understanding of the children's developmental levels. Young or socially inexperienced children may require specific teacher suggestions about how to work or play together, because they may not have many of their own ideas about what to do. For example, a teacher might suggest to a child driving a truck through the block area that she deliver some blocks to another child who is building a garage nearby. Alternatively, a teacher might refer children to each other for help, saying, "Maybe Maryanne can help you take that painting over to the drying table. You could ask her to carry the other end of the paper."

Influence of friendship relations on cooperation

Friendship is an important factor in the social life of young children. Even toddlers as young as 1 and 2 years of age can develop close friendships with peers (Bronson 1975; Lee 1975; Mueller & Lucas 1975). Mutuality and complex interactions between friends increase as children grow older (Hartup et al. 1988). Children who are friends tend to engage in conflicts of less intensity and more equitable outcomes than do children who are not friends. When friends argue, they usually continue socializing with each other after the argument, whereas nonfriends are likely to stop their interaction after a quarrel (Hartup et al. 1988).

Children are most likely to become friends when they have shared a pleasant experience or worked together successfully to achieve a common goal (Heber & Heber 1957; Sherif et al. 1961; Blau & Rafferty 1970). Structuring cooperative classroom experiences in which children are likely to develop friendships can have an impact on the way conflicts are resolved and set the stage for helping children learn nonviolent conflict-resolution skills.

Competition and cooperation

In addition to fostering the development of friendship, experience with activities that require cooperation tends to reduce children's aggression and conflict. Children who have prior experience performing planned cooperative activities (e.g., drawing group murals or digging a class garden) are more likely than others to respond to frustrating situations by behaving cooperatively. On the other hand, children who have experienced playing games that are highly competitive (e.g., seeing who ends up in the winner's spot on the floor when a buzzer sounds) tend to act aggressively when they are frustrated (Davitz 1952). Competitive activities for children are generally much more conducive to aggression than are noncompetitive activities (Hartup 1983). In an experimental study of unsupervised group play, low

group cohesion and high competitiveness within the group were predictive of aggression (DeRosier et al. 1994).

Providing rewards to an entire group rather than to individual children can also be effective in encouraging cooperative behavior. For example, the class as a whole can earn a special activity or privilege for completion of a group project. Children rewarded as a group tend to be friendlier, more cooperative, and less antagonistic toward each other than children who are competing for individual rewards. In fact, direct competition for rewards can foster hostility and lead to aggression. The likelihood of aggression occurring increases as competition becomes more intense and promised rewards become bigger (Christy, Gelfand, & Hartmann 1971; Perry & Perry 1976; Rocha & Rogers 1976).

One of the first ways that young children all over the world learn about the social values and behavioral expectations of their culture is through the types of games they themselves play, the games they observe older children and adults playing, and the way these games are played. Although people in many cultures (e.g., the Inuit Eskimos of Canada) have for centuries played games with cooperative goals, genuinely cooperative games with no losers are extremely rare in the Western world (Orlick 1978). Even games for young children, such as "musical chairs," are often based on elimination down to one winner. In a country that places so much emphasis on winning and on athletic stars, many children drop out of sports at an early age and become spectators. In the late '70s and early '80s, a New Games Movement gained popular-

Children are most likely to become friends when they have shared pleasant experiences or worked together to achieve a common goal.

ity, promoting and publishing many wonderful games that focused on prosocial values, such as all players working toward a common goal, providing for valued participation by all players regardless of ability levels, and the absence of competition between individuals or teams (Sobel 1983). These games, which include imaginative child-tested games for children as young as 3 years of age,

present physical challenge, excitement, and fun. They are, therefore, a highly motivating way to foster cooperative skills and encourage prosocial behaviors (Bryan 1975).

Competition is an unavoidable part of our society. Although competitions can promote aggression, aggression is not a necessary result. The problem, as many see it, is what people allow competition to do to themselves and others (Weinstein & Goodman 1990). For example, striving to win at any cost is often done at the expense of full participation, self-esteem, and fun for all. At its worst, excess competitiveness can lead to cheating and hostility or violence between competitors. One sports commentator observed, "There is nothing wrong with competition in the proper proportion. Like a little salt, it adds zest to the game and to life itself. But when the seasoning is mistaken for the substance, only sickness can follow" (Leonard 1973, 47). Cooperative games can serve as an antidote to the excessive competitiveness in our society.

Preschool children usually have not yet formed strong competitive habits and expectations with regard to games. They can be very receptive to the introduction of genuinely cooperative games and to the positive social learning these games can provide. If we start young children off with a solid foundation of experience in cooperative games, they may later have a better chance of engaging in competition with good sportsmanship and with some perspective on the relative importance of winning.

Teaching guidelines

The more opportunities children have to actively participate in joint-venture cooperative activities in class, the more likely they are to behave cooperatively in a broad range of situations. The following suggestions for classroom activities all incorporate the principle of encouraging a *we* orientation rather than an *I* orientation. For example, children building a structure together can say, "Look at what we are doing," whereas children working on individual puzzles will talk about "Look what I did." The teacher's comments can encourage this feeling of group spirit and shared participation and can help children understand the advantages of cooperation and helping (e.g., "By working together, you made an amazing playhouse" or "When you helped each other clean up, everybody got to have their snack on time").

In the most valuable form of cooperative play, each child actively contributes to group decisions about what to do, how to do it, and who should do what. Thus, truly cooperative activities involve more than sharing resources or working individually on the same project (e.g., a group collage). Spontaneous cooperation often occurs when children find that their self-determined goals cannot be achieved without teamwork (Goffin 1987). A teacher's goal, therefore, might be to set up opportunities for such self-directed group activities and to encourage and support the cooperation when it occurs.

The richness of cooperative activities depends on the extent to which two or more active players

- share mutual goals,
- make decisions,
- share ideas and materials,
- negotiate and bargain,
- coordinate actions to accomplish goals, and
- evaluate their own progress (Goffin 1987; Salyer 1994).

The teacher may give some initial instructions or ideas. However, too much subsequent teacher direction or interference can take away from the cooperative nature and benefits of the activity. If a child seeks teacher input or assistance, she can encourage that child to go instead to a peer to ask questions and talk over ideas. It is important to allow children as much independence as possible in finding ways to continue and direct their own activities. Young children may need greater support, just as serious conflict situations may require teacher intervention. Even in conflict situations, the teacher's role can be to assist children to negotiate solutions between themselves, rather than to impose decisions upon them (see chapter 6).

Provide open-ended activities that invite cooperation

Providing space and materials that are set up to be used by two or more children facilitates cooperation. Open-ended activity areas (e.g., family-living areas, block-building centers, and water and sand tables) provide opportunities for cooperation. Some programs find it useful to designate one space (preferably a semi-enclosed space) for periodically changing particular types of dramatic play. For example, the children may decide at different times to outfit the area as a hospital, a restaurant, a tropical village, or a zoo.

The teacher can also encourage children's joint use of equipment that is often used by only one child at a time. For example, she can present standard play materials (e.g., Legos or formboards that allow creative designs) with the comment, "Let's see what you two can think of to do together with these." Teachers can also modify activities to require cooperation: two children can hold on to one basket to catch a ball, or a peer partner can guide a blindfolded child to pin the tail on the donkey (Goffin 1987).

Promote cooperative free play by using prop boxes

The most complex social interactions that occur during free play in preschool and kindergarten classrooms usually take place in the dramatic play area (Charlesworth & Hartup 1967; Quay, Weaver, & Neel 1986). Using props to suggest a variety of roles surrounding a common cooperative theme can encourage children to engage in interactive fantasy play and to practice cooperation as a natural outgrowth of their play.

Teachers might set up a classroom restaurant by providing props (e.g., menus, tablecloth, dishes, aprons, chef's hat, trays, money box, and credit-card imprinter) and by suggesting roles (e.g., cook, waiter, customer, and cashier). The teacher can then allow children to create their own restaurant play scenes. The cook might prepare food and give it to the waiter, who in turn serves the customer. Disagreements or conflicts might also arise (e.g., the waiter might make a mistake or the customer might not like the food). Developing these themes independently allows children to practice taking reciprocal roles and giving materials to others, as well as to explore mutual decisionmaking and ways of dealing with social conflicts.

Alternatively, a garage theme allows the mechanics to help or otherwise interact with customers, who ride by on tricycles or bring their cars or trucks for repair. Garage props might include a real gas nozzle, auto repair tools, mechanics' shirts, gas pump (e.g., created from

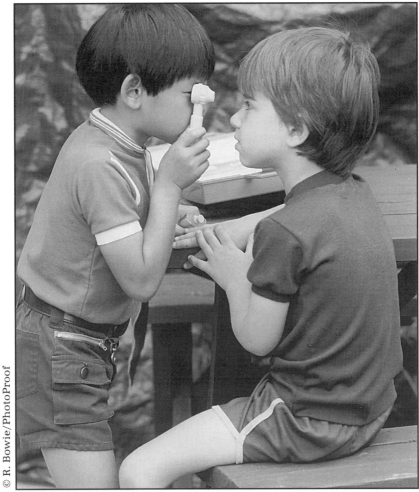

© R. Bowie/PhotoProof

Taking a set of props outside can encourage cooperative play on the playground, where high levels of physical activity sometime lead to aggression.

cardboard boxes or wood), flashlight, and repair-work order forms. Taking a set of garage props outside can encourage cooperative play on the playground, where high levels of physical activity sometime lead to aggression. Teachers can also bring in props to elaborate a theme that comes from the children themselves and reflects their experience or interests.

Including real objects in these prop sets enhances the value of the play and encourages children to act out the roles suggested by the material. The persistent teacher can request donations of real-life materials from hospitals, gas stations, restaurants, post offices, and stores. Materials can often be found at garage sales and surplus shops. Changing the materials as teachers observe children losing interest in the area encourages exploration of new cooperative roles (Howe et al. 1993).

Select or develop games that elicit cooperation and avoid competition

Cooperative or collaborative games, previously described, can be valuable and popular additions to a preschool or kindergarten curriculum. These games engage children in playing *with* each other rather than *against* each other, often toward a common goal. For example, various parachute games require many children to lift the chute together in different exhilarating ways. In a collaborative lotto game, all of the children participate in helping to fill up all lotto boards, rather than in competing to see which child completes his own board first. In three-legged running or back-to-back lifts (two children with linked arms try to rise from a sitting position), children must coordinate their efforts to achieve the goal. In a game called "blanketball," groups of children coordinate their efforts to keep a ball up in the air or to pass it to another group, using an outstretched blanket (Goffin 1987).

A teacher or program interested in cooperative, noncompetitive games can make use of the many available resource materials that prescribe a wide variety of socially constructive games children love to play (Fluegelman 1976, 1981; Orlick 1978, 1982; Adcock & Segal 1983; Sobel 1983; Parry, Walker, & Heim 1990). One particularly useful resource that presents a variety of games for young children is *Everybody Wins* (Sobel 1983). Some games are more suitable for use outdoors or in a gym because they involve considerable physical activity, while others can take place within the typical classroom. Most of the games allow for flexibility and adaptation to the wishes and needs of the group. Starting with ideas from resources such as these, teachers can encourage children to cooperatively create and carry out their own versions of games.

Certain games can be used to increase children's responsiveness to the play ideas of their peers. For example, children in a small group can each be given four to six identical square blocks. One child at a time has a turn as the "leader" in creating a structure or pattern that the other children copy, using their own sets of blocks. The followers are encouraged to check with the leader to find out if their designs are a match. Everyone following the leader gets a turn to be the leader. There are many other games in which one child chooses an action (e.g., an animal sound, a creative movement) that other children imitate. These games provide a structured and supportive setting for children to practice both taking the lead in activities and following the lead of others. These skills can then be encouraged in spontaneous play situations.

Structure group projects with a common goal

The teacher can promote activities that result in a joint product or other consequence for the group as a whole rather than individual rewards or achievements. For example, preparing a stew can be a project that allows cooperation over several days. On one day, the class might take a trip to the store to buy the vegetables, with each child participating. Two children might cooperate carrying a shopping bag with two handles. On another day, the children might work together to cut up the vegetables and put them in a Crock-Pot to cook to provide a meal for the entire group. Children's active participation in deciding what to cook, what to buy, and how to coordinate roles enhances the cooperative value of the project.

Carrying out a task that is important to the group also provides opportunities for cooperation. If a heavy "magic box" needs to be moved in preparation for a special show, several (supervised) children may work together to push the box into place. In thanking them, the teacher can point out that by working together they accomplished something that no one child could have done alone. On a daily basis, small groups of children can work together on common classroom tasks (e.g., setting the table, making playdough, or covering the sandbox). Another popular task that involves negotiation and coordination of effort is washing various items of school property (e.g., tricycles, plastic furniture, or dolls) (Adcock & Segal 1983).

In addition to working toward goals that benefit the children as a group, teachers can devise projects that benefit the larger community or others outside the class. Such projects might include working together to make gifts for children in a homeless shelter, performing for residents of a nursing home, or participating in neighborhood cleanup or recycling efforts. For example, a teacher might take the children on a trash-pickup walk around the school grounds. Children can collect the trash, separate items to be recycled, and make a group collage to show the results of their effort. The learning experience might be enhanced by recording a list of the children's words as they discuss the experience and their descriptions of the way the yard was before and after they cleaned it up. The teacher can help the children realize and be proud of their joint efforts and the benefits to their schoolmates and the community. Young children, thus, begin to experience the gratification that comes from cooperative efforts aimed at the greater good or at helping those in need. Such activities also help children to develop a larger sense of responsibility for the consequences of their individual actions. For example, one teacher found that after the children in her inner-city program participated in a strenuous project collecting recyclable trash from the neighborhood, they were less likely themselves to litter.

The teacher who is attempting to institute an antiviolence curriculum may consider choosing a cooperative group project that directly relates to real-life violence. For example, the class might decide to respond in some way to a child in their community who has been the victim of violence. Children might make something together to send to the hospitalized child or to her family. In addition to providing a cooperative and altruistic experience for the class, such an exercise gives children an opportunity to know that there are real-life consequences of violence and that they can show their caring in a tangible way. The experience may allow for discussions of gun and safety-related issues that are more personal and meaningful. Such projects might be considered controversial. Teachers should inform and consult parents. Their involvement will enhance the potential beneficial effects for their children.

When children cooperate to accomplish a common goal, point out that by working together they accomplished something that no one child could have done alone.

Early Violence Prevention

Set up group art or construction projects

Teachers can challenge groups of children to collaborate in creating structures of their own design (e.g., spaceships, boats, or mazes), using construction toys, art supplies, or recycled materials. These projects can be especially valuable if they follow interests or ideas raised by the children themselves or relate to class discussion of a topic of particular interest (e.g., dinosaurs or space exploration). Collaborative art sculptures offer another medium for cooperation. For example, a pipe-cleaner structure offers an ongoing classroom collaboration using hundreds of colored pipe cleaners. Children can twist the pipe cleaners together, creating a larger and larger structure that can be worked on over several days. Other group art projects include creating a mural of expressive colors that show how the children feel when listening to a piece of music, decorating a large box to be used as a playhouse, or making a group thank-you card to send to community members who hosted children's field trips.

These collaborative activities are most valuable if the children themselves determine the goals and procedures. For example, in decorating the playhouse box, if the teacher assigns each of four children one side of the box and one color of paint, children lose the chance for a truly involving cooperative experience. On the other hand, if she gives a group of children a variety of art materials to choose from (including three-dimensional objects to attach) and lets them determine how to decorate the box, a cooperative activity may result. Focusing the children's attention on the cooperative aspects of the project will increase the effectiveness of the activity. The teacher can comment on how well the children work together, how pleased they must be with their group effort, and how their cooperation results in a wonderful product they can all enjoy. The most meaningful group projects emerge from children's own interests and activities, and the children themselves help to shape the direction that the project takes (Katz & Chard 1989).

While encouraging cooperation during creative group projects, as well as during dramatic play and cooperative games (as described previously), the teacher will want to be as flexible as possible about boundaries of time and space and about "neatness," to allow ongoing group processes to proceed and develop in creative directions.

Model cooperation

When the teacher actively cooperates with the children in helping them achieve their goals (see chapter 12), she provides them with a powerful model for cooperative behavior. She can be especially aware of seeing the children's perspective, sharing ideas in an open-ended way, and coordinating her own efforts with the children's as much as possible. She can also comment on the value of her own cooperation (e.g., "I'm glad I can help you figure this out").

Points to Remember

Set up free-play activities that elicit co-operative behavior and provide opportunities for children to practice helping, sharing, and working together. Prop boxes enhance the opportunities for children to play cooperatively together around common helping themes.

Modify selected activities to require or encourage cooperation. Many individual or competitive activities can be converted into cooperative activities.

Select and develop cooperative, non-competitive games. Children play *with* rather than *against* each other, and there are no losers. Cooperative games promote prosocial behavior.

Provide group, rather than individual, rewards. Children can work together toward earning a desired outcome rather than competing for rewards.

Structure group activities in which children work together to accomplish a common goal. Cooking activities and group art or construction projects work well. Create group projects that reach out to others in need or that benefit the larger community.

Encourage joint-venture cooperative activities in which children make decisions, share ideas, coordinate actions, and evaluate progress. Provide support and initial direction, if needed, but minimize subsequent adult direction or interference.

Point out the specific advantages of co-operation and helping. Show children that these behaviors are valued and beneficial.

Model cooperation by working cooperatively with children. Demonstrate respect for their perspectives, goals, and decisions.

6

Responding in Effective Ways

Kevin grabs the truck from Justin, kicking and hitting to make him let go. The teacher grabs Kevin and says, "Kevin, why did you do that? Give that back to Justin." She talks to Kevin for a long time, reasoning with him and urging him not to hit. But 10 minutes later, Kevin is hitting Tanya with a wooden block, Tanya is crying, and the teacher is again talking with Kevin. **How could the teacher respond more effectively to help prevent a recurrence of Kevin's aggressive behavior?**

Children learn, in large part, from the *consequences* of their behavior. Whether children behave aggressively or cooperatively is often related to the particular responses they have experienced themselves or observed others experiencing. Children's social behaviors produce consequences from others, whether or not the consequences were planned by the teacher. The routine ways that teachers respond to children's behavior can have beneficial or detrimental effects. For example, attention from teachers and peers has a strong effect on children's behavior in the classroom. Teachers can use the powerful tool of *planned attention* to increase the likelihood that children will behave cooperatively and nonviolently rather than aggressively.

One way to minimize aggressive behavior in the classroom is to analyze the existing consequences for aggression and eliminate or reduce rewards for that behavior, including submission by peers and attention from both teachers and peers. Teachers can vigilantly watch for and respond to instances of children demonstrating cooperation, constructive problem solving, and nonviolent responses to conflict or provocation. They can point out the concrete benefits of the cooperative or nonviolent act for the children who are directly involved, as well as for others. In addition, teachers can motivate children to want to make changes in their own behavior. They can also use planful strategies in responding to aggression, including applying meaningful consequences and coaching children to use their social skills at the scene.

What research tells us

Researchers have studied extensively the effects of peer and teacher responses to children's violent and nonviolent actions. The nature and timing of responses from people—not only the deliberately applied consequences but the unconscious reactions—have proven to be extremely important in changing children's behavior patterns.

The ways consequences work

Consequences of behavior affect children in two distinct ways. In one way consequences serve to *inform* children of whether they are doing the "right" thing. Consequences are most effective in providing this information when they immediately follow the child's behavior. Young children quickly forget what they have done and find it difficult to make connections between events that are separated in time. A second way that consequences function is to *motivate* children to perform the action again or to avoid performing it. In many instances a single event provides both informational feedback and a pleasant or unpleasant experience that can influence the child's desire to repeat the behavior. When a teacher comments in a positive tone, "I see that you are working together; you both look like you're having fun sharing the blocks," the children not only receive information about the value of sharing, but they also may feel good for having earned the teacher's attention.

In most cases, young children (a) want and welcome teacher attention and (b) prefer to get positive rather than negative attention, once they know how. Of course, a child who dislikes a particular teacher or wants to rebel may try to avoid doing things the teacher approves. A child who wants attention from a teacher and lacks experience in gaining positive attention may try to do things that will upset her. The actual effect of any consequence depends upon the child's interpretation, not the teacher's intent. A big hug may serve as a reward for one child but as a punishing consequence for another child who doesn't like being hugged by the teacher.

The teacher's positive comments in the example of sharing blocks are designed to focus the children's attention on the intrinsic fun to be had working together rather than on the teacher's approval. One goal of prosocial-skills education is to help children realize that prosocial behaviors can be self-rewarding. In the long term, the pleasure derived from cooperative play will make teacher attention relatively unimportant. A social skill such as offering to trade can be very useful in gaining a desired object, thereby providing a natural reward for using the skill. However, children who initially lack the skills to play cooperatively with enjoyment and effectiveness may require specific teaching, in addition to teacher attention, to learn and use the skills that will eventually become rewarding in and of themselves (see chapters 5 and 9).

Teachers encourage desirable behaviors when they remind children of the natural, positive consequences that can be expected or when they offer related positive consequences (McGinnis & Goldstein 1990). For example, the teacher might say to a child, "When you ask in a friendly voice, then you may have a turn." Or she might say to a group of children, "If you all work together to clean up quickly, then you may have 10 extra minutes of storytime." Aggressive behaviors can often be discouraged by offering positive consequences for alternative behaviors. The child who habitually hits at snacktime might be told, "If you have quiet hands today at snacktime, then you can be my special helper to clean up." Offering positive consequences in this form can be a powerful way to encourage specific behaviors, especially from a child who is defiant, while avoiding the confrontation of stating a direct requirement.

Tangible rewards in the form of objects, activities, or privileges are also frequently used to recognize instances of prosocial behavior or the absence of aggression. This type of positive consequence has often been shown to be effective in changing behavior, both experimentally and in classroom practice (Hopkins & Mawhinney 1992). Many early childhood educators, however, oppose the use of tangible reminders (e.g., stickers) or material rewards to encourage positive social behavior in the typical preschool or kindergarten setting.

One anticipated problem with providing tangible reminders or rewards is that after children learn how the system works, they may begin to act cooperatively only to receive their reward. The concern is that by focusing on the sticker or prize, children may not pay as much attention to the intrinsic rewards of cooperative and nonviolent behaviors and may instead become dependent on the tangible rewards. Concern about potential detrimental effects of rewards on the development of children's self-reliance and internal motivation has been widely voiced (e.g., Schwartz 1990; Sutherland 1993).

While these issues are important to consider, the stated concerns about the use of tangible rewards seem overstated and generally unsupported by the body of research evidence. A recent large-scale metanalysis (i.e., cumulative analysis) of the results of all relevant studies in this area indicates that in most instances rewards do *not* decrease internal motivation (Cameron & Pierce 1994). The only adverse effects were found when children who were already highly motivated to engage in a task, such as coloring with markers, were promised a tangible reward ahead of time (rather than receiving it unexpectedly) and were rewarded simply for doing the task (regardless of their level of performance). Under this highly specific set of circumstances, children spent less time on the task after the reward was removed, although their expressed attitude about the task was unchanged. A very different set of circumstances apply when using rewards to help motivate a child to change established aggressive behaviors, increase infrequent cooperative acts, or begin to use a new social skill.

We do not recommend the routine or casual use of tangible reminders or rewards for social behaviors, but suggest instead that teachers rely principally on the kinds of "rewards," or positive consequences, that occur naturally in children's interactions with others. However, in light of the substantial body of research evidence, we believe that there are circumstances within the early childhood classroom for which the teacher may want to consider the short-term use of tangible reminders or incentives as part of an individualized plan to break a dangerous cycle of aggression. These circumstances, as well as the use of procedures designed to avoid possible dependence on incentives, are discussed in chapter 7.

Effects of teacher and peer reactions to aggression

Aggressive behavior is learned or strengthened when children are rewarded, as is often the case, for aggression. With a single aggressive act, a child may gain a toy or a turn; cause other children to cry, shout, or run; make adults move quickly and talk loudly; and make an object fly through the air and crash with a satisfying thud. Even if a child receives no tangible benefit from an aggressive act, causing a pronounced disturbance, with the accompanying peer and teacher attention, can be rewarding in itself.

In preschool classrooms, most aggressive acts result in the victim of aggression surrendering an object, crying, or running away. When this happens, the aggressor is more likely to launch an attack against the same child in the same way again. Other children in the classroom who observe this successful aggression, or who become victims of aggression, are likely to begin initiating attacks themselves, and their attacks are also likely to be rewarded. If aggression is allowed to continue in the classroom, it will increase dramatically over the course of a school year. The combination of observing peers acting aggressively and being rewarded themselves for their own aggressive activities will teach even initially nonaggressive children to behave aggressively (Patterson, Littman, & Bricker 1967).

Often a well-meaning teacher comforts a child aggressor or engages in extended reasoning and other "processing" of the episode immediately after it occurs. This type of response often functions as a reward for the child's aggressive behavior. Similarly, when the teacher's response is to rebuke or lecture the aggressor, the attention, even though negative and intended to stop aggression, may instead increase the likelihood that the aggressive act will recur (Risley & Baer 1973; Combs & Slaby 1977). Even simple teacher attention to aggressive words can increase aggressive acts (Slaby 1974; Slaby & Crowley 1977).

On the other hand, simply ignoring aggression can be equally detrimental. An adult who stands by and does not interfere in an aggressive situation may convey approval of aggressive behavior. Aggression in the presence of a nonresponding adult is likely to increase over time, presumably because children interpret an adult's nonresponse as tacit approval of their aggression (Siegel & Kohn 1959; Berkowitz 1993). Physical aggression against other children simply cannot be ignored; safety considerations and the rights of all children in the class to protection from *any* degree of physical harm require the teacher to intervene in some way. The question becomes how can she intervene in a way that minimizes the potentially rewarding effect of her attention, helps to reduce the chance of future aggression, and encourages the children to use alternative, nonviolent solutions to meet their needs or resolve conflicts.

Using teacher attention effectively

Giving attention to cooperative behavior increases the chances that children's cooperation will recur, but this is not a simple task for the teacher. Children who behave aggressively and disruptively are excellent attention getters, whereas children qui-

© Barbara Tyroler

Although some young children engage in disruptive behaviors to get teacher attention, they prefer to get positive rather than negative attention, once they know how.

Chapter 6—Responding in Effective Ways

etly involved in constructive, cooperative activities are easy to overlook. In addition, different forms of teacher attention are rewarding for different children. The effective teacher carefully observes children's responses to discover which forms of attention are most valued by each child. Attention means the most to children who have a friendly relationship with that teacher. The first priority of a teacher should be to build a relationship with each child in the class by being helpful, friendly, and generally supportive.

Teachers can adapt a variety of verbal and nonverbal forms of attention to suit individual children. Verbal forms of attention include the many types of conversation between children and adults, such as general comments about the day, suggestions, questions, invitations, challenges, or jokes. Especially positive forms of verbal attention include praise, encouragement, compliments, and expressions of affection.

Some nonverbal forms of attention include making positive gestures, laughing together, showing interest in the child by watching and listening attentively, and looking toward the child while smiling, winking, or clapping. Some children enjoy sharing a hug with a teacher, but others prefer less direct forms of physical contact. Assisting the child with a task, complying with the child's request, giving the child special materials, participating with the child in an activity, or waiting for the child to finish an activity are other ways of giving attention. The creative teacher will discover forms of attention that feel natural and are appropriate for each child in the class.

Giving encouragement instead of evaluative praise

Praise is perhaps the most widely used form of adult attention in the early childhood classroom, extended to bolster self-esteem and reward desirable behavior. The appropriateness, as well as the effectiveness, of many of the most common forms of praise has, however, been challenged, based on particular theoretical considerations and selected research findings (e.g., Hitz & Driscoll 1988). Critics claim that statements of praise may have detrimental effects when they express the teacher's approval or admiration, provide general commendations on the value of achievements, or set up comparisons between children. These forms of evaluative praise are thought to focus children's attention on approval from others, on external rather than intrinsic rewards, and on competition about achievement, rather than on personal development and the value of the activity itself. Frequent use of evaluative praise is said to work against the generally accepted educational goals of fostering positive self-concept, autonomy, self-reliance, and internal motivation. Striving to give high levels of evaluative praise can lead teachers to make unrealistic or noncredible statements and to overuse pat phrases rather mechanically (e.g., repetitions of "Good job") (Brophy 1981).

These are important issues that deserve careful consideration; yet, it should be noted that the factual basis for some of the claims is questionable. Most importantly, research does not support the claim that traditional praise reduces internal motivation. On the contrary, a recent large-scale metanalysis of all relevant studies revealed that verbal praise *increases* children's intrinsic motivation, as measured both by the time they spend on a task and their favorable attitude about the task (Cameron & Pierce 1994). Other strong claims against the use of praise seem subjective rather than based on evidence (e.g., the statement that children who observe others being praised will feel "manipulated") (Hitz & Driscoll 1988).

Even those who caution against the excessive use of evaluative praise recognize that supportive teacher comments and acknowledgments are very important for young children. Instead of evaluative praise, they suggest a form of verbal statement that has been called "effective praise" or "encouragement."

Encouragement . . . refers to a positive acknowledgment response that focuses on student efforts and/or specific attributes of work completed. Unlike praise, encouragement does not place judgment on student work or give information regarding its value or implications of student status. (Hitz & Driscoll 1988, 10)

The following are some of the key aspects of encouragement, as spelled out by its proponents:

• Encouragement is specific rather than general. The teacher might notice that a child worked on a painting for a long time or used a lot of blue but does not describe the painting as "great" or "beautiful."

• Encouragement focuses on improvement of process and on the child's efforts rather than on evaluation of a finished product. "You traded those cars all by yourselves" or "You're learning to let your friends know just what you need" may be preferable to "You're great at trading" or "Nice job."

• Encouragement involves sincere and direct comments delivered with a natural tone of voice. Being more specific and honest helps teachers avoid overused pat phrases or overstated praise that may lack credibility.

• Encouragement does not set children up for failure by applying laudatory labels that children cannot consistently live up to. "Jose, I noticed that you shared the playdough today with Alice" is preferable to "Jose, you're such a nice boy."

• Encouragement helps children develop an appreciation of their own behaviors and achievements and of natural consequences, rather than focus on teacher approval. "You must feel proud of how you all worked together to finish that project" or "Tonya looks happy that you asked her to play" are preferable to "I like the way you . . ." or "I'm so proud of you."

• Encouragement avoids comparisons or competition between children. "I noticed that you helped Mandel put away his puzzle" is preferable to "You are the best helper in the class." The context for any comparison is the child's own prior behavior. Statements such as "You are getting faster at calming yourself down" may help the child recognize change and progress (Brophy 1981; Hitz & Driscoll 1988).

Suggesting that teachers should never use verbal praise that expresses some form of evaluation or approval of children's behavior would be an overreaction not supported by research findings. Nevertheless, specified characteristics of the encouragement—and the rationale for encouraging rather than praising—are important correctives for the tendency to overuse evaluative praise.

For violence-prevention efforts to have lasting effectiveness, children must come to know that nonviolence is preferable to violence, based on their own experience and judgment—not just because the teacher says so or shows approval. A situation in which a child acts violently is not equivalent to a child's drawing a picture; it is not value free. A nonviolent solution to conflict is *better* than a violent solution. Teachers convey this value judgment when teaching nonviolence and when responding to the actions of particular children. The specificity of adults' comments, emphasized as a key feature of encouragement, is likely to be useful for children in the process of learning new behaviors and attitudes. For these reasons, encouragement in the form of simple, positive statements acknowledging specific aspects of prosocial and nonviolent behaviors and pointing to the intrinsic benefits of these behaviors can be very effective in promoting the objectives of violence prevention. Throughout this book we include examples of encouragement.

Teaching guidelines

This chapter offers suggestions for reducing and responding to the relatively mild forms of aggression most commonly found in preschool and kindergarten classrooms. Approaches to working with children who display more dangerous and persistent forms of early childhood aggression will be presented in chapter 7.

Convey the changeability of behavior

Meaningful violence prevention requires much more than imparting an understanding of the nature and consequences of violence (as discussed in chapter 2). It requires that children learn new behaviors and ways of thinking and, often, that they change existing behaviors. Introducing the concept of *habits* is a way to help children understand the changeability of behavior and, therefore, the changeability of violent behaviors. Young children can understand, given some examples, that a habit is something that you do over and over again without thinking about it. Encouraging them to give examples of "good habits" (e.g., brushing their teeth, saying "Thank you") and "problem habits" (e.g., yelling, hitting) advances children's understanding. Problem habits, which some people call "bad habits," cause trouble for the person with the habit and sometimes for others. Teachers can explain to children that everyone—even grownups, even *teachers*—has some good habits and some problem habits. Adult problem habits, such as smoking, might even be mentioned as an example. Children can be taught that people can learn new good habits and change problem habits, but that to do so takes time and practice. Someone with a problem habit is not a bad person, but rather just has a habit he needs to change.

Engaging children in understanding and working toward changing their own habits is one of the key components of programs designed to change children's aggressive behavior. When behavior change is determined and imposed from the outside, with little choice or participation by the child, legitimate concerns about manipulation and authoritarianism arise. However, if the child is included in the process and put in charge (to the extent possible) of wanting to change and control her own behavior, then behavior-change methods can be among the most powerful tools available to empower children to reach those goals. The teacher and the child then become partners, working toward the same goals, rather than adversaries in the process of behavior change.

Children may be more highly motivated to work on changing their own aggressive habits once they are convinced through educational violence-prevention efforts that stopping violence is necessary and personally valuable. As a group, children can lay out a set of consequences for violent acts, and they can be encouraged in a variety of ways to value the goal and the process of changing their own habits and to see doing so as a major source of accomplishment and pride. Statements of encouragement by the teacher help to acknowledge children's progress in learning or changing a given behavior. Within this context all of the strategies described in this book to bring about behavior change—including the use of attention, consequences, coaching, role playing, and training in self-control and problem solving—can be understood by children as ways to help them "change habits" and gain control. For example, when children accept the consequences that the group has established for violent acts, they do so in order to learn to change their own habits. When they respond assertively and refuse to submit to an ag-

gressive classmate, they also help the peer learn to change a problem habit.

When this idea of "habits that are changeable" is carried out consistently, young children take it to heart, thus making lasting behavior change. One troubled 5-year-old boy changed remarkably in his aggressive behavior by actively participating in a program that emphasized changing one's own behavior. He became very proud of himself for being "good at changing habits" and as a result was highly motivated to change other problem behaviors, such as taking too much time getting dressed in the morning. When asked what helped him most to change his habits, he said, "Doll playing!" (his term for role playing with a doll that was used as a skills-training tool in his classroom). He was later heard to say to an adult who was angry at a younger child, "She's little and has to learn to change habits, so don't get mad at her" (Arezzo 1978). In this case the boy's motivation to change his own behavior and his growing belief in his ability do so, combined with the teacher's methods for encouraging change, resulted in enduring changes in his behavior, self-esteem, and sense of control over his world.

Avoid encouraging the venting of anger on substitute "victims"

Teachers should not assume that anger is always behind children's aggression. If the teacher routinely tells children who act aggressively, "You must be feeling angry," he may be redefining other feelings the child is experiencing, such as frustration or impatience. The child is cued to feel angry when he might not otherwise, or he learns to use anger as an excuse for aggression. Even worse, if the teacher directs children to "get the anger out" by hitting something else (e.g., a "hitting pillow" or an inflatable punching doll), this procedure *increases* the likelihood of children subsequently behaving aggressively toward peers (e.g., Davitz 1952; Mallick & McCandless 1966; Berkowitz 1993).

The idea of offering a child a substitute target for aggressive behavior is a highly popular notion in our society and may be appealing to some teachers as an immediate response for a difficult situation. However, teachers need to know that the momentary redirection of aggression under these circumstances is short-lived. While the child may momentarily divert her kick from a peer to a doll, the tendency for that child to hit or kick another child at a later time is increased by the experience of hitting or kicking a material substitute. Rather than reducing the child's aggression, these substitution techniques usually contribute to increased aggression in the long run (Bandura 1973).

The attention the child receives from the teacher and peers while being given special equipment may also serve as a reward for aggressive behavior. Giving presumably angry children padded bats with which to hit each other or an inflated doll, as some counselors unfortunately suggest, is particularly ill-advised. This conclusion is not a mere extrapolation from theory. A substantial body of research has consistently demonstrated that children who play aggressive games, use aggressive toys, or practice aggressive behavior with inanimate objects are likely to behave more aggressively toward other chil-

dren afterwards (Feshbach 1956; Bandura 1973; Berkowitz 1993).

The suggestion is often made, based on the same theoretical model that encourages the "venting" of aggression, that children can work through and gain control over past violent traumatic events by acting out in play the role of the aggressor (e.g., Wallach 1993). The assumption is that children will feel empowered and will overcome feelings of fear and helplessness when they play the aggressor role (e.g., the violent burglar who had broken into their apartment).

There are a number of serious problems with encouraging children to play out aggressive roles, for any reason. For one thing, the observer can never be sure of the source of the aggressive play. It may reflect real-life experience or derive from imitation of a violent television hero. Secondly, when a child acts aggressively, even in fantasy play, some playmates may be victimized in that play. Other children may be caught up in the action and may imitate the aggression or retaliate, thus contributing to an escalation of real aggression. Research also tells us that role playing aggressive scenes is likely to serve as "rehearsal" of aggressive acts and lead to subsequent increases in real aggression (Berkowitz 1993). And suppose the child does feel "empowered" by acting out the role of the violent burglar. Is this the way we want children to feel empowered? Do we want them to think, even for a moment, that the only way to overcome violence is to become violent?

Young children do reveal in their play very important information about violent events and related feelings that they may be unable to verbalize. The sensitive teacher can be

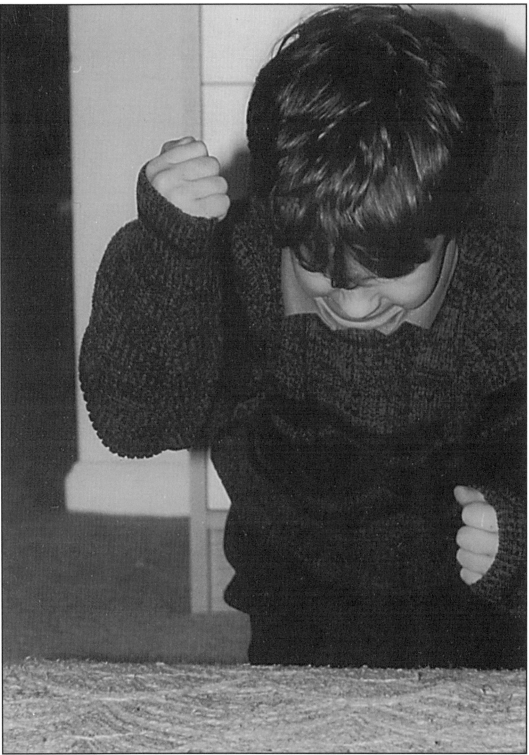

Encouraging a child to vent his anger on a substitute object, such as a punching doll or pillow, may momentarily divert him from hitting a peer, but this tactic often increases the child's tendency to use violence against others.

attentive to such information and use it to help her understand and guide the child. However, despite the popularity of the idea, there is no empirically based reason to think that encouraging the child to act out the role of the aggressor is therapeutic or helpful. Instead, using information revealed in the child's play, the teacher can help him learn ways to stay safe, get help when needed, or feel empowered by acting in a strong but nonviolent way (see chapters 2 and 10).

Intervene constructively while minimizing rewards for aggression

In considering and applying the research findings in this area, teachers will want to pay attention to consequences in their own classrooms: Do children succeed in obtaining toys by grabbing them from other children? Do some children in the classroom fill a victim role—crying, giving in, and running away from the offender? Do the adults in the classroom give attention to an aggressor by engaging the child in lengthy conversation about the incident at the time it occurs? All of these events can serve as rewards for aggression and increase the likelihood that the aggression will continue and possibly increase. The teacher's challenge is to prevent aggressive acts from being rewarded by either peer submission or teacher attention and to intervene, when necessary, in a constructive way.

One successful technique in achieving this balance when one child can be clearly identified as the aggressor is for the teacher to step between the children involved in the incident, ig-noring the aggressor but paying attention to the victim (Allen, Turner, & Everett 1970; Pinkston et al. 1973). Attention to the victim might include comforting a hurt child, giving the victim something interesting to do, or suggesting assertive, nonaggressive ways for the victim to deal with the aggressor. Depending on the developmental level of the child, the teacher can stand by the victim and prompt her with words such as, "Tell him no hitting!" or "Tell him, 'I'm playing with this now,'" or "What can you say to make him stop?" Some curricula recommend teaching children to say something such as, "That hurts. I'm not going to play with you!" and then to walk away from the aggressor (e.g., Parry 1993). The teacher at the scene could support the victimized child in his responding in this way. In certain circumstances the teacher might also encourage other children to support the victim and, perhaps, leave the scene with the victim. Children thus learn to avoid contributing to the escalation of violence that can occur if they join with the aggressive child (as children sometimes tend to do) and, instead, join with the victim and leave the aggressor unsupported following his aggression.

In using such techniques, the teacher would strive to eliminate rewarding the aggressive behavior with teacher attention, victim submission, or bystander support. When the teacher tells the victim, "*No* one is allowed to hurt you for *any* reason; you can tell him to stop kicking," the aggressor also hears the teacher describe the rules and responses to aggression, but without receiving immediate and direct teacher attention himself. In addition, the victim receives direct support and practice in coping assertively with conflict. Finally, the other children in the room observe that aggression is not successful, that the teacher supports assertive responses to conflict, and that the appropriate response to a victim is concern and support (see chapter 12). Encouraging the victim to be assertive while showing victim concern teaches an important lesson, whereas only giving sympathy may reward helplessness in the victim (see chapter 10).

When one child engages in minor and recurrent aggressive incidents apparently aimed at gaining attention, the teacher might choose to limit her intervention entirely to attending to the victim, thereby withholding all teacher attention from the aggressor. However, in other cases an aggressive incident can provide another type of learning opportunity for the aggressor. Once the teacher has assisted the victimized child in responding assertively and not submitting to the aggressive child, she might turn to the aggressor to explore the child's perception of the problem and guide her in practicing an alternative solution.

For example, if a child shoved a classmate and grabbed a book away from him, the teacher could first assist the victim in speaking up and taking back the book. Then, the teacher might talk to the aggressor and discover that she wanted that particular book for a special reason. The teacher might then say to her, "I understand now why you really wanted that book. But in this class no one is allowed to get something by hurting someone else. If you still want the book, one thing you can try

is to ask your classmate to trade books with you." The teacher can then assist the child in appropriately asking to trade. In carrying out this procedure, the teacher recognizes the child's feelings, suggests an alternative solution, and offers practical help in achieving the solution. Although the child who had acted aggressively does not receive immediate teacher attention following the aggressive act, her needs and feelings are ultimately attended to in a constructive way.

When more children than one are simultaneously acting aggressively toward each other, the teacher can intervene as quickly as possible to stop the aggression in a low-key, matter-of-fact way and then coach the children in resolving the conflict nonviolently (see chapter 8). If the aggression has escalated to the point that the children are highly agitated and are having difficulty controlling their aggressive actions, the teacher may choose to separate the children initially, saying simply, "There is no hitting in our school. Hitting hurts. When you are ready to talk calmly, I'll help you work it out." The teacher can ensure that the children are physically separated, avoid further discussion with them until they are calm, and then bring them back together to help them negotiate a nonviolent solution to their conflict. The goal here is to give minimal attention to the aggressive incident itself and to focus instead on the problem solving that follows the teacher's cue for the children to calm down first. If self-calming strategies have been introduced to the class (see chapter 8), the teacher might help support children in using these strategies in this situation.

Use reasoning effectively

Using reasoning with children is important in helping them to understand the reasons behind the rules and ultimately in fostering their own development of moral judgment (Galinsky & David 1988). Reasoning, as compared to other disciplinary techniques, generally fosters the long-term achievement of self-control and self-regulation, even in toddlers (Chapman & Zahn-Waxler 1982). However, although using reasoned discussion can effectively increase self-regulation of aggression in the long term, it is important for the teacher to avoid engaging in extended reasoning while aggressive or destructive behavior is occurring or has just occurred. It is best to apply such reasoning efforts at another time when the child is more receptive and the teacher would avoid inadvertently rewarding aggressive behavior by giving attention to it.

After initially responding to an aggressive incident by attending to the victim, the teacher might engage the aggressor and the victim together in a discussion a few minutes later when they have calmed down. Children generally respond best to reasoning that focuses on the harm caused by aggression, emphasizes the feelings of both the victim and the aggressor, and engages them in discussions of what else they might have done (Zahavi & Asher 1978). It is often ineffective to ask the child *why* he hit a classmate. Rather, the teacher should draw the focus to the painful effects of the aggression on all of the children involved. The teacher might say, "You know hitting hurts. You both were really upset when Keisha grabbed the shovel and you began hitting each other. What could you have done differently that would have worked out better for both of you?" In some cases it may be appropriate to have the children act out a better alternative, with teacher guidance and encouragement. Many teachers find it effective to briefly acknowledge the apparent feelings of the aggressive child and follow with a statement of the rule or contingency that applies. For example, the teacher might say, "I know that it's hard for you to wait for a turn, but hitting is not allowed."

A particularly good time to use reasoning is when the child is demonstrating the desired alternative behavior. For example, for a child who deliberately and repeatedly rides too fast and crashes his tricycle into playmates, the teacher might set a classwide contingency that, because crashing is dangerous, anyone who crashes a tricycle will have to give it up for the rest of the playtime. If the child then crashes, the teacher can briefly tell her, "No crashing—you have to get off the tricycle," without further reasoning. The next time the same child is noticed riding carefully at a reasonable speed, the teacher might want to specifically encourage her to continue this behavior and discuss with her the benefits of riding carefully. In this way the teacher rewards nonviolent behavior with his reasoning attention and is essentially saying, "Let me tell you why what you are doing is right," rather than the more typical, "Let me tell you why what you are doing is wrong."

Do your reasoning with a child when she is showing nonviolent behavior. When a child is careening around and crashing her tricycle into other children, be brief ("No crashing—you have to get off the tricycle"). Wait until you notice her riding safely and then explain why safe riding is best.

Another effective learning experience for a child who is often aggressive is to hear the teacher comment on the positive behavior of another child ("Dan is riding his trike safely"). In using this strategy, the teacher wants to avoid any direct or implied comparison between children. The approach provides a useful way for teachers to convey rules, values, and approval of particular behaviors, while avoiding lecturing the misbehaving child.

When a child inadvertently hurts another, it is appropriate for the teacher to encourage the child to apologize and tell the other child that he did not mean to hurt him. However, the common practice of forcing the aggressor to give a verbal apology to the victim following a deliberate act of violence is not recommended. In addition to providing attention to the aggressor, the apology is forced and not sincere, as both the aggressor and victim usually know. Furthermore, both children may get the idea that it's OK to hurt someone as long as you say you're sorry afterward. In fact, some young children learn to apologize profusely after a deliberate violent act and seem to expect adult praise for apologizing. Teachers can use reasoning, instead, to teach both the aggressor and the victim that deliberately hurting others is *not* acceptable, is not made right by a simple verbal apology, and will result in meaningful consequences.

Design meaningful consequences

Teachers may want to apply one of the following types of meaningful consequences to specific aggressive behavior:

- related corrective consequences,
- reparations, and
- immediate practice of alternative behaviors.

These consequences should *not* be thought of or applied as punishment. Rather, they provide the means by which to help children take greater responsibility for the consequences of their own behavior and learn to follow reasonable rules about that behavior. These are learning tools and can be explained to children as such. Whenever possible, children might participate in setting up class rules of behavior and related consequences for breaking those rules. Involving children in this way can increase the educational benefit of using consequences, children's understanding of how consequences help one learn, and their willingness to follow the procedures they helped to design. Before applying any new rules or contingencies, children need to know the reasons behind them. Demonstrations and role playing with puppets or dolls may be useful in achieving this purpose.

When a new consequence is being applied or a problem is new for a given child, using one clear reminder/warning helps the child avoid the problem behavior and its consequence (e.g., "Remember, crashing is not allowed; if you crash again, you will have to get off the tricycle"). Once a rule and consequence are established and known to the children, the consequence can be stated and applied in a matter-of-fact way immediately following an aggressive behavior, without blame, criticism, or extended discussion. Since the consequence itself is designed to teach responsibility and reduce the occurrence of aggression, strong teacher displays of disapproval or anger are unnecessary and may be detrimental to the learning process. Teacher anger may be very upsetting to some children, and other children may enjoy the power of making the teacher angry.

If the concept of changeable habits has been introduced, children can understand that the aggressive behavior is unacceptable and that the *only* purpose of the consequence is to help them change that problem habit. When discussing a particular aggressive behavior, teachers can help children understand the problems it produces for them and others and the real benefits of changing the behavior. As a result, children may be more highly motivated to work on changing their own aggressive behaviors in a variety of ways, including the accepting of meaningful consequences. The application of consequences works best when both teacher and child see it as a useful learning tool and not as a form of punishment or shame.

Related corrective consequences. In many circumstances aggressive actions lend themselves to the application of related corrective consequences, such as having toys or privileges removed or not being allowed to participate in play. Whenever possible, these consequences should be applied immediately so that the child can most readily associate them with his own misbehavior. If a girl belligerently breaks the rules or hurts others in the course of a game, she may be required to lose her turn or, if the problem persists, to be out of the game. If a boy repeatedly kicks others with his new pointy boots, he may be required to remove his boots for a period of time. In this case the consequence also immediately reduces the risk of further injury. If a child aggressively cuts in line by pushing ahead of other children, she may be directed to go to the end of the line instead of back to her previous place.

A consequence might involve taking away a toy or piece of equipment that the child has used in a dangerous way. For example, the class might help the teacher set a rule that in order for children to stay in the block area, they have to use the blocks in a safe way that does not hurt or endanger themselves or others. Teachers might use examples of safe and unsafe behaviors to help the children clearly understand the difference. Then, if a child deliberately hits a classmate with a wooden block, he may be told, "If you use the blocks to hurt others, you have to leave the block area for the rest of free play" or "for five minutes." If the child does not leave voluntarily, he may need to be physically guided out of the block area. It would not be effective to give him a choice about leaving or to argue with him about his behavior while he remains in the block area. Once the consequence is applied and the child is out of the block area for a brief period of time, the teacher may want to help him problem solve about alternative behaviors he could have used. However, if hitting with the blocks is a repeated occurrence for this child and it has been discussed before, the teacher may want to avoid following a repeated incident with even *this* much teacher attention and, instead, elect not to discuss it at all, letting the consequence speak for itself. She may seek other ways to help this child that are not directly linked to the block-hitting incidents.

Another possible meaningful consequence for aggression is a brief separation from activities or from activities and classmates. Such a consequence has been referred to as "quiet time," "sitting-out time," or, most commonly, "time-out." In helping children understand how time-out is related to aggression, the teacher might explain in the following way: "Hitting someone is not allowed when we are playing in this class. If you hit someone, you need to spend time not playing." Because time-out is both controversial and potentially problematic in its application, we present a more detailed discussion of its use in chapter 7.

Reparations. Having children attempt to "repair the damage" caused by their actions is another form of meaningful consequence that might be considered in some instances of hurtful or destructive acts (Azrin & Besalel 1980). The use of this procedure supports a violence-prevention philosophy by teaching children to recognize how their own actions can hurt others and to take responsibility for those actions. The child who has caused another person pain, injury, or loss through destructiveness can be called upon to repair or "make up" for the harm she has caused, sometimes by doing something extra for the person she hurt. Directing the aggressor to assist the injured child (e.g., by getting ice to put on the bruise) is one means of reparation for deliberate physical violence. Reparation for acts that destroy or damage property might include having the child expend considerable effort to clean up, repair, or replace the damaged objects. For example, the teacher might say to a child, "Because you knocked over the other children's structures on purpose, you will need to help put away all the blocks in the block area." Reparation is not always practical for every minor incident, but it could be used when problem patterns develop. In those cases the children in the class, particularly the victim and the aggressor, might participate in determining what kind of reparation would be fair and helpful.

Immediate practice of alternative behavior. Guiding a child in practicing an alternative appropriate behavior can be instructive, especially immediately after a hurtful act. For example, some children have a tendency to hurt others because of careless or hurried actions. If unchecked, unintentional injury to others can escalate into conflict and violence. When the injury is unintentional, an adult can cue the child to apologize (e.g., "I'm sorry; I didn't mean to bump you"), thus reducing the chances that the injured child misinterprets his action. Then, the child might be directed to practice the previous activity in a slow and careful way so as to avoid hurting anyone. For example, if Louie knocks over Pedro by running past him roughly in a confined space, Louie could be asked to practice walking up to Pedro, saying, "Excuse me" or "Please move over," and walking slowly past him without knocking into him. Teacher guidance could include giving directions, cuing, or modeling the appropriate behavior, as needed. For persistent problems, the child might be directed to practice the appropriate behavior more than one time following each problem incident (Azrin & Besalel 1980). Guiding the child through appropriate behavior in this way, even once per incident, is likely to be more effective in helping him learn how to avoid hurting others than would be giving him a reprimand or simply requiring him to apologize.

Defuse conflicts before they escalate

One of the best times to coach social skills or to involve children in problem solving about how to deal with conflicts is during a disagreement *before* aggression has occurred. Teachers can defuse potential aggressive confrontations by helping the children define their problem and come to an agreement (see chapter 8).

To help younger or less-experienced children develop these skills, the teacher can offer specific suggestions, such as, "You can *ask* Maria to move over," "Tell Peter, 'I'm playing with this now,'" or "You can *ask* Joan to trade with you." When a teacher sees that a child is becoming frustrated or angry with a classmate, he can intervene quickly to help calm the child (if necessary) and to remind that child about how to use words to express her feelings and needs to her peers. The likelihood of aggression will decrease if the teacher then also guides the children to follow these suggestions by providing verbal cues and modeling to help the children work the problem through to a nonviolent solution. In addition, the children gain experience in learning new conflict-resolution strategies for future use.

Once children have practiced prosocial strategies with this type of teacher guidance, they can be encouraged to think of solutions themselves and eventually to negotiate differences in coming to an agreement. However, even when young children reach this point, it can be critically important for the teacher to intervene in tense situations before aggression occurs and play a mediating role in order to help the children stay calm, express themselves, and listen to each other. In situations in which physical aggression is not imminent, the teacher might observe unobtrusively and allow the children to work things out as independently as possible.

A teacher may be able to avert aggression by closely watching a child with a history of aggressive behavior, such as roughly grabbing toys or barging into other children's play. By anticipating from the child's actions when he is about to have a problem with other children, the teacher could possibly head off trouble by reminding him of specific actions he can take, for example, by suggesting ways that he could ask for an object, for inclusion, or for a trade. Children are more likely to cooperate voluntarily with a child who asks for something than with a child who takes aggressive action (Spivack & Shure 1974). However, learning to ask nicely carries no guarantee of acquiescence and is only the beginning of the process of learning to negotiate and respect the rights of others. By actively guiding the child before an anticipated aggressive act, the teacher has a chance to help him and his classmates gradually build these complex skills. If results of the child's efforts are disappointing or frustrating to him, the teacher is there to offer sincere encouragement for his efforts and to help him find another rewarding activity. Thus, when a teacher arrives to mediate a potential conflict before violence occurs, children receive the guided support they need to develop and practice nonaggressive problem-solving skills. As children develop these skills, teacher mediation will become less necessary.

Attend to cooperative behavior

Because cooperative behavior generally is incompatible with aggression, teachers can control aggression by directing their attention and encouragement to specific instances of sharing, cooperating, and helping, as well as to specific instances of nonviolent responses to conflict. A group of children working well together, negotiating

Teachers foster prosocial development when they focus their attention on children's cooperative, nonviolent social interactions rather than on aggressive behavior.

problems, sharing materials, and carrying out joint projects has so much fun that the interaction itself provides its own reward. The teacher can comment briefly on how much fun the children are having by playing together, thereby strengthening their feelings of positive involvement. Introducing additional materials to the group without disrupting the flow of play can extend the play and provide teacher attention, making it more likely that these children will behave cooperatively in the future. Children building in the block corner, for example, might welcome additional small cars, miniature furniture, or play people.

One effective teaching technique for increasing cooperation is to suggest a specific cooperative behavior and to give the child positive attention—a smile or simple comment of acknowledgment—when the suggestion is followed. For example, two children both want to play with a prized gold car. The teacher suggests that Keisha may use it for five minutes (or "until the big hand on the clock reaches 3") and then Jamal may use it for five minutes. Jamal may need a reminder or assistance in appropriately asking for the car when the five minutes is up. The teacher can then reward their cooperative turn taking by smiling, by making a comment such as "You both remembered that it's Jamal's turn," or by bringing additional toys for the children to play with together (Doland & Adelberg 1967; Hart et al. 1968).

Specifically noticing children's prosocial verbal comments can also be effective. Children who are encouraged to say nice things to each other are more likely to behave cooperatively with each other as well. When a child has made a positive verbal statement to another child, simply noticing it and making a nonevaluative comment (e.g., "I heard you say, 'Thank you,' to Carlos" or "I heard you tell Gina that you are her friend") helps increase children's verbal and physical cooperation and decrease their verbal and physical aggression (Slaby & Crowley 1977). This type of specific and nonevaluative teacher encouragement is more effective than pat phrases of evaluative praise, such as "Good girl!"

As the teacher watches for instances of cooperation and nonviolence for which to give encouragement, other children in the group hear her remarks—"You all look like you're having fun" or "When you asked if you could use the red marker, Talia gave it to you." Hearing such comments about how much fun cooperative play is or how nonviolent approaches work, children will be more likely to cooperate and act nonviolently themselves. Interacting with peers without conflict and receiving positive attention from the teacher combine to make children feel happy and good about themselves. The positive cycle continues because children are most likely to share and cooperate when they are in a positive mood (Staub & Sherk 1970; Moore, Underwood, & Rosenhan 1973; Galinsky & David 1988).

Attention from peers can also serve as a powerful reward for positive social behavior. Asking children to comment on instances of helping and sharing that happened during the day calls their attention to these actions and highlights their classroom value (Eisenberg & Mussen 1989). Some classrooms have used an approach in which for a few weeks children are encouraged to drop a plastic chip into a clear jar whenever they hear or see a "kind act," simply to help children begin noticing and appreciating kindness by others. The goal of this exercise is not primarily to single out the behavior of individual children but rather to have the whole class appreciate and perhaps discuss the many ways they have been kind to each other, as they see the jar filling up.

* * *

All children's behavior results in responses of some kind from others and from the environment. Often, aggression and other problematic behavior in a classroom get rewarded without the teacher's awareness. By noticing consequences and planning for responses that support positive social interactions and discourage aggression, teachers have a dramatic influence on the social climate of the classroom, on the behavior and adjustment of individual children, and on the extent to which violence is a problem in the classroom.

Points to Remember

Emphasize that behavior can be changed and motivate children to want to learn new habits and change problem habits. Encourage children to value the goal and the process of behavior change and self-control.

Avoid encouraging the venting of anger or the use of alternative targets for aggression. Such practices usually increase the likelihood of subsequent aggression. Recognizing that anger is only one of many reasons for aggression, do not assume that a child who acts aggressively does so out of anger.

Analyze classroom interactions and eliminate or reduce rewards for aggression. Do not allow children to gain toys or unnecessary attention from either peers or adults by behaving aggressively.

Intervene in aggressive episodes by prompting and supporting assertive behavior by the victim, without paying direct attention to the aggressor. Step between two fighting children and suggest to the victim specific words and actions to use.

Involve children in discussions about alternative solutions to problems and their consequences at times when aggression is not occurring. Remind children that hitting hurts and fighting makes people unhappy. Help them discover alternative, nonviolent actions that would make them feel better.

Structure meaningful consequences for aggressive acts that help children take responsibility for their actions and control aggressive impulses. These consequences can include actions specifically related to the behavior, reparations to the victim, or immediate practice of alternative behaviors.

Intervene in conflicts before violence takes place and guide children toward mutually agreeable resolutions. Coach children in asking for what they want, listening to each other, and finding ways to resolve conflicts nonviolently. Phase out teacher mediation as children learn the skills to solve problems on their own.

Focus teacher attention on cooperative and nonviolent social interactions. When children are playing cooperatively, encourage them by noticing and pointing out the benefits of such play for the children. Comment on how specific nonviolent behaviors (e.g., expressing strong feelings verbally) are effective ways to achieve their goals.

7

Helping Children with Aggressive Behavior Patterns

Four-year-old Chris has started biting Tony. Sometimes Chris bites during conflicts, but other times he does so with no apparent provocation. The teacher has tried to find out what might be bothering Chris, and she has explained to him that biting hurts. But Chris's biting has increased. Tony has become fearful and withdrawn, and now he is strongly resisting coming to school. The teacher's reassurances fail to comfort Tony. **What are the teacher's responsibilities to Chris and to Tony? How can she best meet these responsibilities?**

Physical aggression in young children has many contributing causes. The child who shows severe or persistent patterns of aggression may be demonstrating behaviors that were learned by experiencing victimization, being encouraged and rewarded for behaving aggressively, witnessing powerful violent models, or watching portrayals of violence on television. Emotional problems, traumatic experiences, or deficits in social skills can also be contributing factors. Some children may have temperamental tendencies that predispose them to high impulsivity, and these tendencies can combine with learned factors to contribute to the development of aggression. Considering the level of violence that many American children face, it is not surprising that aggressive behaviors are commonplace and often reach serious proportions in early childhood program settings.

Whatever the source of their aggressive behavior, young children can seriously hurt peers, staff, or themselves by throwing heavy objects, using sharp objects as weapons, punching, biting, scratching, kicking, or pulling hair. Biting can be particularly problematic because of the high risk of infection from human bites. Spitting is another aggressive behavior that children and adults often perceive as an extremely offensive and provocative personal attack, although it is not usually physically harmful. In addition to possibly sustaining physical injury, other children may become emotionally upset, fearful, or even traumatized by repeated violent behavior or threats from a peer. When any such aggressive behaviors occur, the teacher's paramount responsibility is to control or stop those behaviors and prevent their recurrence—for the sake of the children who act aggressively, the potential victims, the children who witness the events, and the program's overall goal of promoting nonviolence. Beyond applying routine strategies described in other chapters of this book, teachers can design specific strategies to help children deal with extreme levels, unusual forms, or persistent patterns of aggressive behavior.

What research tells us

Any attempt to help young children cope with violence in their lives must include a highly effective program for preventing and stopping children's violent behaviors in the classroom. There are a number of reasons for this.

First, if we allow young children to use violent and destructive behaviors to express feelings or to gain attention and other rewards, they are likely to show continuing and escalating patterns of violence as they get older. Early aggressive behavior is a strong predictor of later violence, antisocial behavior, and other serious adjustment problems (APA 1993; Pepler & Slaby 1994; Yoshikawa 1994). Stopping children's early violent behavior helps to prevent their developing aggressive behavior patterns that may lead to later severe violence.

Second, if violence is permitted in the early childhood program, other children may learn to accept and imitate it. Alternatively, they may learn to fear and submit to violence, thereby perpetuating a cycle of increased violence and victimization (Patterson, Littman, & Bricker 1967; Schwartz, Dodge, & Coie 1994).

Third, if we want children to learn the message that violence can be stopped and replaced with nonviolent alternatives, then we must demonstrate these principles in children's social world. If violence is allowed to continue in classrooms or child care centers, how can we expect children to believe that it can be stopped elsewhere?

This chapter focuses on children with persistent or severe patterns of aggressive behavior. In order to help these children become cooperative, nonviolent members of the group, the teacher may routinely employ a broad set of general strategies described in this book. In some instances, however, these strategies will not suffice. Both research and practice show that more focused methods are sometimes needed to change well-established habits of aggression in individual children. For example, the common practice of pointing out that aggression hurts others, while effective with many young children, may be ineffective or even counterproductive with children who regularly show high levels of aggression. Although most children respond to a victim's pain and distress by stopping or reducing the level of their hurtful acts, some children with high levels of aggression respond to their victim's pain by laughing and increasing the aggressive attack (e.g., Patterson, Littman, & Bricker 1967; Perry & Perry 1974). With these children, repeating the message that aggression hurts provides neither new information nor a persuasive reason for changing the behavior.

If something more than business as usual is needed to confront the very aggressive behavior of some children, what kind of additional intervention should be used? Research and classroom experience suggest that by applying individualized programs of behavior change, along with their usual guidance strategies, teachers are able to help children who otherwise cannot be reached. Effective behavior-change programs are based on observation and tailored to the actions and needs of individual children. They may encompass a range of positive incentives and corrective consequences and, in some instances, tangible-reminder or reward systems and time-out procedures (e.g., O'Leary & O'Leary 1972; Kazdin 1975; McGinnis & Goldstein 1990; Hopkins & Mawhinney 1992). If teachers choose to use such behavior-change strategies, in most cases they should see results within a limited period of time. They can then reduce or even discontinue use of these procedures as naturally occurring social consequences come into play more strongly. Thus, these strategies need not be viewed as ongoing methods of behavior *control* but rather as short-term methods of behavior *change*.

Many early childhood educators are reluctant to use structured behavior-change procedures and believe that these procedures are unnecessary, if they conscientiously apply tried-and-true methods for helping children to develop self-control and positive social skills (e.g., by setting clear limits, modeling and encouraging expected behavior, and reasoning with children). Teachers are justifiably concerned that behavior-change techniques may be overused, misused, or used in harsh or punitive ways (Greenberg 1988). They also fear that children— and perhaps they themselves as teachers—may become overly dependent on these methods, which are viewed as an external and authoritarian means

of controlling behavior. These concerns deserve careful consideration. Yet, they must be weighed against the pressing needs and rights of the young child who is highly aggressive to receive the most effective and timely intervention possible, as well as the equally important needs of classmates to be protected from that child's aggression.

For example, if a child showing serious levels of aggression does not receive effective intervention in the regular early childhood setting, then she may be referred for special education services, based solely on the aggressive behavior. Special education services are limited and costly, and the labeling and tracking that often accompany such placement may be detrimental for a child with no other special needs beyond changing her aggressive behavior. It is surely preferable for early violent behavior to be "nipped in the bud" within the early childhood program setting whenever possible. Behavior-change techniques, applied with sensitivity and safeguards against possible misuse, offer an effective means of changing serious childhood aggression that other conventional classroom methods fail to alter.

Violence-related traumatic experiences or emotional disturbance may contribute to violent behavior for some children. In such cases the children and their families may need additional support, intervention, referral services, or even an eventual change of placement. However, as long as the child remains in the group, it is important for the teacher to consistently use teaching and behavior-change strategies that help the child to stop and replace violent behaviors.

Even if the teacher suspects underlying emotional problems, she needs to maintain clear expectations, teach and support nonviolent behaviors, and apply effective consequences for destructive behaviors. In fact, it has been argued that providing firm but appropriate limits is particularly important with young children who come from chaotic or violent environments, in order to maximize their sense of security and safety (Wallach 1993).

Teaching guidelines

Aggressive behaviors often are well established, even in young children, and rewarded in many different ways that cannot be completely controlled. Therefore, effective intervention to reduce aggression requires a range of general teaching strategies, including the use of meaningful consequences, to offset previous learning and uncontrolled rewards (as described in chapter 6 and throughout this book). When working with children who display high levels of aggression, supplemental strategies beyond those already described may be needed. Key supplemental strategies include (1) designing individualized behavior plans, (2) using tangible reminders and rewards, (3) initiating a particular corrective consequence—time-out, and (4) providing additional support for children who act aggressively.

Design a plan for the individual child

The early childhood teaching and administrative team should approach systematically the challenge of helping a child who shows severe or persistent patterns of aggression. They might make a plan that includes the following steps:

• Observe the child's behavior and related circumstances.

• Develop and implement an individualized behavior-change program.

• Record and review the results of the program on an ongoing basis.

• Revise the program as needed.

It is also helpful for program staff to have regular contact with the child's family to exchange information, discuss progress or problems, and work together in a consistent way to help the child.

In the observation phase, program staff can make an effort to determine both the circumstances that tend to promote aggressive behaviors and the consequences for the child that most frequently follow aggression. If time and resources permit, it can be useful to list briefly a number of aggressive incidents on a page with three columns, labeled Antecedent—Behavior—Consequence (or A—B—C). Briefly describe the child's aggression in the middle column under Behavior. In the Antecedent column list the location and the events that immediately preceded the aggression. In the Consequence column note any immediate results (including responses by teachers and peers, as well as material gains or losses) that follow the aggression. Looking over the list, perhaps reviewing it with a supervisor or behavioral consultant, is helpful in determining patterns affecting aggression. Understanding the situational factors that elicit aggression, as well as the consequences that serve to reward it for the child, is important in designing a plan for change tailored to that child's needs.

For example, if the teacher observes that a child appears to engage in violent behaviors as a way to avoid an undesirable activity, he might teach the child to request a break or change of activity in an acceptable way. If a child is observed using certain aggressive behaviors to gain attention, the behavior plan can be designed to minimize the attention received for those behaviors and at the same time to help the child learn appropriate ways to gain attention. Further, noting a situation in which a child frequently engages in aggression (e.g., during free play at the swings) alerts the teacher to be vigilant about this situation and thereby enables her to intervene more often *before* aggression occurs and to help the child work out a nonviolent solution at the scene.

The behavior-change plan need not be sophisticated to be effective. It may consist of specifying (a) prosocial behaviors for the staff to attend to, encourage, or teach; (b) behaviors to ignore; (c) contingencies or requirements; and (d) related consequences for various behaviors. For some children, staff may choose to use a system of concrete reminders (such as stickers) or incentives, or a time-out consequence, as described below. What makes the program individualized is that the specifics are determined on the basis of observation and judgments about the unique behavioral patterns and needs of the child. The plan needs to be well understood by *all* program staff who work with the child. Putting the plan in writing is important to ensure consistency among staff members and across work shifts and to allow for review and revision.

In attempting to produce behavior change, program staff might think of themselves as practical experimenters. They start off with their best efforts in designing a plan for change. Then, as they observe the child's reactions and any behavioral changes, they reassess the plan—keeping and improving what seems to work and dropping or changing what does not. In order to assess the effectiveness of a behavior plan, it is necessary to keep a written record of key behaviors, for example, by counting specific aggressive incidents. Staff members should not expect immediate improvement, because behaviors sometimes get worse before they get better (e.g., O'Leary & O'Leary 1972), particularly when children challenge or react to a new set of procedures. But a plan should not continue unchanged if there are no positive results within a reasonable amount of time (e.g., several weeks). For early childhood programs in school settings, a school psychologist or counselor may be available as a consultant in this process.

Consider short-term use of tangible-reminder or reward systems

Stickers and other material rewards for social behaviors are not recommended for routine classroom use, as explained in chapter 6. However, when a child has entrenched habits of aggressive behavior that are resistant to change, as well as few positive social behaviors, short-term use of these methods can provide a "jump start" in initiating change.

Some children are relatively indifferent to teacher attention, approval, or other attempts at encouraging prosocial behaviors. For other children, the excitement and peer attention resulting from their aggressive behavior outweigh the effect of the teacher's attempts to encourage constructive behavior. If a child's aggressive or disruptive behaviors far outnumber her positive social interactions, she may not have had enough opportunities to experience the natural joys of playing cooperatively. In order to help such children over the hump of making a major behavior shift, teachers may consider the temporary use of tangible reminders or additional positive incentives.

Tangible reminders, such as stickers or washable stamps, can be used to help children identify, learn, and practice specific cooperative and non-violent behaviors, as well as to refrain from specific aggressive behaviors. A child might be able to receive a sticker for a positive social behavior (such as cooperating with other children in cleaning up the block area) or for the absence of aggressive behavior over a period of time. In the process of explaining and carrying out a sticker program, the teacher would also use reasoning to focus the child's attention on the naturally occurring results of his behavior. The teacher could say, "I will help you learn not to hit and how to play nicely with the other children." The child can assist, to the extent possible, in designing a reminder system. The teacher should make the child aware, from the beginning, that the reminder system is only to help him remember the expected behavior and begin to change a "problem habit"; once he learns, he won't need

reminders anymore. While giving the child the stickers, the teacher also points out the natural benefits of the child's changed behavior, such as everyone feeling happier and the child making new friends.

Teachers may sometimes use rewarding consequences for each of the children in the group or for the group as a whole in order to encourage certain behaviors, as described in chapter 6. However, if individual incentive systems, such as sticker charts, are used for only one child or a few in the class, the issue of the other children's reactions arises. One concern is that the chart itself could stigmatize the child as different; but when a child is accustomed to behaving in a highly aggressive and antisocial manner, he is already perceived as different. If an incentive system is presented in a positive way, it has the potential of enabling the child and even his classmates to see the "different" behavior as changeable. In special education settings, where individual incentive systems are routine, nonaggressive peers tend to be accepting—and even actively supportive—of programs designed to reduce the aggressiveness of their classmates. They are genuinely happy and relieved to face less aggression in class.

There is now a strong movement toward "inclusion" (i.e., integrating children with various special needs into typical educational settings). Ideally, in inclusion settings, all children learn to accept a variety of equipment, procedures, and services needed to meet individual children's needs. Just as some children need individualized help to develop fine-motor or language skills, others may need individualized help to develop behavioral

© R.Bowie/Photo Proof

Whenever possible, teachers need to respond to aggressive acts with meaningful consequences; for example, if a fight between two children results in a spill, have them clean it up.

Chapter 7—Helping Children with Aggressive Behavior Patterns

alternatives to aggression. An incentive system may be thought of, and presented, as a specialized, individual learning tool. If Jake acts aggressively, it is explained to him and his classmates that his sticker chart is designed to help him learn to play cooperatively and avoid hurting others. Other classmates do not have a chart such as his because they have no need for one with that purpose, although they may be working on other individualized goals. The chart is but a temporary, specialized tool to meet Jake's particular needs.

One method of reminding both teacher and child to be alert to positive interactions is to give the child a card or badge to wear. The teacher provides a sticker on the badge if the child has been a "good friend" and refrained from hurting others during a specified period of time. This use may be reserved for particularly problematic times, such as in outdoor play, or it may be applied more broadly. Sending the sticker card or badge home when completed, with a note saying, "Nelson is learning to be a good friend!" gives parents an update and increases the incentive value of the stickers. Gradual increases are made in the time that the child needs to avoid aggressive behavior to earn a sticker.

The use of stickers reminds the teacher and others to regularly notice and encourage good behavior. For the system to be most effective, the teacher needs to watch behaviors carefully and to ensure that the child receives stickers in a consistent and planful manner. For some children, the stickers themselves serve as rewards. In other cases, additional rewards may be needed to initially mo-

tivate the child. For example, when the child has received a specified number of stickers (e.g., enough to fill the boxes drawn on the card or badge), she could be allowed to pass out the snack at group time, use a special piece of equipment, engage in a special activity, or have some time alone with a favorite teacher. Increasing the number of stickers required to earn the extra reward may be appropriate as behavior improves.

One expressed fear of teachers is that in providing tangible reminders and incentives, children may quickly learn the rules and begin to act cooperatively only to receive stickers. Another common concern is that by focusing on the sticker or reward, children may not pay as much attention to the intrinsic rewards of appropriate behavior, and, therefore, when the stickers or incentives are stopped, the desired behavior may also stop. The body of research evidence, as discussed in chapter 6, does not support these fears about the use of tangible rewards. Overall, rewards have not been found to reduce intrinsic motivation (Cameron & Pierce 1994). In addition, precautions can be taken to minimize possible overdependence on tangible rewards. One approach is to avoid giving the rewards every time the child shows the desired behavior and, rather, to space them at irregular and gradually increasing intervals. At first, many stickers may be needed to encourage the child's nonaggressive play. Later, as the child begins to be more accepted in children's play groups, the need for stickers can gradually disappear as they are spaced out over longer and longer intervals. As the child's behavior improves and aggression is substantially reduced, naturally occurring social rewards and self-esteem increasingly serve to maintain the improved behavior pattern.

Another key to avoiding overdependence on stickers and encouraging self-motivation is preparing the child, from the beginning, to view the stickers as a helping tool, secondary in importance to learning. The teacher may say, for instance, "The stickers are to help you at first, but what's *really* important is that you are learning to be a good friend." Later, the teacher helps the child see the ending of the system of receiving stickers as a goal and a personal accomplishment (e.g., saying, "You're doing *such* a good job of being a good friend that soon you won't need the stickers to help you anymore—you must feel very proud of yourself"). When the system is framed in this way for children, they sometimes volunteer that they don't need the stickers anymore.

Although such reminder systems take some planning and effort, they often are effective (sometimes quite dramatically) in reducing violence and disruption, as well as in producing other benefits for the child with behavior problems. In some cases a successful sticker or reward system can be helpful in engaging the child's family. If family members can see the benefits of noticing and keeping track of the child's prosocial behavior, they may become interested in trying this strategy for dealing with aggressive behavior at home. Such consistency between home and school greatly benefits the child.

Consider using time-out as one in a range of consequences

The rationale for using a variety of meaningful consequences designed to reduce aggressive behavior and help children take responsibility for their actions is described in chapter 6. A range of consequences for various forms of aggression can be determined by program staff, with as much input as possible from the children. These consequences can be discussed with the children in advance and then applied with little discussion as situations arise. The range of consequences might include the child's giving up a toy, leaving an area when she has been playing in a hurtful way, or sitting out of play entirely for a time. The consequence of sitting out is usually referred to as "time-out." Time-out was introduced in chapter 6 but was not discussed in depth. A high level of controversy surrounds the use of time-out in the field of early childhood education. Some educators have called for an outright ban on the procedure (e.g., CEASE 1993). To assist teachers in weighing the issues with regard to managing classroom aggression, this chapter addresses the potential uses of time-out, the concerns that have been raised, and some of the safeguards that might be taken.

Meaningful consequences that are intrinsically related to specific characteristics of the problem behavior are desirable when possible. In some cases, however, intrinsically related consequences may not be appropriate or readily available. In addition, intrinsically related consequences cannot always be applied immediately or in an entirely consistent manner from incident to incident. For example, the children and their teacher might decide that the consequence for throwing blocks is to leave the block area for the remainder of free play. However, if a child violently throws a large block at someone's head when she is not in the block area or when free play is just ending, application of the consequence becomes inconsistent or impossible. For young children it is important that the consequence be applied immediately following aggression and with maximum consistency. For these reasons the use of a brief time-out procedure may be useful in combination with other consequences and methods.

Giving the child a short time-out at the moment of aggressive behavior has been shown to be effective as part of a program to help a child learn to control aggression (Patterson & White 1970; MacDonough & Forehand 1973; Risley & Baer 1973; Hobbs & Forehand 1977). The purpose of this procedure is to remove the child briefly from rewarding events, including attention from adults and peers. Time-out allows the teacher to interrupt and prevent the continuation of aggressive acts, while at the same time giving minimal immediate attention to the aggressor. Time-out is best applied by the teacher in a matter-of-fact way, without reprimands or anger. Using a structured time-out following an upsetting violent incident sometimes gives teachers a chance to control their own emotions and, thereby, to better consider their next move. Time-out provides a separation and a break that allow both the aggressor and the victim to calm down following what most likely was an emotionally charged moment. Children learn to compose

themselves independently in time-out before returning to the group. As children grow older, they can be encouraged to ask for a brief "quiet-time" break in order to separate themselves from others, calm themselves, and prevent emotions from getting out of hand.

Early childhood programs differ markedly in philosophy about the use of time-out for dealing with aggression. Some do not use time-out at all. Others use it in extreme cases and only as a last resort after other behavior-change techniques prove ineffective. Still other programs choose to use a brief time-out procedure on a regular basis for deliberate, nontrivial aggressive acts by any child. If time-out is to be used, all staff members need to carefully consider how and under what conditions they will do so, including defining the type and severity of aggressive incident for which time-out will be used and specifying the procedures that provide consistency and adequate safeguards.

Using time-out effectively. Some programs report two different procedures: a sit-and-watch time, in which the child briefly moves to the edge of an area or activity, and a time-out, in which the child sits in an area of the classroom away from ongoing activities and other children. Time-out procedures for young children should never involve isolation in a closed room. As with other consequences, when time-out is applied for a certain behavior for the first time, or when a child first displays a particular aggressive behavior, the teacher should give a warning that the child will need to take a time-out if the behavior is repeated. Except for unusually severe incidents, individual children should receive this first-offense warning even if a classwide warning has been given. Once the procedure is established for a certain behavior and child, further warnings are not given. When initiating time-out, the teacher firmly and clearly labels the aggressive behavior (e.g., "No hitting; you have to take a time-out"). Children usually learn to take time-out by going to the designated place themselves, but the teacher's physical guidance may be required, especially in the beginning. The teacher usually refrains from talking to the child until the time-out is over; any comforting, reasoning, questioning, or debating by the teacher provides adult attention that could undermine the purpose of time-out.

Teachers need to limit time-out episodes for young children to one or two minutes of quiet behavior. Using a ticking kitchen timer is one way to help the child understand the time limits and to ensure that the busy teacher sticks by these limits. If the child is disruptive during time-out, it is more effective to extend the time-out until he is calm for a brief period (30 seconds to one minute), rather than ending time-out while he is being disruptive (Hobbs & Forehand 1977). While taking time-out, the child should receive as little direct attention as possible. Even being watched attentively can be rewarding for the child. The teacher needs to direct and guide the child's classmates to avoid interacting with the child in time-out. As soon as the time-out is over, the teacher takes special care to accept the child back into the group, as well as to watch for instances of appropriate, positive behavior to notice and encourage.

Safeguarding against misuse. Time-out is viewed by some as intrinsically punitive, harsh, and damaging to a child's self-esteem and as a technique for externally controlling children rather than helping them develop. As with other disciplinary techniques, teachers and administrators want to be alert to the possible harsh, inappropriate, or excessive use of time-out. Instituting a regular supervisory and peer-review process helps guard against such misuses. Time-out can be used in a focused and caring way as part of a behavior-change philosophy that involves children in the process of understanding and changing their own behavior, as described in chapter 6. Explaining time-out to children as one way for them to learn to "change a problem habit" puts the procedure in a positive frame. Explaining, demonstrating, or even role playing the time-out procedure before it is actually implemented helps children understand which behaviors will result in time-out and why, what to expect, and how they must behave to end a time-out.

As for the criticism that time-out does not teach self-control or other appropriate behaviors, this claim is valid as far as it goes; it constitutes a good argument for not counting on time-out *alone* to change aggressive behavior. Time-out becomes a valuable part of a plan that includes the simultaneous use of other approaches to encourage desirable behaviors. For example, the teacher might respond to a child's aggressive act by first using a brief time-out procedure and subsequently taking time to help the child figure out and practice a nonviolent alternative (an example of such an approach is given on the next page).

In using a tangible-reminder system, such as stickers, to help a child break out of an aggressive-behavior pattern, the teacher can offset sticker dependence by focusing his attention on the natural results of his behavior, saying "When you use words instead of kicking, no one gets hurt, and your classmate knows why *you're mad."*

What time-out does is to provide the child with an immediate consequence for aggression: the brief removal of social attention. Without time-out as an intermediate step between the aggression and teacher interaction, an aggressive act often is followed immediately by an *increase* in potentially rewarding social attention from adults and peers. The effective use of time-out, thus, is in complementing other educational approaches, not replacing them.

It is important for teachers to avoid overuse of time-out. Its use should be reserved for clearly aggressive, dangerous, or destructive behaviors that require a response. Reserving time-out for such behaviors, and not using it for any other type of problem, conveys the message to children that hurting others is especially serious. Time-out use is inappropriate for accidental roughness or other infrequent behaviors resulting from excessive excitability or impulsivity, particularly in the case of toddlers and younger preschool children. Other approaches (e.g., reasoning, anticipating problem situations, and having children practice alternative behaviors) should be used in such cases. Time-out should not be used until after the child receives an explicit warning that a particular behavior, if repeated, will have this consequence.

For example, if a child with no history of aggression or defiance becomes overexcited in play one day and throws an object in a potentially dangerous way, it is not appropriate to use time-out. Instead, for that child the most effective response may be for the teacher to simply explain that throwing is not allowed because it could hurt someone. Another child may benefit from additionally being reminded of consequences that would result if throwing were repeated. For a child displaying a pattern of deliberate and forceful throwing of objects at people in defiance of previous warnings, an immediate time-out or other behavioral consequence is appropriate as part of that child's behavior plan.

Teachers need to guard against becoming so vigilant in watching for behavior requiring a time-out that they forget to attend to the child's positive actions. Time-out for any child is most effective when adults also give a great deal of attention and active encouragement to the cooperative and nonviolent actions of that child and other children in the group. Using time-out is certainly not always easy or effective. Children may resist, become silly, or even ask for it. Time-out procedures should be modified or discontinued if they are ineffective. If a teacher finds that she is using time-out frequently with one or more children without seeing a reduction in aggressive behaviors, or if she notes problematic reactions to time-out by any child,

she should discuss the situation with a supervisor or a specialist in behavior and consider other alternatives.

Handling retaliation or severe behaviors. Children need to understand that *no one* is allowed to hurt anyone else, for any reason, including retaliation. Whatever the consequences used for deliberate aggression, these should also be applied to the child who strikes back. As an alternative to physical retaliation, children should be taught to respond assertively to peer aggression (as described in chapter 10) by firmly telling the aggressor, "No hitting!" or "No kicking!" and by seeking adult help if necessary. Children can learn that if they hit back instead, the teacher will apply the consequences that are designed for aggression. By strongly discouraging physical retaliation in this way, teachers help to interrupt the cycle of escalating violence that can otherwise easily develop. It is important to explicitly state that grownups, as well as children, are *never* allowed to hurt anyone in the classroom.

Severe agitation or dangerously violent behavior by a child may require the teacher to use physical restraint to ensure the child's safety and that of others. Restraint should be used only when absolutely necessary and as a last resort since it is a highly intrusive intervention with complex potential ramifications. Teachers facing the need to use restraint should secure professional consultation and receive training on how to use minimal-force restraint techniques that are appropriate, effective, and safe in given situations (CPI 1994). Once the restrained child is calm, and considering the circumstances, the teacher may enforce a time-out before the child's return to normal activities. Most school systems and child care programs require that every incident involving physical restraint be documented and reported to a supervisor, as well as to the child's parents. Any child who requires physical restraint may need referral for additional services beyond what the program setting can provide.

Provide extra support to the child who behaves aggressively

The young child with a pattern of aggressive behavior very much needs support, understanding, and assistance. She may require extra individualized help in learning the prosocial and self-control skills described in this book. Support in the form of family involvement or outside referral services can make a critical difference for some children. Most important, the child needs emotional support within the program setting in conjunction with any behavior-change plan. Just as the child must understand that violence toward others will not be allowed in class, she also needs to know that her feelings and needs are important, the teacher cares about her, and she can learn new ways to solve problems. Although, in most cases, the teacher will want to avoid prolonged discussion with a child immediately following an aggressive act, coming back at another time to interact warmly and provide understanding and guidance is very important.

* * *

The various components of a behavior-change plan and its effective implementation can be seen in the case of a kindergartner, Alex, who had a history of persistent aggressive and disruptive behaviors (Arezzo 1991). At the beginning of the year, the teacher involved the children in creating a set of general rules and consequences for a variety of aggressive behaviors. The consequence for playing with blocks in an unsafe way was to leave the block area for the remainder of free play. This consequence had been used with Alex a number of times but had not been effective, perhaps because Alex was not especially fond of playing with blocks. Similarly, other routine classroom strategies to reduce aggression (e.g., reasoning, attending to cooperative behaviors, and prompting peer assertiveness) had not changed Alex's aggressive behavior. The teacher had contacted Alex's family to discuss his behavior, hear their concerns and suggestions, and discuss the need for a plan to help Alex control his aggression and replace it with other behaviors. She carefully observed Alex and designed an individualized behavior plan for him. This plan included a list of positive behaviors to encourage, minor problem behaviors to ignore (e.g., making animal noises), and other specific contingencies and consequences. The plan included a brief time-out separation for each serious aggressive incident, as well as a sticker chart with stickers to be earned for successful periods of playing nicely with others. For Alex to earn a sticker, the amount of time that he needed to play without aggression was brief at first (only 15 minutes) to allow him to succeed, with longer periods required as his behavior improved.

This plan and each of its components were explained to Alex as a way of helping him change problem habits that could hurt others and as a means of learning new habits so that he could be a good friend to others (as described in chapter 6). In a check of his understanding, Alex showed that he knew which behaviors would result in time-out and why these behaviors could not be allowed. He understood the time-out procedure after it was concretely demonstrated. His teacher increased Alex's involvement in the process by letting him select the type of stickers he wanted to earn and by having him design the sticker chart (shaped like the Seattle Space Needle, with sticker boxes forming the elevator shaft). Alex knew that when he had filled the boxes with stickers, he could take the chart home with the teacher's note on it saying, "Alex is learning to play nicely with others!" Since Alex was observed showing excess body tension and excitability, as part of his plan he participated in small-group relaxation games designed for children his age (Cautela & Groden 1978). He also enjoyed participating in classroom role-playing activities, using a doll to practice social problem-solving skills (see chapters 8 and 10). The teacher sometimes selected hypothetical situations for group practice specifically because Alex had demonstrated difficulties in those situations.

An incident occurred in the block area several weeks after Alex's plan had been in effect and some progress had been made. During free play Alex forcefully kicked over Matt's tall block structure, without warning, sending blocks flying and very nearly injuring classmates. The teacher firmly told Alex, "Kicking blocks is not allowed. You need to take a time-out." Because the dangers of kicking or throwing blocks had been thoroughly discussed with the children earlier, there was no need to repeat them here. Alex sat in the classroom away from the activities for two minutes, and then he rejoined his peers. At this point his teacher drew him aside and asked him if he had a reason for kicking Matt's structure. She did not make guesses. Alex said that he was real mad at Matt because Matt had pushed Alex's friend Tanequa.

Teacher: "I think you were trying to be a good friend and help Tanequa, but did kicking the blocks help Tanequa?"

Alex: "No."

Teacher: "And when you kicked the blocks, did Matt know *why* you were mad?"

Alex: "No."

Teacher: "Do you want him to know why you were mad?"

Alex: "Yeah!"

Teacher: "OK! Well, then, let's think of a better way you could help Tanequa and also let Matt know why you were mad. Let's think of a way that wouldn't be dangerous or hurt anyone."

The teacher helped Alex to think through the situation and to arrive at the solution that he could tell Matt in a strong voice not to push Tanequa. Alex even initiated the idea of role playing, saying, "Get the doll!" Using the doll to help Alex role-play appropriate words, body language, and tone of voice, the teacher then accompanied him as he walked over to Matt and said, "Don't push my friend Tanequa. That makes me mad." The teacher encouraged Alex by talking about the progress he was making in learning to use words to say what he was feeling. In this way his teacher showed concern, acknowledged Alex's feelings, and directly assisted him in meeting his own needs effectively and nonviolently.

The child who behaves aggressively does not, of course, always have a reason that lends itself to this type of intervention, or he may have a reason that he is unable to articulate. In these cases the teacher should avoid probing or prompting. However, whenever the teacher can help the child in this way to identify a goal and practice meeting that goal constructively, she strengthens his ability and motivation to use nonviolent strategies.

The child with aggressive behavior patterns presents a serious challenge and responsibility for the teacher as she attempts to meet the specialized needs of that child while also attending to the needs of the rest of the class. In addition to applying the general planning and teaching strategies suggested throughout this book, the teacher will want to consider supplementary management techniques, such as those described in this chapter. Creating special adaptations of the classroom routine in order to help individual children who behave aggressively to learn positive social skills and to control their aggression is well worth the teacher's extra time in planning and implementation. If successful, a teacher will more than make up for the extra time by spending less time monitoring aggression and dealing with classroom flare-ups. More importantly, she will be helping the child to break a behavior pattern that otherwise may continue and become increasingly destructive.

Points to Remember

Recognize that teachers have a responsibility to prevent or stop violent behavior in their classrooms. Doing so is important both for children who behave aggressively and for other children in the class.

Follow the basic strategies for handling aggression when children show severe or persistent patterns of aggression, even if you decide to use more intensive and individualized methods as well. Using proven educational strategies, as suggested in this book, are especially important in these cases.

Design individualized behavior-change plans to help children who behave aggressively. Base the plans on careful observations, put them in writing to maximize consistency, and revise them as needed, depending on results.

Consider a system of concrete reminders or incentives for children who require extra support to begin the process of change. Let children know that these systems are temporary. Help children focus on self-control and the naturally occurring social consequences of behavior change.

Consider using a brief time-out procedure for aggression as one in a range of corrective consequences. Explain and demonstrate to children the rules and procedures of time-out and the reasons for its use. Guard against excessive use or the misuse of time-out.

Provide extra support to children who show aggressive-behavior patterns. While maintaining consistency and following the behavior-change plan, let the children know that their feelings and needs are important, that you care about them, and that you can help them to make changes in their habits.

8

Fostering Social Problem-Solving Skills

Things have finally calmed down after a morning of turmoil in the classroom. The teacher is talking to Ben about the fights he got into with several of his classmates. Each time she asks him what other things he might have done to resolve the conflict without fighting, he says, "I don't know." **What should the teacher do next?**

The early childhood setting provides children with important opportunities to learn the skills needed for interacting competently with others. Besides the social skills related to making friends and playing cooperatively, children need to learn skills that permit them to resolve conflict effectively and nonviolently. Social conflicts occur when one person objects to what another person does. The skills needed to manage social conflict successfully are often called *social problem-solving skills.* Children usually develop these skills primarily by interacting with and observing other children in the same age range. However, teachers can foster the development of problem-solving skills by directly teaching them to children, demonstrating and modeling their effective use, and guiding children's interactions with peers.

Much of children's aggression with peers derives not from an excess of meanness, hostility, or aggressive energy but rather from a *lack* of fundamental skills in solving social problems effectively and nonviolently (e.g., Dodge 1986; Rubin & Krasnor 1986). Fundamental problem-solving skills can be learned and practiced by children in early childhood settings, thereby resulting in reduced levels of aggression (e.g., Spivack & Shure 1974; Krasnor & Rubin 1983; Denham & Almeida 1987). Children with well-developed problem-solving skills are less likely to resort to aggression to solve their social conflicts. They are also better equipped to achieve their own goals, negotiate mutually beneficial solutions, and avoid becoming victims of other people's aggression.

What research tells us

Through relations with their peers, children learn many important social skills. Informed by research, teachers can help young children develop positive peer relations and useful social problem-solving skills.

The importance of peer relationships

In the United States, infants and very young toddlers often interact more with adults than with their peers (LeVine 1991). However, as children move through the early childhood years, their interactions with peers usually become increasingly frequent, complex, and important in their development of a wide range of social skills. It is primarily through their peer interactions and observations that children learn skills related to social problem solving, sharing, assertiveness, and perspective taking.

Children's relationships with adults are fundamentally different from their relationships with peers. Although children learn through their interactions with adults from the beginning of life, the adult–child relationship involves vast differences in status, power, perspective, and motivation. Adults can often regulate interactions in ways that avoid social conflict. Children also react to adults very differently than they do to peers. If a child is frustrated or angry with an adult (especially a nonfamily member, such as a teacher), he is likely to use passive coping responses, such as crying, becoming distant from the adult, or ignoring the adult. In contrast, if the child is angry with another child, he may yell, tattle, retaliate by taking something the other child values, or hit the other child (Fabes & Eisenberg 1992).

Children's interactions with their peers provide a unique opportunity for learning because many reciprocal social skills develop primarily through interactions with social equals. Children often show more active problem-solving responses with peers than with adults because peers engage them at similar levels of status, power, size, and social skills (Brownwell & Carriger 1990). Similarly, children are better able to learn both to share voluntarily and to respond assertively to unreasonable demands, provocations, or threats when they practice these responses with peers, rather than with accommodating or directive adults (see chapters 9 and 10). Interactions with peers also provide children with direct challenges to the *egocentric thought* (characterized by a failure to see things from another's perspective) that often guides young children's actions (Piaget 1932; Rardin & Moan 1971; Kohlberg 1976). The conflicts that arise when equally egocentric children interact tend to provoke children into considering each other's perspectives. Being able to take the perspective of others is an important step in the development of empathy, a skill that helps children inhibit aggressive responses (see chapter 11).

Fostering positive social skills and peer relations

A child who lacks social skills is greatly disadvantaged. For example, a child who wants to join a group activity but does not know how may charge into the group and disrupt the other children's play. Children with poorly developed social skills tend to become socially disruptive when stressed, and they often fail to cope effectively with their own and other children's feelings and demands (Coie, Dodge, & Kupersmidt 1990).

Helping children to gain social skills reduces classroom aggression because socially adept children are better prepared to achieve their goals and cope with frustration peacefully.

Chapter 8—Fostering Social Problem-Solving Skills

Helping children to become more socially skilled reduces aggression in the classroom because socially skilled children are better prepared to achieve their goals peacefully and cope with frustration in direct and active ways that minimize further conflict or damage to social relationships (Fabes & Eisenberg 1992). Children with well-developed social skills tend to initiate more-positive social interactions with peers; behave in a friendly, nurturing, and helpful manner; have fewer conflicts; show more cooperation; and use less aggression in resolving conflicts (Hazen, Black, & Fleming-Johnson 1984; Shantz & Shantz 1985; Denham et al. 1990). Socially skilled children are less likely to be targets of aggression, social rejection, and victimization by their peers (Spivack & Shure 1974; Perry, Kusel, & Perry 1988).

Children learn from their interactions with and observations of peers, whether or not a teacher intervenes. Some children learn patterns of behavior that contribute to aggression, victimization, or bystander support for aggression (Patterson, Littman, & Bricker 1967; Slaby & Stringham 1994). These aggression-supporting behavior patterns may interfere with later learning of more-effective social behaviors. Because socially skilled children often choose to play together and avoid playmates who have poor social skills, these less-adept children may have inadequate opportunities to learn from interaction with socially skilled peers (Kohler & Fowler 1985).

Teaching children specific social skills provides them with the tools they need when facing conflict situations that might provoke aggression. A child who aggressively grabs toys from others and hits, for example, may not be showing excess hostility but, instead, may simply lack prosocial skills that would allow appropriate access to toys, such as waiting until the other child finishes playing with an object, sharing it, taking turns in using it, or trading it for another toy. The more diverse and highly developed children's social skills are, the more freedom they have to choose an appropriate response in a variety of social settings. Reduction in children's aggression is often an important side effect of programs designed to teach prosocial skills, such as problem solving, sharing, assertiveness, and perspective taking.

The development of social problem-solving skills

We can evaluate children's attempts to solve a social problem in terms of *effectiveness* (e.g., the extent to which the child succeeds in getting what he wants) and *acceptability* (e.g., the extent to which the child's methods are socially sanctioned). In the short term, a child's aggressive actions sometimes allow him to attain something he wants, yet in the longer term, aggression causes problems for the child because the victim and others find it unacceptable. If the child accomplishes his immediate goal by means of aggression, he may feel successful and be more likely to use aggression again in the future. However, children who use aggressive solutions to solve problems may soon find themselves with few friends and excluded from group play.

Children's social problem-solving skills generally increase together with their developing competencies in the areas of thought, language, and emotion. For example, when *2-year-old children* attempt to solve problems with their peers, their problem-solving strategies are often limited, inflexible, and not well adapted to the specific circumstances and individuals involved. Two-year-olds are generally able to see only their own perspective in the conflict, and they seek an outcome that achieves only their own goals. If their first attempt at getting what they want fails, they usually have very few, if any, alternative strategies to fall back on.

Three-year-old children generally show much more complex problem-solving strategies related to their rapidly developing verbal abilities. These abilities often lead to more social communication and cooperative play, as well as to more quarrels and verbal aggression. Children of this age usually begin to verbalize what they want or how they feel in a conflict, to respond to the requests and demands of other children, and to ask questions. They also begin to realize that their requests and demands need to be supported. They may start using strategies for refusing requests that supply reasons for their refusal, even though the reasons are usually self-referenced (e.g., "No, you can't have it, because I want it"). However, most children at this developmental level still tend to be inflexible and adhere to only a single strategy to resolve problems.

Four-year-old children generally add a variety of problem-solving strategies to their repertoire, reflecting their growing skills in communicating clearly and their increasing appreciation of what others need to understand in order to resolve the conflict. At this level children make greater use of both positive and negative compliance-gaining strategies. For example, many children at

this age are capable of recognizing that they may need to restate their request to give the other person additional information rather than simply restating the request and remaining at a stalemate. Four-year-old children may use several different strategies to support their positions (e.g., demand an object from the other child, soften the demand by saying "please," and offer to trade something for what they want). They may also use negative strategies, including bribes, insults, and threats. Once a conflict moves into threats and counterthreats, it can easily escalate into physical aggression.

By *age 5* many children have mastered sufficient self-control to rely primarily on verbal problem-solving strategies. These children also begin to individualize their responses to others, based on their knowledge of them from past social experiences, even though they may not be highly skilled in identifying others' intentions, motives, and perspectives. As children develop further, they may eventually acquire the skills to negotiate resolutions to conflict that are mutually beneficial, based on what they know about the other person, past experiences with the person, and understanding of one another's perspectives (see chapter 11).

The ways that children respond to conflict

Most young children respond to simple conflict in one of several ways. Since the vast majority of conflicts center on the possession of an object, an example of such a conflict will be helpful. One child approaches a peer who is playing with a toy car and says, "I'm going to drive the car." In this situation a young child's *first response* is most likely to be one of the following (Garvey 1984):

• Refusing to comply by using a simple negation (e.g., "No," or "No, you're not!")

• Offering a reason for opposing the demand, with or without a negation (e.g., "No! It's mine" or simply "It's mine!")

• Postponing compliance (e.g., "Later you can have a turn")

• Evading the demand (e.g., "It's not a car, it's a van")

By far, the most common verbal response among young children is simply refusing to comply, often followed by a reason for this refusal if the conflict persists. "No" is much more likely to be accepted if it is accompanied by a reason or explanation. A simple "No" without an explanation often results in the continuation and possible escalation of the conflict, because the child who is after the toy is not deterred.

If the child's first response to a demand fails to deter the other child, *follow-up responses* to each other can take a variety of forms (Garvey 1984). Continuing with the toy car example, these responses might include the following:

• Compromising, such as sharing the toy or taking turns (e.g., "We can take turns driving the car")

• Agreeing under a particular condition (e.g., "I'll let you drive the car if you'll drive me to Grandma's house")

• Making a counterproposal or substitute plan (e.g., "You play with this ball")

• Providing an explanation or justification for refusal (e.g., "I have to drive the car, because I have to go to work")

• Requesting an explanation (e.g., "Why do you need it right now?")

• Weakening or strengthening the previous statement (e.g., softly repeating, "No," or shouting, "You are not!")

• Refusing to acknowledge the other's position (i.e., giving no noticeable response)

• Using a threat or verbal attack (e.g., "If you don't let me drive the car, I'll hit you" or "You poophead!")

• Using physical force (e.g., grabbing the car or pushing the child off the car)

Children's choices of responses can affect both the way the problem gets resolved and the way the children treat each other afterward. Strategies in which neither child has to give in completely to the other generally have more positive outcomes (i.e., children continue to play together after the conflict) (Garvey 1984). The first four follow-up responses listed (i.e., compromising, agreeing under a particular condition, making a counterproposal, or providing an explanation) involve the use of *conciliatory gestures,* with neither child having to submit completely to the other. These responses often lead to positive outcomes because they enable the child who is trying to get a toy or achieve some other goal of her own to get past the initial opposition and to begin to negotiate. By far, the most successful strategy is compromise, perhaps because it permits a concession to the child making the request, while not requiring the other child to subordinate herself.

Young children generally use insistent behavior far more often than conciliatory behavior, although conciliatory gestures are more likely to be used between friends (Laursen &

Hartup 1989). Insistent responses (e.g., using threats and physical force) almost never lead to a positive outcome for both children. In fact, the use of physical force often escalates into a fight. Even very young children understand the concept of the right of prior possession. Therefore, an attempt to take an object from a child who already possesses it has a high probability of resistance that may escalate to aggression. In early childhood centers, these kinds of aggressive struggles are usually brief and often escalate rapidly into protests, screams, or crying. These aggressive encounters are usually resolved through the intervention of an adult. However, teachers can prepare children to resolve their own conflicts effectively and nonviolently by having them learn, practice, and use social problem-solving skills to deal with peer conflicts.

Key social problem-solving skills

When tempers flare in a social conflict, children often behave impulsively for a variety of reasons: (1) they do not understand or know how to regulate their own emotional reactions, (2) they do not listen carefully to others, (3) they do not use their own verbal skills to help themselves stop and think through the situation, (4) they do not think of the alternative solutions and anticipate the consequences, and (5) they do not evaluate the aggressive solutions as harmful and inappropriate. They default to whatever automatic and stereotyped response they have learned, rather than thoughtfully choosing an effective response that is appropriate for the situation. For many young children, yelling and hitting is their de-

fault response, and for other children it is crying and submitting. Learning to solve social problems effectively involves a variety of skills that children can begin to build in the early years.

Programs designed to teach social problem-solving skills usually contain variations of the following set of skills, commonly representing sequential steps in a process of solving social problems:

• Keeping calm (maintaining self-control, remaining "cool-headed," being reflective)

• Listening carefully (to understand what the other person wants)

• Gathering information (about key facts, circumstances, motivations, intentions)

• Defining the problem (with objectivity, rather than hostile bias)

• Setting goals (for self, for others, for mutual benefit)

• Generating alternative solutions (What other actions could be taken?)

• Anticipating consequences (What might happen next?)

• Choosing the "best" solution (deciding what to do by prioritizing the possible solutions and their anticipated consequences for self, for others, for mutual benefit)

• Enacting the chosen response (What do you need to do? What is the best way to do it?)

• Evaluating the response (Did it work? What might work better next time?)

This entire set of skills is far too complex for young children to learn as a whole. However, they can begin to learn and apply each of these fundamental skills one at a time and then begin to make connections between them. For example, several programs begin by focusing on generating solutions, anticipating consequences, and connecting the solutions to the consequences. Each of the fundamental problem-solving skills can be taught in the context of ongoing activities or through specially designed activities, such as demonstrations, role playing, and storytelling.

Teaching guidelines

Children sometimes resort to aggressive actions because they lack the problem-solving skills to get what they want in more acceptable ways. Among the many benefits of children's development of social skills, then, is reducing aggression. Together these benefits provide a strong impetus for the early childhood teacher to know the most effective strategies for helping young children to develop their social problem-solving abilities

Teach skills at the appropriate developmental level

At specially prepared developmentally appropriate group activities and throughout the day, teachers can help young children begin to learn and apply fundamental problem-solving skills in ways that reduce aggression and lay the foundation for preventing violence in the future. Although young children often have difficulty dealing with abstract presentations and the inclusion of several factors at once, they can often learn these skills if they are presented more concretely

and individually. Teachers can make the skill concepts concrete and understandable through activities that make use of pictures, stories, dolls, puppets, props, videos, dramatizations, and role playing. For example, in one of the earliest related studies, preschool children observed an adult acting out alternative solutions to conflicts, using a set of dolls and some props (Chittenden 1942). A typical incident involved two children who both wanted to play with the same wagon. In the aggressive solution the two children fought, the wagon broke, and both children were unhappy. The alternative involved taking turns with the wagon, which satisfied both individuals. Preschool children who observed these little dramas and participated in discussing the alternative solution became generally less aggressive and more cooperative in their play.

Teachers can help children to transfer the individual skills they have learned from hypothetical to real situations. The problems depicted in the hypothetical situations can be drawn from events that have occurred in the program setting. The skills learned in the hypothetical situations can then be applied in daily program activities. Within the framework of a small group, children might hold the puppets and act out possible actions and consequences. While role-playing, children might talk about how they feel when they solve a problem cooperatively, in contrast to how they feel when they fight. Using puppets to demonstrate or role-play cooperative solutions suggested by either the children or the teacher will help children to understand and remember those solutions. Reminding children of the puppet demonstrations during ongoing spontaneous play helps them transfer the learned skills to their daily activities in the program setting. In fact, teachers who regularly use this technique report that children sometimes ask for the doll or puppet to be brought into a conflict situation to help them work out a solution (Arezzo 1991).

Help children understand their strong feelings

Throughout the day and also at specially designed group activities, teachers can encourage children to talk about which events cause them to feel various emotions and how they can communicate their desires to others (Shure 1992). Children are able to learn to identify their own strong feelings of frustration, anger, fear, and sadness and to know that when they have these feelings, it is important to make a choice about how to act, not just react (Moore & Beland 1991). Children begin learning that strong feelings, including anger and frustration, are normal and OK, but acting violently is *never* OK no matter how they are feeling.

Understanding and dealing with strong feelings can be adopted as learning goals for the class as a whole. Children who have particular problems controlling strong feelings and explosive emotional outbursts may benefit from specialized assistance and practice in self-calming and self-control strategies. Such intervention has a much better chance of succeeding if the child begins by practicing in role-play situations when he is not actually in a rage. The teacher should intervene as early as possible in real, emotionally charged situations to support the child in applying the learned

strategies. In cases of extreme behavior, the teacher should ask for the assistance of another staff member or specialist or consider referring the child for counseling.

Encourage good listening and communication skills

Children who are able to resolve conflicts in mutually satisfactory ways are generally both clear and assertive in communicating their own wishes and are attentive to the wishes of the other person. In a conflict situation, even among adults, each person may be so focused on bolstering her own arguments that she never really hears the points the other person is making. Beyond identifying the other person's feelings (e.g., angry, sad), successful listening requires attention to the meaning of the other person's words. Some curricula provide exercises to build children's skills in listening attentively and clarifying their perception of what the other person says and means (e.g., Kreidler 1984; Shure 1992).

Teachers can also help children practice using their listening skills when they are involved in conflicts. For example, when Bret and Dominick are yelling at each other, the teacher might separate them and ask what each child wants. Bret says, "I want to build the tower myself, and he knocked it down!" Dominick says, "He was taking all of the blocks, and I wanted some!" The teacher asks each boy to restate what the other boy said he wanted, and then she checks to see if each agrees with that perception or wants to clarify it ("Dominick, what does Bret say?" and "Bret, why was Dominick upset?"). This procedure

To help children improve their listening skills, the teacher intervenes and asks each child to say what he wants; she then asks each to restate what the other child said he wanted.

may help each boy to understand what the other boy said and actually did want, as a first step toward considering the other's point of view and finding a peaceful solution to the problem (see chapter 11).

Help children to achieve self-control

Children who behave aggressively often have a rapid-response style and fail to use verbal skills to talk to themselves and to talk to others about what they want and what they can do (Camp 1977). Many problem-solving curricula for older children

begin by having children practice strategies to "Think first," "Stop and think," or "Think aloud" when faced with social conflicts and strong emotions (Camp 1977; Crary 1979; Slaby, Wilson-Brewer, & Dash 1994). Even young children are capable of learning to tell themselves, "Stop," when they feel angry or upset and to use such self-calming strategies as taking one or two deep breaths or slowly counting to 10 on their fingers (Moore & Beland 1991). Relaxation procedures have been adapted and used successfully with children (Cautela & Groden 1978). Young children will initially need con-

siderable cuing and guidance to follow these procedures, and they will
probably continue to need adult
support periodically. The skills they
practice, even with adult help, provide a foundation for more independent self-control skills in later childhood and adulthood.

Self-calming, self-control, and relaxation procedures are aimed at reducing those impulsive reactions
that lead children to automatically
provoke, attack, retaliate, or submit
to others. The next step is for children to learn what specific nonviolent actions they can take when they
have strong feelings or face conflicts
(e.g., cool down, talk to a friend or
an adult, listen carefully to the other
person, assert your own needs, try
to solve the problem, negotiate an
agreement, get help from others). By
using various strategies, some described in this book and others in a
variety of resource materials, teachers can help children learn nonviolent responses to strong emotions
and to support the children in using
these responses at critical times.

Provide practice in generating and connecting solutions and consequences

Young children can learn to generate their own solutions to a problem (e.g., "What else can we do?"),
to think of consequences of various
behaviors (e.g., "What might happen
next?"), and to connect solution-
consequence pairs (e.g., "What might
happen if I do that?") (Shure 1992).
In a 10-week program using stories
and puppets to encourage young

children to think of their own alternative solutions and consequences,
children's skills improved and so did
their behavior adjustment, as rated
by teachers (Spivack & Shure 1974).
The longer children participated in
the program, the fewer aggressive
solutions they offered.

Some of the first curricula in this
area were designed to encourage
children to generate as many alternative solutions and consequences
as possible without placing a "value
judgment" on these solutions (e.g.,
Spivack & Shure 1974). But simply
generating a large quantity of solutions may not be sufficient to reduce
aggression. Although children who
behave very aggressively can benefit
from learning to generate more solutions to social problems, they often also come up with more solutions that are aggressive (Sharp
1981). Less socially competent children may demonstrate as many different types of problem-solving strategies in their behavior as their more
competent peers, but more of their
strategies include aggressive acts
(e.g., pushing, threatening, and taking without asking) (Sharp 1983).
Thus, children need to learn to critically evaluate the ways in which violence is harmful and avoidable, as
well as to generate a variety of solutions and consequences. More recent
curricula take steps in the direction
of encouraging children to critically
evaluate their answers. For example,
the newest version of the *I Can Problem Solve* curriculum (Shure 1992;
see "Resources" for a description of
this curriculum) encourages children to think of reasons why certain
activities are not a good idea. This

process can be applied in evaluating solutions that involve aggression (e.g., "Tell us why this is not a good idea").

Teach children to critically evaluate violent and nonviolent consequences

Although research on young children's beliefs about violence is limited, violent behavior among older children has been found to be related to their beliefs supporting the use of violence (Perry, Perry, & Rasmussen 1986; Slaby & Guerra 1988; Guerra & Slaby 1989). Children's aggressive behavior can be reduced by changing their violence-supporting beliefs (e.g., aggression is legitimate, it increases one's self-esteem, it is needed to avoid a negative image) in combination with developing their problem-solving skills (Guerra & Slaby 1990; Slaby, Wilson-Brewer, & DeVos 1994).

Children in our society often acquire unrealistic and superficial beliefs about violence that go unchallenged unless adults teach them to critically evaluate these beliefs. For example, American television often portrays violence as prevalent, legitimate, justified, socially approved, rewarded, effective, clean, heroic, manly, funny, and even pleasurable (Slaby 1994a). Young children are particularly susceptible to adopting these lessons of violence uncritically (Donnerstein, Slaby, & Eron 1994) and acting them out in their behaviors in the early childhood program (Carlsson-Paige & Levin 1987; Singer & Singer 1981). Teachers can help young children to build skills in critically evaluating the ways in which violence portrayed on television is unrealistic and in real life is harmful, destructive, and unacceptable; and to understand, as well, the ways in which nonviolent alternative solutions may be more useful and effective (see chapter 13).

Use available resources

Various curricula and other materials may be helpful in fostering children's social problem-solving skills (see "Resources" for some ideas). The school or child care center may want to develop a procedure for systematically reviewing available resources and selecting those that would best suit the needs of their children. These deliberations might also address the need for consistency of application and the opportunities for focused inservice training and staff support.

Effective social problem solving consists of a set of skills that children need to learn and practice. Through a combination of planned curricular activities and spontaneous interventions in children's ongoing activities, teachers can help children to develop each of these fundamental skills, combine their skills, and apply them flexibly and appropriately in conflict situations (e.g., Yarrow, Scott, & Waxler 1973).

Points to Remember

Prepare yourself by drawing on the most promising available resources. Review, discuss, select, and adapt developmentally appropriate curricular materials for fostering social problem-solving skills. Some ideas for promising resources are listed under "Resources" at the back of this book.

Find concrete ways to teach children skills needed to solve the problems they face. Although preschool children often have difficulty understanding abstract presentations, they readily understand concrete presentations of familiar problems. Demonstrations, dramatizations, puppet role plays, and illustrated stories can help to make the presentation understandable.

Divide social problem solving into component skills and focus on building one skill at a time. Preschool children who might otherwise become confused with the complexity of the problem-solving process are able to learn one skill at a time.

Help children transfer the skills they have learned in hypothetical situations to real situations. Identify real-life situations that offer children opportunities to apply the skills they have developed in hypothetical situations and support them in applying their skills.

Teach problem-solving skills that relate directly to reducing violence. When problem solving, select realistic situations for discussion and practice.

Help children understand and deal with their strong feelings. Show them that strong feelings are OK, but violence is never OK. Help them learn nonviolent ways to express their feelings.

Provide children with practice in using their listening skills. Attentive listening is needed to understand what the other child wants and why.

Encourage impulse control and self-calming. Children are able to learn self-control, self-calming, and relaxation techniques to deal with strong feelings, such as anger and frustration.

Provide children with practice in thinking of solutions, anticipating consequences, and evaluating the harmfulness of aggressive solutions. The combination of thinking of alternative solutions and consequences, together with learning that violence is harmful, can help children avoid aggression.

9

Encouraging Voluntary Sharing

A preschool class is on a field trip to a children's museum. In an exciting and crowded activity room, the children struggle over the use of limited equipment. Within a short time period, one can hear their teacher and other adults repeatedly admonishing: "You need to share," "It's nice to share," "Why don't you share?" "Let's share, OK?" **What specifically do these statements help children learn about sharing? What might the teacher do to be helpful here?**

Most of the conflicts in early childhood settings involve children fighting for possession of an object or toy. Such conflicts can easily lead to physical fights. Helping children learn the value and skills of sharing works to decrease aggressive behavior in the center or classroom and encourages the children to use nonviolent solutions to problems.

Sharing has two primary meanings. One is "to divide and distribute," and the other is "to partake of, use, experience, occupy, or enjoy with others" or "to have in common." Furthermore, "Sharing implies that one [person] as the original holder grants to another the partial use, enjoyment, or possession of a thing, though it may merely imply a mutual use or possession" *(Merriam Webster's Collegiate Dictionary* 1993,

1077). This chapter focuses on the voluntary nature of sharing—the willingness of the "original holder" to share her possessions and available resources with others—rather than merely on children's mutual use or possession of resources. In other words, the concern is the development of children's willingness to independently accept and initiate sharing. Accordingly, the teacher's primary goal in fostering sharing would be for children to voluntarily choose to distribute or jointly use resources with fairness and generosity, rather than for them to give up or divide resources at her directive. Aspects of sharing that involve jointly participating in activities or jointly experiencing feelings will not be emphasized here. These issues are addressed in chapters 5 and 11.

What research tells us

To the extent that children engage in sharing resources voluntarily and independently, one of the primary sources of childhood conflict is removed. If the values and behavior of sharing are learned early and well, later serious violent conflicts over possessions and resources may also be reduced. In addition to sharing being a desirable alternative to fighting over resources, studies of "social reciprocity" among young children indicate that it is a way for children to increase the level of their social acceptance by peers (Hartup, Glazer, & Charlesworth 1967) and the level of "social reinforcement" they receive from peers (Charlesworth & Hartup 1967; Gottman, Gonso, & Rasmussen 1975).

Share is a word and an admonition that is well known to young children. But children receive mixed messages on the subject, especially in a society that emphasizes individual rights over the common good and status gained through the ownership of possessions. Children usually learn that most things belong to somebody, that material acquisition is highly desirable, and that they need to protect their own possessions and territories. Commercial television programming and advertising often emphasize the benefits of individual ownership; associate owning toys with having friends, pleasure, and self-esteem; and even justify aggressive retaliation for violations of individual ownership rights.

The need for children to learn to share and work cooperatively may ultimately be critical to human survival in a world of limited and diminishing resources. Moreover, sharing can expand our humanity, making play or work a fuller and more rewarding experience. Young children's difficulties in sharing and their frequent forceful attempts to control resources may reflect not merely social immaturity but also the influence of living in a possession-oriented and highly individualistic society. Children's difficulties in sharing may also be related to a reduced sense of "community" and the diminishing resources faced by many families. The resulting challenge that early childhood educators face is how to teach sharing and the cooperative management of resources to children in such a way that children may apply these values and skills in their lives in the world beyond the classroom walls and in the years ahead.

A double standard for sharing

Adults tend to apply a completely different standard of sharing to young children than they use for themselves. The norm of sharing one's possessions is generally promoted as a universal good for young children, but this is not the case for adults. Adults take their own property rights very seriously, and they limit their own sharing, according to particular circumstances (Furby 1978). In contrast, adults often trivialize the property rights of children and lecture them frequently about the need to share (Ross et al. 1990). In the unlikely event that an adult were to forcefully push a co-worker aside and take over use of an office computer without asking, no one would suggest to the co-worker that he should give up his use of the computer because "It's nice to share" or "He hasn't had a turn yet"

Children should not be expected to hand over a toy the minute another child asks for it; knowing that they have the right to decline—to not share in a given instance—enables children ultimately to develop the capacity for voluntary sharing.

Chapter 9—Encouraging Voluntary Sharing

or "You have another one at home." Yet, some parents and teachers make such suggestions to young children, disregarding the children's possession and ownership rights in the name of keeping the peace or promoting "sharing." In one study, when mothers intervened in a conflict between two toddlers, 90% of the time it was to tell their own child to let the other child have the toy, regardless of ownership, possession, or the way in which one child tried to get the toy from the other. Giving up a toy was typically described as "sharing," even if it was done under duress (Ross et al. 1990). However, it is the voluntary and cooperative aspects of sharing that we most want to encourage. We degrade the concept if we use it to justify yielding to an aggressor.

The desirable goal of encouraging children's voluntary sharing is not advanced by denying the basic rights of children to be treated fairly, to make choices, and to respond assertively when necessary. Teaching children to respect reasonable ownership and possession rights for themselves and others is a matter of justice, and it can serve as a foundation for the development of mature prosocial behaviors. The approach presented here includes deemphasizing possessiveness and materialism, while at the same time extending to the world of young children our society's affirmation of legitimate rights of ownership or possession.

Although most classroom materials are not owned by any of the children, reasonable possession rights require that a child who wants something that is being used by another ask the other child for it, rather than merely taking it. A peer's use of verbal or physical aggression in attempting to take something, as is often the case, is an even greater violation of the child's rights. The child who is faced with a peer forcefully trying to take something from him certainly has the right to defend against that aggression and to refuse to submit. Allowing or encouraging a child to submit to the unreasonable demands of another may promote the formation of bully–victim relationships (Olweus 1993a). Instead, even when overt force is not involved, a child can be encouraged to politely defend his right not to have something taken from him. Facilitating voluntary sharing in the classroom involves teaching children to respect the possession rights of others and to defend their own rights, when necessary, in an assertive and nonaggressive way.

Cultural and socioeconomic factors

The challenge of promoting children's sharing is heightened in the United States, because babies and toddlers in this country have traditionally been isolated from their peers to a greater extent than they are in other cultures (LeVine 1991). A trend toward decreased family size also means that many children have little or no experience with siblings. Although a growing number of children in working and professional families are in group care before the age of 2, and many live in large, extended family groups, the majority of very young children receive a great deal of one-to-one attention from a primary caregiver, are surrounded by toys that are just for them, and acquire little or no social experience with a consistent group of agemates (Willer et al. 1991). They therefore begin preschool having had very little experience sharing either material objects or adult attention.

In most early childhood settings, children are told that the materials belong to everybody and must be shared. This can raise new issues for young children who have previously played primarily at home with their own toys. Aggressive conflicts are especially common for children who have lacked group care experience prior to preschool, as they try to apply rules of sharing.

Some children may claim ownership of certain toys and defend against their use by others. Other children may be unsure about which objects they are allowed to use. Children may get upset when they are not allowed to take school or center toys home with them. This confusion for the child is heightened if parents send their children to class with toys and a warning not to lose or break them, while teachers tell the children that they must share toys. Children sometimes use a toy of their own to gain social power by controlling who gets to play with it and by trading its use for promises of friendship and attention.

In dealing with issues of sharing and possessiveness, teachers need to be sensitive to socioeconomic differences between children and the sometimes vast differences in their access to material items and privileges at home and in their communities. When a child has trouble shar-

ing at school or at the center, a contributing factor may be that he has very limited access to toys, books, or constructive activities outside the child care facility. If this is the case, it may be helpful to assist the family in gaining access to community resources. For example, activities and materials for young children may be available, at little or no cost, through libraries, museums, churches, recreational centers, service agencies, or other community organizations. At the opposite extreme, family consultation of a different nature may help a child who has trouble sharing because her parents buy or give her nearly everything she demands. Understanding the child's family and community circumstances allows the teacher to respond with greater sensitivity and effectiveness to the child's particular needs.

Developmental levels of sharing

Some teachers attempt to teach sharing and cooperation by repeating variations of the principle that sharing is "nice" and that selfishness and uncooperative behaviors are "not nice." Yet, the skills involved in sharing, and the specific situational requirements, are far more complex than this dichotomy implies. Children receive differing and sometimes inconsistent messages from adults about sharing. When told to "share," preschool children have been observed to show very different interpretations of the meaning of sharing and the conditions under which they would comply with a request to do so (Hoffman & Wundram 1984).

The type of sharing behaviors that children display and their understanding of the concept of sharing change across successive developmental levels. Children's capacity for sharing generally increases with age, especially since young children may have limited ability to accurately perceive and react to the needs of others. Although the age at which different children reach any given developmental level varies considerably, the development of sharing skills generally proceeds in the following steps for most children (Krogh & Lamme 1983).

• *Egocentrism (ages 3 to 4)*. At this level it is difficult for most children to distinguish between their own viewpoint and that of others. Children tend to share according to their own likes and desires. For example, a child who is given several pieces of candy may give one to another child in order to gain teacher approval. Children may engage in the cooperative use of art materials for the same reason. The goal of children at this level is centered around their own feelings, rather than the other person's feelings, and their desire for adult attention and approval is stronger than their desire to please a peer.

• *External egocentrism (ages 4 to 5)*. Children's perspective at this level usually continues to be self-centered, but sharing and cooperation may now also be based on observable external characteristics of others. For example, a child may ask a new child to play because the new child looks sad and lonely. On the other hand, children may engage in what looks like sharing because another child is bigger and can therefore enforce his or her wishes through physical aggression; in such instances the motivation for the behavior still stems from the child's own needs, in this case for self-protection.

• *Rigid equality (ages 5 to 6)*. As children begin to gain perspective-taking skills and an understanding of other people's feelings, sharing comes to be based on the concept of strict and rigid equality. For example, children at a birthday party may say that it is not fair unless everyone has a piece of cake of exactly the same size. Children engaged in a cooperative game to build a cardboard castle may demand that if one child gets to use a special object, everyone else must have a chance to use it, too.

• *Merit (ages 6 to 7)*. As children continue to develop the ability to understand that others have their own perspectives, they also develop an understanding that people may be more or less deserving of rewards or attention, depending on how they act. For example, they would support the idea that a child who worked for a longer time on a school project might get a bigger share of the reward or an important role in displaying that project.

• *Moral relativity (ages 7 to 8)*. Children begin to see that everyone has a different viewpoint because everyone has his or her own individual set of values. More advanced compromise and negotiation skills begin to develop. For example, if one child forgets to bring a snack, she may be seen by other children as deserving to have a share of all their snacks because she has nothing to eat. A child who is new to a group game might be allowed a second turn because she is unfamiliar with the rules.

Teaching guidelines

Based on this research, teachers will find several guidelines useful in fostering children's development of voluntary sharing.

Deemphasize possessions and individual control of objects

Sharing is less likely when strong emphasis is placed on individual ownership and the value of material possessions. Teachers can deemphasize material possessions and focus instead on experiences, relationships, creative solutions to material needs, and aspects of the natural world (see chapter 4 for specific suggestions about how this can be done).

Teachers sometimes settle children's conflicts over objects by providing each child with a similar object and telling them, "Now you both have one, so you don't need to fight." This strategy, although expedient and sometimes appropriate for children younger than age 3, may have the effect of discouraging sharing. It not only removes the need for the children to find cooperative ways to use limited resources but also conveys the message that individual control of objects is important. Furthermore, in real-world situations there is rarely a benefactor available to provide extra materials.

Similarly, when teachers routinely assign turns, they may be inadvertently encouraging children to focus on gaining exclusive (if only temporary) use of a toy, rather than on more cooperative and interactive options. Alternative solutions for allocating resources include joint use of a toy by more than one child and complementary use of different toys in imaginary play scenes (see chapter 5).

Set guidelines about bringing toys from home

Toys brought from home often stimulate conflicts and reinforce the relationship between possessions and power. It is difficult for young children to adhere to different rules for toys that are owned by an individual child and those that are owned by the school. A child who brings a toy from home might be given the choice of letting others play with it in the classroom or leaving it in her cubby. Teachers can talk with parents to set limits or rules about bringing toys from home. They can also be alert to children trying to use possessions to "buy" social acceptance.

Certain items brought from home, however, are particularly conducive to shared activity, and teachers might welcome these items specifically for that purpose. Such items include a child's favorite book for the teacher to read to the whole class, a tape to which everyone can listen or dance, or a game for several children to play together. To respect each child's ownership rights, teachers may find it useful to label these items with the child's name, keep them in a special place, and send them home after a limited time. At the same time, teachers can encourage classmates to express appreciation directly to the child for his sharing a valued possession and activity with them.

Help children to negotiate the shared use of resources

For young children the first step in learning to negotiate the shared use of materials is practicing how to address each other directly, instead of turning to the teacher. Getting children to do this consistently takes persistence on the part of the teacher, because young children often have already learned to count on adults to solve their problems and meet their needs. At the same time, in their attempts to be helpful, teachers tend to speak for children, expressing the children's presumed feelings and making requests of other children for them. For example, a teacher might be inclined to say, "Anna, please give Hector some of your blue paint, because his is almost used up." The teacher might even take some of Anna's paint herself and give it to Hector, explaining that the children need to share.

Instead, the teacher could consider speaking to Hector, saying, "If you need more blue paint, you can ask Anna for some." If Hector is just learning to make peer requests, the teacher can even give him the phrases to use, saying, "You can say, 'Anna, can I please have some blue paint?'" Anna may begin to hand over the paint when she hears the teacher's comment, but the teacher can ask her to wait, saying, "Thank you, but let's give Hector a chance to practice asking first." Hector would be learning to speak for himself (instead of relying on adult help), and Anna would be responding to a peer request (instead of to an adult directive). Rather than focusing on an equal division of paint, the aim of this procedure is to give children a chance to ask and respond to each other about using materials together.

Teach children that the decision to share is a real choice

Children need guidance to learn how to ask each other for things, wait for an answer, and respect that answer (whether yes or no). For sharing to be meaningful, children should have the freedom to choose not to share, as well as the opportunity to play alone at times. Giving up things under the pressure of aggressive peer demands or unreasonable adult expectations (the "sharing lecture") is counterproductive to the development of prosocial behaviors.

If a child knows that it is OK to say "No," even when she is asked nicely by peers to give up a toy, she is more likely to develop a willingness to share because the choice is under her own control (Arezzo 1993). The child's right to say "No" to immediately giving up a toy deserves to be respected. The requesting child can be taught to accept the "No" by responding, "OK." It would not, however, be reasonable to allow any child to monopolize a valued or limited object indefinitely. Therefore, in such instances the teacher might say to the child who asked, "Gabriel's not ready to give it to you right now. But since you asked so nicely, you can have a turn in five minutes, when the big hand is on the number 6 or when the timer rings."

When this approach is used consistently, the child possessing the toy will often volunteer, before the time is up, to give it to the one who asked for it; perhaps, on learning that the toy has to be given up shortly, the child prefers to take control of the tim-

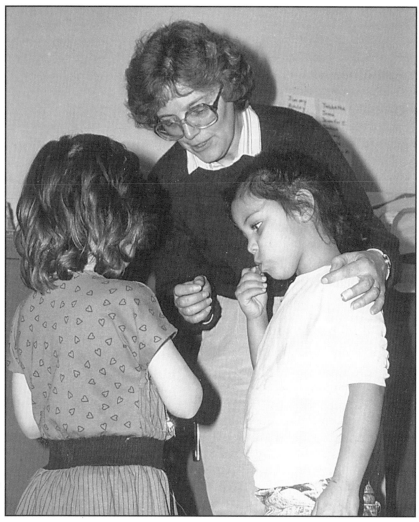

Young children's first step in learning to negotiate the shared use of materials is practicing how to address each other directly, instead of turning to the teacher.

ing and give it up voluntarily (Stocking, Arezzo, & Leavitt 1979). When they do so, the teacher can acknowledge this as genuine sharing and encourage the recipient to show appreciation.

When children learn that they will have a chance to get the toy, they are more willing to calmly accept "No" and to wait. Because the system is fair and predictable, even children with behavior problems are likely to follow

the rules (Arezzo 1991). As they learn to trust each other, children become less dependent on teachers for reminders or time limits. In programs that systematically use this approach, it is not unusual to see the following spontaneous exchange between children 3 to 7 years of age:

Child 1: "Can I have that?" (or "Do you want to trade?")

Child 2: "I'm still using it" (or "You can have it when I'm done.")

Child 1: "OK."

Child 2: (Several minutes later) "You can have it now" (handing it over to the first child).

(See chapter 10 for suggested ways to teach these skills.)

Add extra incentives to share

Some children consistently say "No," even when being asked nicely by their peers for an object or for a chance to play together. The teacher might consider providing such a child with special incentives to share, without forcing him to do so. In this way the teacher attempts to increase the motivation or ease with which the child begins to share. For example, a kindergarten child playing with a valued airport toy might be told, "Maria asked you if she could play with you. You can choose to play with the airport by yourself for five more minutes, and then it will be Maria's turn to use it; or, you can choose to let her play with you, and then you can both use it until recess." The child might agree to share, primarily to have longer use of the toy; nevertheless, he can be acknowledged for including Maria. Most importantly he will have an opportunity to begin to experience the intrinsic rewards of sharing and playing with others. The goal is to reduce or eliminate teacher-facilitated incentives as soon as they are no longer necessary.

Teach children to trade

Agreeing to trade with a peer is usually more acceptable to young children than giving up an object out-right. Trading is a valuable social strategy in itself, and it can also serve as a first step toward more interactive or altruistic sharing.

Teachers can design activities that require or strongly encourage trading, exchanging, or rotating materials. For example, in an individual art project, each child might be given a different-color marker or a page of geometric stickers that are all one color. In order for any child to make a multicolor project, that child would need to trade materials with other children. Alternatively, each child could be given only some of the materials needed to complete a project. These situations would be conducive to sharing, since each exchange of materials could help each child develop a more complete or varied project.

It might be a useful first step for the teacher to instruct the children to exchange or rotate use of the materials. However, she would eventually want to guide the children in recognizing trading opportunities themselves and in asking *each other* to trade or take a turn to use the materials. In allowing them to make real choices in responding to each other and teaching them to respect each other's choices, the teacher thus helps the children learn to deal with their peers directly rather than to count on an adult to make sharing happen.

Working with children individually or in small groups, teachers are able to demonstrate and provide guidance for learning specific trading skills, such as how to ask a peer to trade, answer clearly, follow the wishes of the trading partner, and respond assertively if someone is breaking the rules of fair trading. Opportunities for trading fit easily into classroom activities.

For example, the teacher might pass out different-colored hats in preparation for a game or song and give children the opportunity to trade hats before the game begins. When children learn the skills of trading in these structured group activities, they will find many opportunities to trade in free play. The teacher might then encourage and guide trading in free play, while pointing out the mutual benefits.

Teach children to take turns fairly

Taking turns is a way to share materials. Although it should not be overused as a substitute for more interactive forms of play, turn taking is sometimes necessary, as in many structured games or when only one child at a time can use a particular piece of equipment (e.g., a swing). Turn taking provides opportunities for practicing various sharing skills. For example, instead of the teacher consistently assigning turns, she can help the children learn to ask each other for turns in a way that lets them initiate and participate in the process. If the teacher observes that a boy is finished with a toy before his turn is up, she can suggest that he offer it to the girl who is waiting for it. The boy will have little resistance to making the offer in this case, and the girl will happily accept the offer. Such a situation provides social skills practice and a positive social experience for both children. In this real-life context, the teacher assists the children in learning to offer things to others and to show appreciation.

Turn taking also presents an opportunity to address issues of fairness, since it often involves clear-cut rules and is aimed at providing equitable access to resources or activities. It is important for children to be able to give a turn to a peer and to avoid becoming overly possessive about their turn (i.e., to avoid "hogging" a turn). It is also important for children to be able to stand up to someone who attempts to take unfair advantage in a turn-taking situation (i.e., to resist allowing another child to preempt their turn). The teacher has an opportunity to create an environment in which fair play is the norm and unfair treatment toward others is not tolerated—by either the teacher *or* the other children.

Model and acknowledge sharing behaviors

Teachers are powerful role models when they display empathy and prosocial behaviors in the classroom toward other adults and toward children (see chapter 12). Children are likely to imitate the sharing and cooperative behaviors they observe, especially if they know and like the person who is modeling the behavior (Yarrow, Scott, & Waxler 1973). When teachers describe the prosocial intentions behind their actions, they enhance the effect of role modeling. For example, a teacher might say, "I'm going to give some of our red paper to Ms. Jones. I know she'll appreciate it. Ms. Jones and I like to help each other out."

Teachers can make a point of noticing, commenting on, and showing approval for children's spontaneous sharing behavior. They can comment on the positive consequences of sharing and cooperation occur-

Besides learning to give other children their fair turns, the child needs to learn to stand up to anyone trying to take her turn.

ring in the classroom. In group activities or projects, instead of focusing on the individual performances of children, the teacher can emphasize how well the children work together and how well they share materials. In addition to generally encouraging all children in this regard, the teacher would want to specifically acknowledge particularly good examples of spontaneous sharing. For example, she might say, "Pedro, that was very nice of you to give Jamie some of the blocks you were using. Because you shared the blocks with him, he could help you build that awesome tower. Nice teamwork." The teacher might also follow up by encouraging Jamie to specifically express appreciation to Pedro for sharing the blocks. Such teacher and peer acknowledgments not only serve as social rewards but also point out the naturally occurring benefits and good feelings that sharing can provide.

Points to Remember

Deemphasize possessions. Emphasize instead the value of experiences, relationships, and aspects of the natural world.

Encourage complementary use of materials, and deemphasize individual control of objects. Avoid simply providing extra resources or routinely assigning turns.

Set guidelines about toys from home. Limit the type and number of items that can be brought from home, and ensure that they are used in a socially constructive way.

Encourage independent negotiation about the use of materials. Teach children to ask and to make offers to each other in a way that respects one another's choices.

Recognize a child's right to choose not to share. Avoid forcing a child to give up an object in the name of "sharing." Teach children that saying "No" is OK and help them learn how to accept "No" for an answer.

Add extra incentives to share. If necessary, set up contingencies that increase the motivation for children to begin to share.

Teach children the skills of voluntary and fair trading. Encourage such trading during routine activities.

Teach children to take turns cooperatively and fairly. Guide them in asking or offering turns to each other and in assertively responding to unfair treatment.

Model and acknowledge sharing. Demonstrate, comment upon, and recognize sharing behaviors that occur in the natural setting. Point out the real-life benefits of sharing for all.

10

Teaching Assertiveness Skills

Rachel and Devin were happily playing with a new batch of homemade playdough that they had helped to make. Mark came to the table, loudly said to Devin, "Give me that," and took all the playdough Devin was using. Devin looked down and quietly left the table. Then Mark said to Rachel, "I want the rolling pin," and he grabbed it away from her. Rachel ran, crying, to tell the teacher that Mark had taken the rolling pin from her. **Which of these children lacks respectful assertiveness skills? What can the teacher do to help?**

ssertiveness consists of effectively expressing one's own needs and feelings and defending one's rights, while respecting the rights and feelings of others. For children, as for adults, assertiveness represents a socially desirable alternative that stands between the extremes of *aggression* (where the rights of others are disregarded) and *submission* or passivity (where one's own rights are disregarded). It also provides children with an alternative to excessive dependency on adults to solve social problems. In the context of violence prevention, assertiveness training for children serves three important functions: (1) it offers a nonaggressive and socially responsible way for potential aggressors to achieve their goals; (2) it provides potential victims with a nonaggressive way to avoid victimization; and (3) it prevents aggressive acts from being rewarded by peer submission. Teaching young children to use and value assertive behaviors can help to prevent aggression and victimization, both in the present and in the future, as children develop increasingly mature social behaviors.

What research tells us

Research has demonstrated the potential value of assertive behaviors in preventing violence and indicates specific skills that are important for children to develop.

Rationale for teaching assertiveness skills to children

It is no surprise that children often lack assertiveness skills, considering that many parents and teachers lack these same skills. Yet, young children are more likely than adults to find themselves in face-to-face situations that call for assertiveness—as when peers attack them, intrude on their play, or grab toys from them. Different assertiveness skills are needed when children want to enter into play with others, have a turn, or get help.

In one study, toddlers in group care experienced more than nine peer conflicts per hour, mostly over possessions (Ross et al. 1990). In another study of preschoolers' behavior, about 80% of all observed aggressive acts were directly rewarded by such victim reactions as giving up objects, crying, or running away (Patterson, Littman, & Bricker 1967). Yet, children typically receive very little guidance in learning appropriate and effective ways to act or respond in these situations. The aggressor may be scolded for hurting someone but not taught what to do instead (e.g., how to ask the other child for a turn instead of pushing her off the swing). The victim is most often rewarded for being helpless and dependent instead of being taught to stand up to the aggressor. When she cries or "tattles," the adult often gives her sympathy, speaks *for* her, and solves her problem (e.g., by telling the aggressor, "You hurt her feelings," and taking the aggressor off the swing).

Another common problem is that adults may allow the aggressor to prevail, or they may tell the victim to yield to an unreasonable demand in the name of keeping the peace or promoting accommodation. In the study cited above, when toddlers had a conflict over a toy, 90% of the time the mother told her own child to let the other child have the toy, regardless of ownership, possession, or the manner in which one child tried to get the toy from the other child (Ross et al. 1990). The reasons the mothers gave their children for why they should yield to their playmates were completely inconsistent with regard to any principles that might help the children understand their own rights or the rights of others. Although

mothers often say that they encourage their children to stand up for themselves, such encouragement was rare in this study.

Assertive social behavior in children has been shown to relate positively to healthy school adjustment (Cartledge & Milburn 1980). However, specific assertive skills have not been generally accepted as important for children. In the case of responding to peer aggression, researchers and practitioners have often considered "telling a grownup" to be the most appropriate response for a young child. Little recognition has been given to the fact that refusing to submit to the frequent inappropriate demands of peers is an important social skill. It is also important to know how to say, "No," in an acceptable way, even to appropriate requests. Young children, however, almost universally believe that they are expected by adults to acquiesce whenever they are asked nicely for something (Arezzo 1991).

Social skills training programs typically include learning to say, "No," only in the context of staying out of trouble. In fact, the only widespread child assertiveness training has come from attempts to teach children to say, "No," to drugs and to sexual abuse. To be able to effectively stand up for themselves in such critical situations, children must learn that they have a right to say, "No," and how to do so in a broad range of everyday situations. Adults also must recognize children's fundamental rights to express themselves and to be heard in a much broader range of social contexts than merely protesting against abuse or drugs.

Perhaps we have overlooked the assertiveness needs of young children because we have so highly valued

When children fail to stand up to peer aggression, they not only tend to become victims, they also reward the aggression by their submission.

compliance, acquiescence, and "being nice." But there is no inherent conflict between children learning to assert themselves appropriately and their developing the ability and inclination to cooperate and share. Ironically, by allowing children to choose to say, "No," we may increase their willingness to say, "Yes." By teaching assertiveness skills that recognize children's right to make choices, teachers help children to behave in a realistic and self-reliant manner, rather than have them become either chronic victims or chronic aggressors.

Children who are excessively submissive and unable to stand up to peer aggression become increasingly likely to be victimized. In experimental playgroups of young boys who did not previously know each other, those boys who initially showed low rates of assertive behavior and high rates of submissive behavior were subsequently targeted for aggression and increasingly victimized (Schwartz, Dodge, & Coie 1994).

Children who lack the social skills needed to initiate interaction, ask for what they need, or express their feelings may instead increasingly resort to grabbing objects from peers, intruding on other children, physically attacking others, or withdrawing from playmates. Unless the initial assertiveness deficits are corrected, these negative behaviors can set up a vicious cycle of increasingly poor peer relations, lowered self-esteem, and escalating negative behaviors (Combs & Slaby 1977). For this reason it is important for teachers working with young children to intervene actively to foster assertiveness skills,

especially when initial deficits are most apparent.

With respect to assertiveness and acquiescence, adults do not treat boys and girls equivalently. Girls tend to receive greater adult encouragement toward self-sacrifice and submission than do boys. For example, in the toddler study cited earlier, mothers told daughters to yield to a playmate three times as often as they told sons to do so (Ross et al. 1990). Teachers and parents need to guard against inadvertently reinforcing societal biases about the appropriateness of submissiveness for girls and aggressiveness for boys. To counteract these common gender-role–related socialization practices, it is important to teach assertiveness skills to both boys and girls.

By learning assertiveness, children become empowered to meet their own social goals more effectively. For example, a child is more likely to take an active role in shaping play activities to her own liking when she is able to effectively express her ideas and wishes to her peers. Standing up to aggression or bossiness, as compared to submitting, is likely to result in reduced harassment from others. These beneficial consequences do not depend on the presence of an adult to dispense rewards. Favorable responses from peers and success at reaching one's own goals are the most powerful incentives for promoting the long-term use of these skills.

Teaching assertiveness is consistent with valuing and fostering self-reliance and self-confidence in children. The child with assertiveness skills learns to trust his own feelings and judgment and to avoid excessive reliance on approval from either adults or peers. Assertiveness training is also a tool for teaching children to resist peer pressure to do things that they may feel are wrong or dangerous or that they simply may not want to do. Assertiveness skills may even help young children resist imitating problematic or violent peer behaviors. Teaching children to resist peer pressure and to think and act for themselves on what is right and what is safe clearly needs to be included in any educational violence-prevention efforts.

Valuing assertiveness for children does not deny the teacher's (or parents') authority to set rules and requirements and to make decisions about which the children do not have a choice. By clearly distinguishing requirements from choices, the teacher helps the children accept legitimate authority while also learning assertiveness. To communicate this distinction, teachers should present requirements, rules, and contingencies as clear statements, not as questions or statements that end with "OK?" Questions to which there is really only one right answer can be confusing and unfair to children, as well as contradictory to the intention of giving children real choices. For example, a child may think that she has a choice when she is asked, "Wouldn't you like to hang your coat up?" or "Let's hang up your coat, OK?" To avoid ambiguity the teacher could say, "You need to hang up your coat" (statement) or "When you hang up your coat, then you can join in the game" (contingency). Teachers should give children as many real choices as are feasible—clearly stated as choices—but avoid asking pseudoquestions when there is not a real choice.

In their relations with peers, as well as with adults, children cannot always have a free choice. It is sometimes necessary for teachers to impose rules about dividing up resources, taking turns, or other social matters. These situations should be clearly distinguished for the children from those in which they are allowed to ask each other for things and make real social choices that will be respected by the other children and by the teacher. For example, a teacher might say, "I'm going to divide the playdough so that you will both have enough," rather than asking, "Don't you think you should share with Billy?" and then dividing the playdough, regardless of the child's answer.

Assertiveness as a set of specific skills

Effective assertiveness requires a variety of specific types of verbal and nonverbal behaviors, which need to be adapted for different social situations. These skills are not likely to be acquired by children through everyday observation, because exemplary assertive interactions are rare and those that do occur may be too subtle to serve as effective models for young children. Furthermore, there are many salient models of nonassertive behaviors. For example, *Sesame Street*'s Bert is usually nonassertive and ineffective in dealing with Ernie's audacious behaviors. Primary-school children in one study spontaneously generated very few specifically assertive solutions to social problems; however, once assertive solutions were described to them together with other

Teachers should make a point of giving children real choices (e.g., by providing a small group of children a single bowl of paste and letting them work out how to share it) and then make sure to respect the children's choices.

solutions, they strongly preferred the assertive solutions (Rathjen, Hiniker, & Rathjen 1976). Although children often lack knowledge of possible assertive behaviors that they can use, they are generally receptive to learning these skills.

General admonitions to young children to "cooperate" or "try to work it out" are of no value in helping them learn new social skills, particularly because these skills are more complex than they may first appear. Consider the example of kindergarten children trading toys according to ideal assertiveness principles.

• If Sarah wishes to initiate a trade with Derek, she looks at him, calls his name, and appropriately asks him to trade.

• Derek answers promptly and clearly.

• Sarah waits for Derek's answer before acting. If she does not, Derek politely tells her to wait.

• If Derek agrees to trade, they exchange toys (Sarah is not allowed to take back her offer at this point), and they thank each other.

• Both children understand that Derek has a right to say either, "Yes," or, "No," and that he can say, "No," in a firm but polite way if he chooses to decline.

• If he declines, Sarah willingly accepts his response by saying, "OK."

• If Sarah should try to force the trade on Derek, he firmly repeats that he does not want to trade and holds on to his toy. (In this case Derek talks directly to Sarah and does not seek an adult's help.)

In addition to learning the sequence of steps and the words to use, the children learn body language and tone of voice appropriate to each situation. Even 2- or 3-year-old children, with considerable guidance, can begin to learn the basic aspects and benefits of trading when trading is viewed as a teachable set of specific social skills.

Teaching guidelines

Young children can learn the assertiveness skills listed below, but they need step-by-step guided practice. Teachers can provide this help through proven teaching techniques, which include demonstrating, modeling, coaching, role playing, and providing feedback. Using these techniques together and in complementary ways maximizes effectiveness: (1) during structured practice sessions with the whole group or with smaller groups of two to four children and (2) during "real-life practice" at the scene of naturally occurring social situations.

Recognize key assertive behaviors that young children need

In *proactive* assertive behaviors, the child initiates a social interaction. In *reactive* assertive behaviors, the child responds to the actions of another.

General assertive behaviors

• Speak and respond *directly* to peers (avoid turning to adults, except as backup).

• Use words in addition to gestures and actions.

• Make eye contact; use a clear, firm voice; sit or stand tall.

Proactive assertive behaviors

• Greet others and initiate social contact.

• Make requests in a polite, open-ended way (e.g., for an object, a turn, help, a favor, information, permission, a chance to play with someone). Open-ended requests or offers allow the other person a real choice to accept or decline.

• Offer things in a polite, open-ended way (e.g., to help, trade, give an object to someone, give someone a chance to do something).

• Make friendly suggestions (rather than bossy demands).

• Express your own feelings, opinions, and ideas (without putting down those of others).

• Show interest and give encouragement to others.

Reactive assertive behaviors

• Firmly tell an aggressor to stop hurtful acts (e.g., by saying, "No hitting!" or "Stop pushing me!").

• Resist giving up objects or territory to an aggressor (e.g., say, "I'm still using this" or "I'm not leaving").

• Firmly refuse to accept discriminatory acts (e.g., say, "Stop calling me that name!" or "You can't say that girls are not allowed").

• Stand up for other personal rights and against unfair treatment (e.g., by saying, "You forgot my turn" or "Cutting in line is not allowed").

• Politely ask someone to change an annoying behavior (e.g., say, "Please stop yelling in my ear").

• Ignore routine teasing or other provocative peer behaviors by turning or walking away.

- Don't take orders from bossy peers (e.g., say, "No, I want to do it my own way").

- Politely turn down unnecessary help (e.g., by saying, "No thank you, I can do it myself").

- Respond promptly and clearly to questions, requests, and offers.

- If choosing to decline, say, "No," politely to requests or offers.

- After making a request, offer, or suggestion that is declined, willingly accept "No" for an answer by saying, "OK."

- Show appreciation, when appropriate.

- Firmly and persistently say, "No," to peer pressure to misbehave.

- Firmly say, "No," to the abusive use of power by older children or adults (e.g., sexual abuse, physical abuse, or other maltreatment) and seek help from a trusted adult.

Structure practice sessions for assertiveness skills

Teaching social skills through structured practice and role playing can be very effective. Teachers who are interested but inexperienced in using these techniques might request inservice training or work together to develop methods appropriate to their program. Practicing with one or two children at a time might help a teacher become more comfortable with these methods before trying them with a larger group.

Older preschoolers and kindergarten children can practice assertive behaviors in a teacher-directed group activity using demonstration and role playing. The teacher first sets up a simple, hypothetical situation or story and then demonstrates assertive behavior as well as contrasting aggressive or submissive responses. The demonstration might include the participation of a teacher aide, a child, dolls, or puppets. The observing children practice identifying and explaining why a given behavior is right (with thumbs up) or wrong (with thumbs down). Children usually enjoy and participate very attentively in these dramatic demonstrations (Arezzo 1991).

Once they are familiar with the role-playing idea, the children are able to participate in suggesting responses for the teacher to demonstrate. They might also take a doll or puppet themselves and actively role-play different options, with teacher guidance as needed. The child and the teacher might alternate—one using the doll or puppet to play a role (e.g., child protagonist, reacting peer, or teacher), while the other responds to the doll directly in a reciprocal role. For example, if the situation is about resisting peer pressure to misbehave, the teacher might use the doll first to demonstrate submissive responding (e.g., agreeing to misbehave) and help the children recognize the negative consequences. She could then use the doll to demonstrate assertive responding (e.g., refusing to go along with misbehavior, even under pressure). Next the teacher could use the doll to play the role of a peer urging a child in the class to do something wrong, such as playing with matches or picking on another child. The child then practices firmly telling the doll, "No, I won't do that!" and then ignoring the doll's taunting and pleading by turning her head away. This type of pretending is

Children can learn assertive responses by role-playing them with puppets, with teacher guidance as needed.

© Marietta Lynch

natural and appealing to young children. During role playing, children are given supportive feedback and coaching to help them learn the main features first and then the finer points of assertive responding in a given situation. Role playing allows the children to observe or act out the assertive behaviors, see the possible consequences, and evaluate how well the assertive behaviors worked.

A role-playing demonstration might present a girl puppet (held by a child) playing with a set of small blocks. A boy puppet (held by the teacher) *really* wants to play with the blocks. What can he do? The teacher could demonstrate the boy puppet saying, "Give me those blocks!" and grabbing the blocks. How does the girl puppet feel? (The child could act out how the girl puppet might react).

What do the children think of the way the boy acted? What else could the boy do? The teacher could demonstrate the boy sitting quietly and looking down sadly. Does the girl puppet know that he wants to play with the blocks? The girl puppet might say, "No, I don't know what he wants." What do the children think about the boy saying nothing? What else could he do? The teacher could have the boy puppet ask the girl nicely for some blocks. How does the girl puppet feel about the boy now? What do the children think about the boy asking nicely?

This type of demonstration can be expanded on subsequent days to include demonstration and practice of saying, "No," nicely (in contrast to saying, "No," rudely or agreeing to something you don't want to do); accepting "No" for an answer by saying, "OK" (in contrast to protesting or pleading); or offering to play together, trade, or work out another compromise. Children begin by role-playing with the teacher and progress to role-playing with a peer instead.

When demonstrating the aggressive or rude behaviors, the teacher needs to show some restraint in order to reduce the risk of imitation. For example, the teacher might say, "We'll pretend that the doll is hitting," and only move the doll's arm, making a gutteral sound but not real contact. When the children each take a turn to role-play, the teacher guides them to practice only appropriate assertive behaviors, rather than undesirable behaviors. However, a child might spontaneously act out aggressive or submissive behaviors in the role-playing situation. When this happens,

it is helpful to play out the scene, showing the negative consequences for others or for the child. The child should then always end by practicing a desirable assertive response for the same situation, with guidance from his teacher or classmates if needed. For example, a child might respond to a pretend hit from the doll by hitting back. The group can talk about what might then happen in a real situation (e.g., the two might get into a big fight and get hurt or both get into trouble). The child should then practice, instead, assertively telling the doll, "Don't hit me!" without using physical retaliation.

Making a large display of three cartoon faces can aid children's participation in these exercises at the kindergarten level (Arezzo 1991) (see illustration on p. 135). *Assertiveness* (in the center) is represented by a pleasant face with eyes open and a partially open mouth and is labeled "Good Asking/Good Telling." *Aggressiveness* is characterized by an angry face and is labeled "Rude/Hurting." *Submissiveness,* or passivity, is conveyed by a face with hands covering the eyes and a closed mouth and is labeled "Giving Up/Giving In." The characteristics of the faces and the familiar words labeling these depictions help young children understand the concept of assertiveness and its alternatives.

Children can point to the appropriate face and learn the labels as they identify demonstrated behaviors. Some situations call for proactive behavior. For example, when a person needs help, saying, "Please help me," is an assertive response represented by the Good Asking face. Demanding help in this situation would be represented

Illustrations for use in assertiveness training

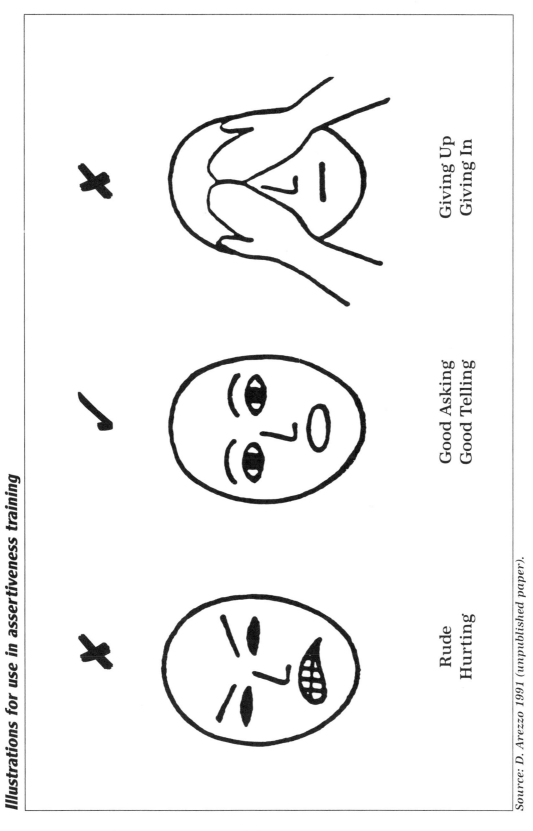

Rude
Hurting

Good Asking
Good Telling

Giving Up
Giving In

Source: D. Arezzo 1991 (unpublished paper).

by the Rude face, and whining helplessly would be represented by the Giving Up face. Other situations call for reactive behavior. For example, if a playmate is trying to take a child's turn, telling that playmate, "It's my turn," would be represented by the Good Telling face; hitting the playmate would be represented by the Hurting face; and meekly letting the playmate take one's turn would be represented by the Giving In face. After the children learn the basics, the teacher might vary eye contact, tone of voice, and body language, as part of the game to help them learn to identify more specifically what is required to achieve the goal of Good Asking or Good Telling.

In their book *Skill-streaming in Early Childhood,* McGinnis and Goldstein (1990) present useful guidance for teaching preschool and kindergarten children prosocial skills and managing behavior problems. A social skills training program of exercises includes the techniques discussed here. The authors use the term *brave talk* in lessons designed to help children learn how to respond to peer pressure to misbehave and how to deal with teasing. They provide cartoon faces to distinguish a "brave look" and a "brave voice" from a friendly look and from an angry look. Other types of assertive behaviors are also presented, including saying "No" and making requests or offers. Cartoon faces are used to depict responses, such as smiling, turning away (i.e., ignoring), thinking, taking a deep breath, and asking a question. Additional training resources that include structured practice of social skills are discussed in chapter 8.

Structured practice sessions might also include activities specially de-signed to allow coaching and practice of particular assertive behaviors. For example, activities that encourage or require trading as a means of teaching assertive trading skills are important (see chapter 5). A group of toddlers can learn to speak up for themselves by each saying, "My turn," in sequence before the teacher enthusiastically tosses a ball to them. When the teacher (deliberately) skips a child's turn, that child can learn to politely correct her. Next, with coaching, each child can ask a classmate to throw the ball to him or ask, "Do you want to catch?" before throwing. For 4- to 6-year-old children, a picture lotto game provides opportunities to practice trading picture boards before the game begins, offering help (e.g., "Can I put this picture on for you?") and politely rejecting an offer (e.g., "No, thanks, I can put it on myself").

Structured sessions are a good place to introduce and practice assertiveness skills, because they are not emotionally charged and allow as much adult support as is needed. Of course, these skills will have lasting benefits only if the children are able to use them spontaneously and effectively in their lives outside structured practice sessions. Coaching and practice in naturally occurring situations can help to accomplish this goal.

Support children in applying assertiveness skills in their everyday interactions

In coaching, the teacher intervenes and gives direct guidance at the scene of social situations as they occur naturally in the classroom. Situations in which real feelings and consequences are at stake heighten children's motivation to learn. Teachers can use such coaching effectively even if they choose not to use structured practice sessions. At first the adult may need to model the exact words for the child to repeat. Later the child may require only a brief cue, and eventually no teacher intervention will be needed. The teacher may intervene either before or immediately after a problem occurs.

Before a problem occurs, the teacher can interrupt a social interaction that seems headed for trouble and suggest assertive behaviors to prevent the anticipated outcome. For example, if a child appears ready to disruptively barge in on a group project, the teacher might interrupt and assist that child in finding a way to be helpful to the group (Hazen, Black, & Fleming-Johnson 1984). If a child appears upset and ready to hit a peer who has taken something from her, the teacher might step between them and say, "You can take it back and tell her, 'I'm still using that. Please give it back!'" The teacher can then help her follow through without aggression. If an overly submissive child seems about to give in to the unreasonable demands of a bossy peer, the teacher might suggest to him that it is all right to say, "No, I won't," and then support him to do so assertively. She could then suggest to the other child how he might change his bossy demand into a friendly suggestion.

A second type of real-life practice might be called *corrective instant replay*. Right after a problematic social interaction has occurred, the teacher can intervene and have the children reenact the scene on the spot to practice alternative assertive behaviors that prevent the aggressor from being rewarded. For example, Katie pushes Jason off his chair, whereupon Jason gives up the chair and stands by, looking dejected. The teacher might say, "Wait a minute. Let's try that again." She would first turn to the victim. After having Jason sit back in his chair, she would tell him, "If someone tries to take your chair without asking, you can *stay* there and tell her, 'I'm sitting in this chair.'" Only after Jason had practiced such an assertive response would the teacher guide Katie to ask him appropriately for the chair or to offer to trade chairs. Jason might need to be reassured that he can say, "No." He would then either choose to give up his chair (this time, voluntarily) or practice saying, "No," politely. Katie would practice either showing appreciation or accepting his "No" by saying, "OK," all with teacher guidance if necessary. Thus, both children have the opportunity to practice and to see the benefits of particular assertiveness skills, just when they have a real and immediate need for those skills.

Immediate reenactment is particularly useful when a novel conflict situation arises, to allow clear demonstration of alternative responses that had not been previously discussed. However, the reenactment may need to be delayed in specific situations if the teacher decides to apply an immediate consequence for aggression—either as part of the classroom rules or when following an individualized behavior plan (see chapter 7).

Some teachers are reluctant to intervene directly in children's conflict situations, thinking it best to "let them work it out themselves," and in some situations a wait-and-see approach is appropriate. However, if the teacher had not intervened in the above example, Katie would likely have benefited from pushing Jason off the chair, and Jason would have presented himself as an easy target by accepting mistreatment. In the absence of constructive teacher intervention, these patterns are likely to perpetuate themselves. In the example given, the teacher did not scold or discipline either child. Instead, she took advantage of a real-life situation to show assertive alternatives to both children and gave them a chance to practice these skills and to see their usefulness. Of course, teachers should avoid excessive or unnecessary intervention and reduce the frequency and extent of their interventions as children learn to use social skills on their own. Rather than intervening immediately, the teacher may want to unobtrusively observe how a conflict situation plays out before deciding whether, and in what way, to intervene. However, when a child shows patterns of serious aggressive behavior, then the teacher will want to respond decisively as part of a plan, not only to interrupt but also to help change the aggressive behavior (see chapter 7).

Often a teacher does not directly observe a conflict, but a child comes and complains to her. Instead of using her authority to solve the problem, the teacher can guide the child in attempting to solve the problem himself. When a child whines to the teacher, "She's in my way," the teacher can say, "Then you need to ask her to move over." If the other child starts to move beforehand, the teacher can stop her and say, "Wait! He needs to practice asking you first." Thus, the teacher encourages social self-reliance, rather than rewards dependency on adults to solve the problem.

Sometimes a child readily allows an aggressor to take something from her forcefully. When urged to resist, she may say, "That's OK. He can have it."

The teacher can then explain, "It's OK to give it to him, but first he needs to practice asking you for it." This practice helps the aggressor learn that he must ask nicely to get the object. Just as important, the potential victim learns that she has a right to be asked and to be given a real choice. In this approach teachers actively discourage giving up objects to an aggressor and never refer to this as "sharing."

A key concept of assertiveness training for young children is teaching them to ask each other directly for what they want and to respond directly and appropriately to each other. Some educators believe that teaching children to "ask nicely" only sets them up for a painful rejection from their peers. This could be true if the teacher goes no further than encouraging children to ask nicely and leaves them with the expectation that the answer will always be "Yes." However, teachers who have systematically used a classroomwide assertiveness-training approach, as described here, have found that young children benefit from learning to ask each other nicely, express their own feelings and choices politely, and acknowledge the rights of others respectfully. Children in these settings are heard spontaneously reminding each other, "You need to *ask*" (Arezzo 1991).

Teach victims to respond assertively to peer aggression

In teaching children assertive responses to physical aggression, the first goal is to have the victim (or potential victim) respond quickly, directly, and firmly to the aggressor, instead of submitting, crying, or telling an adult. Even 2-year-old children can be taught to look straight at a child who hurt them and tell the aggressor firmly, "No hitting!" or "No kicking!" Older children might say, "Stop hitting me! I don't like that" or "That hurts me!" There are several advantages to having the victim directly and firmly tell the aggressor to stop. The victim shows confidence instead of timidity. Furthermore, if the teacher did not observe the aggression, the victim's firm statement serves to alert the teacher about the episode (without the child having to go to her and "tell" on the other child).

Many children call for teacher help and sympathy whenever they are hurt or mistreated by a peer; they may even exaggerate or trump up such charges. When teachers help these children instead to stand up assertively to aggressive peers, they discourage excessive dependency on adult intervention. Of course, in cases in which a child is seriously hurt (either physically or emotionally), the teacher may need to intervene directly and immediately. In other cases, when a child comes to the teacher to report aggression, she can accompany him back to the scene and ask the child himself to tell the other child to stop. Initially, she can support and guide him in this effort. Children need to know that if aggression persists after they have made their best effort to deal with it assertively, they have a right to seek adult help and to expect support in solving the problem. If their initial attempts do not succeed in stopping an aggressive child, children may need to warn that child that they will get help (e.g., "If you

don't stop hitting me, I will tell the teacher").

Role-playing this sequence in structured practice sessions can be very helpful, with these directions: first, you stand up to the child who is hurting you; then, if the child doesn't stop, you ask the teacher for help. By role-playing, children can practice asking the teacher for help, if necessary, in an assertive way (e.g., firmly stating, "I said, 'Stop!' but Derek keeps on hitting me"), rather than acting whiny or helpless. In actual situations that arise in the classroom, the teacher can support the child in responding assertively as practiced.

For children, as for adults, assertive responses to an aggressor do not always work, and children need to understand this fact of life. However, it is important for teachers to help children feel strong and good about themselves in making assertive choices, even when they *don't* work out ideally. Standing up verbally to a child who is acting like a bully doesn't always solve the immediate problem, but the child will feel stronger and more independent than she would if she submits or cries to the teacher. Teachers can lend encouragement, drawing the child's attention to these positive feelings about standing up for herself. Structured role-playing scenarios might include having children practice making assertive nonviolent choices, having these actions *not* work out to solve the problem, and then having the children express good feelings about their choices anyway (e.g., telling themselves, "She didn't stop pushing me that time when I told her to stop, but I'm glad I stood up for myself").

Young children benefit from learning and practicing assertive responses to typical forms of aggression among their peers in the supervised setting of the classroom, center, or playground. However, in unsupervised settings in their communities or at home, where dangerous or even potentially lethal violence may be a serious threat, safety issues must be a first priority. Whenever any weapons or serious violence are involved, the child should avoid confrontation of any kind and, instead, immediately attempt to leave the scene, seek shelter, and get help (as discussed in chapter 2). Attempts to respond assertively to more powerful individuals, or when protective backup is not available, are often unrealistic and may be dangerous for young children. Thus, children need to understand that even reasonable assertive responses may be unsafe to use when they face violence or unfair treatment perpetrated by adults. As educators teach children to act assertively in certain situations, they must also help them to distinguish these situations from others that pose potential dangers. It is important to encourage children to bring dangerous situations to the attention of teachers or other trusted adults instead of trying to handle such situations themselves, so that they might receive realistic assistance or protection.

Teach assertive responses to discriminatory acts

Acts that reflect discrimination or bias are a source of tension, hostility, and verbal violence, and they often produce increasingly serious consequences across the age span. Discriminatory acts, including teasing, exclusion, and name-calling based on any aspect of a person's identity (e.g., gender, race, ethnicity, disability, religion, socioeconomic class, physical appearance), are a form of aggressive behavior potentially as hurtful as physical aggression and must be treated as such. Whatever the method of handling incidents of discriminatory behaviors—and there are many approaches—the purpose is to immediately intervene and stop the behaviors and to guide children's prosocial development (Derman-Sparks & the A.B.C. Task Force 1989).

Discriminatory acts occur in preschool, usually by children who do not fully understand the meaning or the hurtful effects of their behavior. Teachers of young children have an opportunity to discourage bias before it becomes deeply rooted in the child's belief system and behavior. They can help children better understand differences between people and recognize the false nature of bias statements (e.g., "Mexicans are dirty" or "Girls can't run fast"). Children can learn about the power of certain types of verbal insults to hurt people and their own rights to defend against them. As part of a violence-prevention effort, the teacher can set a firm rule that no aspect of a person's identity is ever an acceptable reason for teasing, verbal attack, or exclusion. For example, she might say, "In this class it is never OK to tease someone, to call her a mean name, or to say you won't play with someone because of the color of her skin, because she is a girl, or because she uses a wheelchair" (e.g., Derman-Sparks & the A.B.C. Task Force 1989).

Just as a teacher would not allow one child to continue hitting another, she should not allow a discriminatory act to continue or be repeated. When the teacher intervenes immediately to stop the discriminatory act, she can invoke the classroom rule against it. She can further guide the children's prosocial development in this area in two ways: (1) by supporting the child toward whom the discriminatory act is directed to know his rights, express his feelings to the discriminating child, and firmly resist submitting; and (2) by helping the taunting or excluding child to understand the effects of his behavior and to find alternative ways to treat others in a given situation.

The teaching techniques of structured practice and real-life practice described in this chapter are useful for this purpose. When a teacher first observes a discriminatory act, after intervening by invoking the classroom rule against it, he might assist the target child (or children) in practicing an assertive response right at the scene. For example, he can encourage her to tell the discriminating child, "Don't call me that mean name!" or "I *like* my hair just the way it is" or "You can't say girls are not allowed—I'm staying" or "I *don't* like it when you say that!" Once the rule against discrimination has been established, the teacher might handle subsequent incidents by directly assisting the target child in being assertive, rather than repeating the rule. If a child uses name-calling in a conflict situation, the teacher might help him at the scene to express himself about the conflict in a constructive and nondiscriminatory way instead, focusing on the usefulness of doing so. For example, the teacher might say, "When you called Bridget a name, she got upset, and she didn't know *what* you wanted. But now that you've done such a good job

of telling her what you want, she understands, and we can try to work it out. Way to go!"

Planned demonstrations and role-playing sessions are useful to advance children's understanding of the hurtful nature of discriminatory acts as well as to help children practice specific ways to respond. They can practice using eye contact, body language, and tone of voice to increase their effectiveness in responding to discriminatory acts. Insults and labels that reflect bias should not be used in practice sessions, since their use might stimulate children to imitate these words. If a particular discriminatory word (or phrase) has been an issue in the class or is mentioned by a child, it can be acknowledged as a hurtful word but should not be used in practice. Instead, the teacher should use more generic language. For example, she might say, "If someone calls you a name just because of the color of your skin (or because your family speaks Spanish), what can you say to them?"

Of course, even when children learn to make assertive responses, they will not always be able to solve problems of discrimination on their own. As in the case of physical aggression, teachers need to be vigilant, and children should be taught that when their own assertive efforts are not enough, they should then get adult assistance to stop the discrimination. If a child demonstrates a pattern of persistent discriminatory behavior toward others and does not respond to these types of intervention, then the teacher may want to consider an individualized behavior plan to help that child in a more focused way (see chapter 7). Further

Just as a teacher would not allow one child to continue hitting another, he cannot allow name-calling or other discriminatory behaviors to be repeated.

teacher guidelines for dealing with prejudice and discriminatory acts in the classroom are found in *Anti-Bias Curriculum: Tools for Empowering Young Children* (Derman-Sparks & the A.B.C. Task Force 1989).

Teach children how to ignore routine peer provocation

The problem with teaching children to repeatedly object to any form of teasing or provocative behavior by peers is that such protests are often rewarding for the provoking child and, thus, can encourage the problem behavior. After all, the goal of teasing, sticking out one's tongue, taunting, swearing, chanting "Na Na Na-Na Na," or other provocative behaviors is usually to make others react by getting mad or upset. There-

fore, if the target child repeatedly objects or shows that he is upset, he is really giving the provoker what he wants. Attention from other children (bystanders) can also be very rewarding for a verbally aggressive child. Because successfully and unambiguously ignoring such attempted provocation constitutes refusal to submit, it may be considered an assertive response.

Young children can learn to ignore provocative or disruptive peer behaviors, thus discouraging these behaviors and preventing them from escalating into aggression. In the case of discriminatory teasing, as defined above, children can be taught to respond initially with verbal assertiveness and then to seek adult assistance. However, if children find themselves without an adult to turn to in such a situation, their best reaction to continued teasing might well be to proudly ignore or calmly walk away, rather than to repeatedly protest. Proudly ignoring consists of holding one's head up high while turning or walking away, without showing signs of intimidation or distress. In other cases of attempted provocation—and particularly for common or repeated behaviors—the most effective response may be for the child to ignore the taunting from the start, not even acknowledging the provocation with a protest. In such cases the teacher might also decide to avoid directly correcting the provoking child and, instead, to focus her attention on supporting the target child and bystanders in ignoring the provocation. The teacher would follow up by inconspicuously monitoring the activities of the verbal aggressor in order to give that child positive attention and encouragement as soon as he switches to showing appropriate social behavior.

Young children are generally more willing than adults are to accept "ignoring" as an active and powerful thing to do (Stocking, Arezzo, & Leavitt 1979). The key is teaching them to clearly and calmly turn their heads away from the provoking child and then to avoid reacting in any way. Role-playing exercises help children understand that the teasing is deliberately trying to make them angry and that they can learn how to ignore it. Children can also learn to turn back and play with the teasing child when that child stops teasing. In role-playing games the target child, as well as other children (bystanders), can practice ignoring by sharply turning their heads away from a doll who teases or taunts. The doll mumbles to herself, "Oh, no one's listening to me!" and gives up teasing. Then, when the doll says something nice, the children turn back and respond to the doll. Ignoring is explained as a way of helping the doll learn to stop teasing. When children understand what ignoring means and how it works, teachers can cue them during class activities to ignore a child who is being provocative or disruptive. By participating in the role-playing exercises, the children who might have a tendency to be provocative learn about social expectations and see how the other children respond. Then, in real classroom incidents, they will more readily perceive that their behavior is being ignored and why.

Refusing to show anger in situations that are intended to provoke anger is a nonviolent response that takes considerable self-control. Proponents of nonviolence in the tradition of Gandhi and Martin Luther King, Jr., speak of the strength and courage that are required to be nonviolent. For young children, learning to ignore deliberate peer provocation is an important first step in learning later on to "keep your cool" in peer conflict situations and to avoid being drawn into violent confrontations (Slaby, Wilson-Brewer, & Dash 1994). For all children, when adults are not there to mediate, being able to walk away from verbal or physical provocation may often be the safest and most effective way to respond. Thus, deliberate ignoring is a valuable exercise in controlling one's own emotional reactions that might otherwise contribute to aggression.

*   *   *

Once children learn a range of assertive behaviors through role playing and in guided, real-life practice, they can begin using them more flexibly in new situations with less and less adult guidance. At this point, it is useful to encourage them to generate their own personal variations and to consider alternative types of assertive responses. Children often apply to new situations the assertiveness skills learned in class, because they see that these skills work. If assertiveness is supported consistently throughout a classroom, the children come to expect it, and they begin to cue each other. Positive feedback will be most effective if it downplays adult approval and focuses on social benefits and self-reliance. Don't say, "I'm proud of you for asking nicely," but rather, "You asked her nicely, and she *gave* it to you!" or "I heard you tell her to stop pushing. You're really learning to stand up for *yourself!*"

Points to Remember

Teach children to speak directly to each other, rather than through the teacher. Dependence on the teacher to solve problems interferes with self-reliance.

Teach children to politely ask for and offer things to each other in a way that provides real choice. Peers are more likely to acquiesce when they are asked nicely and given a real choice.

Teach children to say, "No," politely when they choose to decline and to accept "No" from others. Children need to know how to decline a request or offer in an acceptable way, as well as to respect the right of others to do so.

Use demonstration and role playing to teach specific assertiveness skills. Dolls and puppets are helpful.

Take advantage of naturally occurring events to coach assertiveness skills on the spot. Children's motivation to learn is high in such situations.

Teach children to accept legitimate adult authority but also to respectfully stand up for their rights with adults—as long as physical safety is not an issue. Children need to know that they are entitled to fair treatment from adults.

Teach children to use assertiveness skills to avoid submitting to aggression, bossiness, or discriminatory acts. Children can be taught first to stand up directly to an aggressive peer and, only then, to call for adult help if needed. Submission leads to victimization and rewards the aggressor.

Caution children to avoid any confrontation that presents physical danger and to seek adult help elsewhere. Safety is the first consideration whenever weapons are present or a more powerful figure uses physical violence.

Teach children to ignore routine, persistent provocative peer behaviors. By ignoring the behavior, children deny the provoking child the reaction she seeks, and they practice controlling their own emotional reactions.

Teach children to use proactive assertiveness skills to meet their goals. Assertiveness skills can be valuable in helping a child replace habits of aggression or social isolation.

Teach assertiveness to girls and boys equally. Avoid cultural bias toward accepting submissiveness from girls and aggressiveness from boys.

11

Enhancing Perspective Taking and Empathy

Joshua and Aileen push Pat off the wagon. Pat begins to cry. Joshua and Aileen laugh at Pat and run away. **What can the teacher do to help Joshua and Aileen understand that Pat is hurt and sad and help them imagine how Pat feels—and thus be less likely to hurt a child and feel no remorse in the future?**

We each have our own perspective—our own point of view—that shapes the way we think about and react to the people around us. *Perspective taking* is the process of "stepping into another's shoes" and predicting the other person's thoughts and feelings accurately—it is the ability to see another's point of view. Before children can fully engage in this process, they must first understand that other people actually have their own particular thoughts and feelings; which may be different from their own. An individual can understand others' perspectives without having an emotional response to them. *Empathy* involves the capacity to share an emotional response with another, as well as the ability to discriminate the other's perspective and role (Feshbach 1975). Perspective taking and empathy are important skills that may contribute to the development of prosocial behaviors (i.e., intentional voluntary behaviors that benefit others) and to the reduction of violence. Children are less likely to behave aggressively toward someone if they can put themselves in the other person's place and imagine that person's thoughts and feelings.

Children may become involved in aggressive encounters in a variety of roles: as an aggressor, a victim, or a bystander who supports aggression (e.g., through direct instigation, encouragement, or passive support). Alternatively, they may act as problem solvers who attempt to resolve conflicts without violence (Slaby & Stringham 1994; Slaby, Wilson-Brewer, & Dash 1994) (as discussed in chapter 1). For children to stop behaving aggressively, they need not only to learn that aggression is an unacceptable behavior because it hurts others but also to develop concern for the well-being of others. It is important for children to begin to understand what hurting someone means and to care about how it feels from the perspective of each of these different roles.

What research tells us

Our appreciation of the importance of understanding another's perspective has been heavily influenced by the work of Swiss psychologist Jean Piaget. Research has generally supported Piaget's notion that children's social awareness develops from an egocentric perspective to an ability to understand, predict, and respond to others' feelings and points of view (e.g., Borke 1971). However, U.S. research has challenged Piaget's position that, before they reach school age, young children are unable to understand and empathize with another person's feelings (e.g., Iannotti 1978, 1985; Eisenberg & Strayer 1987). Young children are aware of other people's feelings, even when these feelings are different from their own, and they often respond to the distress of others based on their level of empathic understanding (Yarrow, Scott, & Waxler 1973).

By age 3, most children are aware that other people have feelings and that people's feelings vary with the situation, although young children's ability to react empathically to someone's emotion varies greatly with the specific emotional response. Most 3-year-old children can predict very accurately that people will feel happy in a pleasant situation, and they usually respond empathically by laughing or smiling when others appear happy. Children who smile often and seem to be happy are also more likely to prompt these empathic responses in others (Mood, Johnson, & Shantz 1978). Children are better able to show empathy when they feel secure and valued and their own needs are met (Strayer 1980).

Although young children can generally distinguish from among pleasant emotions, they often have difficulty distinguishing consistently from among unpleasant emotional reactions, such as anger, sadness, and fear. Young children's limitations in managing their own distress or in responding to the distress of others may interfere with the accurate recognition of these negative emotions. Nevertheless, most children can easily recognize these negative as well as a variety of positive feelings in another person by age 5 (Borke 1971).

Even before they have the necessary cognitive skills to respond appropriately, young children can experience empathic distress, although they may respond only by showing facial expressions of discomfort or make inappropriate attempts to comfort. Understanding another person's feelings is one thing; acting on this understanding in a helpful way requires more advanced skills. A very young child may be completely at a loss for what to do if she sees another child get hurt. The onlooking child may do nothing or may start to cry in distress at seeing another child upset. A more developmentally advanced child may bring her own mother or a comforting object of her own to the child in distress, offering what she herself has found to be comforting. At higher developmental levels, a child may try to comfort a distressed person or find something or someone that she knows the other person finds comforting. An even more mature child may be able to ask how the other person is feeling later, outside of the context of the immediate situation. Knowing what to do requires not only an understanding of the other person's feelings but the skills to figure out what the other person needs (Eisenberg et al. 1990).

Developmental levels of perspective taking and empathy

Perspective taking and empathy develop at somewhat different rates and times for different children, but this development usually follows a particular sequence. The first steps in the development of these skills will be the ones most easily mastered by most preschoolers. The basic steps in children's development of perspective taking and empathy skills occur in this sequence (Krudek 1978; Enright & Lapsley 1980):

• Children do not consider other people's points of view; they think everyone likes what they like.

• Children begin to realize that other people may think differently from themselves.

• Children become aware that other people have different thoughts and feelings but can't yet think simultaneously about both their own and someone else's perspectives.

• Children can often anticipate correctly how other people will react in situations familiar to the children.

• Children recognize when another person is in distress, but they still may not understand what caused the distress or know what the other person needs.

• Children can judge what someone in distress might need and respond appropriately.

• Children can "switch places" with another person and view themselves from the other's point of view.

• Children can view simultaneously all perspectives in a situation.

In a given preschool classroom, children may be at any of these levels of perspective taking and empathy. Analyzing each child's perspective-taking and empathy skills can help teachers decide how to assist the child to move to the next level. Children are most likely to help someone else if they understand that the other person is in distress, can themselves relate to those distress feelings, feel concern about the other person, and know that helping the other person will make them both feel better. Under these conditions, prosocial behavior rewards both the giver and the recipient and, therefore, is more likely to occur, while aggressive behavior is less likely to occur. A young child's ability to understand another person's point of view and share another person's feelings does not automatically ensure prosocial and non-aggressive behavior. Teaching specific skills that link perspective taking and empathy to appropriate behaviors, however, can produce marked increases in prosocial classroom behavior (e.g., sharing toys, helping a child who is hurt, trying to comfort a child who is upset, and taking turns) and reductions in aggressive behavior (Yarrow, Scott, & Waxler 1973; Feshbach 1974; Ahammer & Murray 1979; Feshbach & Feshbach 1982; Eisenberg & Strayer 1987).

Teaching guidelines

Children move through the same natural developmental sequence in developing empathy, but what they acquire at each level and how quickly they move to the next level varies and can be enhanced by teaching methods grounded in an understanding

Children's simple acts of kindness, such as consoling a friend who is sad or hurt, show their ability to empathize.

Early Violence Prevention

of how children learn and develop their knowledge. Young children construct their understanding through processes including (a) receiving direct instruction (teaching), (b) experiencing consequences of their behavior (rewards and punishments), (c) observing the behaviors and reactions of adults and other children (modeling), and (d) initiating interactions with other people (self-socialization) (Yarrow, Scott, & Waxler 1973). Accordingly, teachers can help young children learn ways to identify and respond to other people's feelings, anticipate how others will feel if they treat them nicely or badly, sharpen their observations of how people respond to being helped or hurt, initiate constructive interactions with others, and decrease destructive interactions.

Encourage children to communicate their feelings

Teachers can encourage children to label their own feelings and to talk about them. For example, if Juan is angry because Keisha and Billy knocked down his sand castle, a teacher might ask Juan, "How do you feel about that, Juan? Tell Keisha and Billy how you feel." This will help Juan to see that he can use words, as opposed to hitting or retaliating in kind, to let other people know how he feels. Teachers can also set examples of this type of communication through statements such as, "I get angry when you push other children" or "It makes me happy when you help me pick up the blocks."

One teacher created a "feeling wheel" in her class to help children recognize and talk about their feelings. The cardboard feeling wheel was composed of drawings of faces showing different emotions and a pointer that children could turn to indicate a particular feeling. When children arrived in the morning, the teacher occasionally asked them to show her how they were feeling that day. Sometimes children who felt uncomfortable starting a conversation about their emotions were able to do so with the help of the feeling wheel; they brought the wheel to the teacher, turned the pointer to the sad or angry feeling, and talked about why they felt that way. Children come to the early childhood center with a variety of feelings, as a result of what happens at home or on the way to the center. Having the opportunity to show their feelings early in the day creates an open, accepting atmosphere that helps children deal with their emotions. This type of interaction also helps children find words to label how they feel so that they can express their emotions verbally to one another and be understood.

Point out the similarities among people

When children see others as similar to themselves in a variety of ways, they may be more likely to anticipate others' needs and responses. With very young children, the many similarities that people share can be emphasized in immediate and concrete ways. By the activities and materials that they provide and the discussions they have with children, teachers also communicate that whatever their differences in individual attributes and group identities, children have much in common: they play, they feel happy and sad, they live in families, and so on. Understanding that all people share certain basic human feelings helps children empathize with those similar feelings. A child is less likely to hurt someone whose point of view she acknowledges and whose feelings she respects and shares (Feshbach & Feshbach 1969; Eisenberg & Strayer 1987).

Present and discuss examples of perspective taking and empathy

Teachers can improve children's naturally developing ability to take another's perspective and to empathize by combining learning through stories, plays, pictures, and real-life modeling, and teaching concrete skills. Stories can provide effective examples, particularly when dolls or puppets are used to act out situations in which the characters experience different feelings. After acting out the story, teachers can encourage children to identify the characters' feelings in the context of the story, emphasizing how the characters' observable behaviors reveal their feelings. For example, the teacher tells a story about a boy who is sad after losing his favorite teddy bear. Children see that the boy is crying because he is sad. The teacher then asks the children what the boy might need in order to feel better (e.g., to find his bear). What could the children do to act on this need they have identified? The children may suggest helping the boy to look for his bear, look-ing for the bear themselves, or asking an adult to help them find the bear. The teacher then asks the children how they would feel if they helped to find the bear and saw that the boy was happy again. Many children's books address problems common in the life of preschool children, such as how to make friends, how to help friends feel good, how children can play together when they have different interests, and how to overcome shyness and fear. Reading stories with these themes contributes to the development of children's empathy.

Remind children of times when they themselves were distressed

Teachers can help young children to develop perspective taking and empathy by encouraging them to think about their own emotional reactions to similar situations. For example, Ying was hit by Todd. The next day, Ying got angry at Marissa and hit her. Because both events were recent, the teacher might enhance Ying's ability to empathize by asking such questions as the following:

• "Do you remember when Todd hit you yesterday? It hurt, didn't it?"

• "How did it make you feel?"

• "How do you think Marissa feels when you hit her?"

• "What can you do to help Marissa feel better?"

This discussion is most effective if it takes place *after* the teacher has coached Marissa to respond assertively to Ying and Ying has stopped the aggression. Engaging a child in a discussion right after her aggressive action is risky because the

Children's ability to take another's perspective and to empathize develops as they listen to or act out stories in which the characters experience different feelings.

teacher attention may reward the child for being aggressive. Teachers need to tailor this type of questioning to the child's developmental level. Some children would be unable to answer these questions. In this case, rather than questioning Ying, the teacher could provide the answers by pointing out Marissa's emotional responses to the aggression. Alternatively, the teacher could ask Marissa to tell Ying how she is feeling.

Model empathic responses

Real-life models make an important contribution to children's learning of perspective taking and empathy. Young children often show increased skill in identifying and relating to another person's feelings in a pictured or hypothetical situation if the teacher first demonstrates perspective taking and empathy for a character in a distressful situation (Feshbach & Feshbach 1982; Shure &

Spivack 1988). Practicing empathetic responses toward another person appears to be relatively easy for preschoolers; responding empathically in real life is usually more difficult. Children may be able to talk about ways to help a character in a story, but they still may lack the skills to translate their feelings and knowledge into actual helping behavior in the early childhood setting.

It is important for children to see the process that adults use to understand another person's feelings. One of the best ways for children to learn is to hear an adult explaining the concrete steps:

• Identify the distress of another person. ("Ardelle is crying—it looks like she's sad.")

• Try to figure out what is happening or what is causing the other person's distress. ("Let's ask Ardelle why she's sad.")

• Figure out what others might do in the same situation. ("Ardelle is sad because she fell off the tricycle. I bet that hurts. I'd cry, too, if I fell that hard.")

• Assess what the other person needs. ("Ardelle, what would make you feel better? Do you need a hug?")

• Try to comfort or meet the needs of the distressed person. ("I'm going to give Ardelle a hug to help her feel better.")

• Experience and demonstrate pleasure at the other person's relief or comfort. ("Ardelle has stopped crying. 'Are you feeling better? I'm glad you're feeling better.'")

These types of concrete statements help children get into the habit of thinking and caring about other people's perspectives and feelings and coming up with nonviolent solutions to problems instead of resorting to aggression.

Guide children to practice empathic responses within conflict situations

Children's understanding of the feelings and behaviors of others may not be sufficient to lead to prosocial behavior if this knowledge is not accompanied by caring about the feelings of others and by practice in directly applying empathic responses. In some cases children may use their understanding of others to manipulate, trick, or otherwise use their skills to their own ends. For example, 4-year-old Anne wants to play with a toy being used by another child, Lisa. Anne is quite adroit at figuring out that if she takes a second toy that she knows Lisa also values, Lisa will drop the first toy and attempt to rescue this other valued possession. Anne then immediately takes the toy she originally wanted.

When faced with a situation such as this, teachers may use it as an opportunity to help build children's empathic concern for and response to others. For example, if Lisa is upset over losing the toy, the teacher might model giving comfort by asking Lisa what is wrong. The teacher might also suggest that Lisa tell Anne that she is upset because she lost her toy. Such guided practice in expressing feelings directly to one's peers within the conflict situation is an important step toward applying these skills independently in real-life settings. The teacher might then ask Anne to describe how she would feel if someone else took her

When a caring adult shows empathy with a child's feelings, he models concern for others and helps the child to develop empathic responses.

Chapter 11—Enhancing Perspective Taking and Empathy 153

toy, what would make her feel better, and what she could do to help Lisa feel better. Most important, the teacher could then encourage Anne to actually help Lisa feel better by carrying out one of these empathic responses and seeing the results.

Points to Remember

Encourage children to label their own feelings and tell each other how they feel. Talk about your own feelings and ask children how they feel in an atmosphere of understanding and acceptance.

Point out ways in which everyone experiences certain basic feelings. Use pictures and stories about a variety of peoples, cultures, and disabilities to demonstrate that individuals who may look different experience universal basic feelings.

Lead children through discussions of feelings and ways to be helpful, using pictures, stories, or puppets. Ask children how they think the character in the picture or story feels, how they can tell, why they think the character is feeling that way, and what could be done to help the character feel better.

Help children learn empathy by reminding them of how they have felt in similar situations. If a child falls down, for example, remind another child of how she felt the day before when she fell and enlist her aid in assisting the child who has just fallen.

Model perspective taking and empathy by talking about ways of identifying others' points of view and feelings and finding ways to respond appropriately. Call children's attention to empathic responses that take place in the classroom or center when either the teacher or other children help and share with each other. Talk about how this behavior makes both the giver and the receiver feel.

12

Providing Role Models

A teacher feels that sometimes the children gang up on her. She deals with each aggressive incident by raising her voice and scolding the children, as she finds this to be effective in getting their attention and stopping them in their tracks. Recently, she has discovered herself needing to scold children more often and in a louder voice. More children have begun to argue loudly and to threaten each other. **Why has children's aggression increased in the classroom despite her escalating efforts to stop it?**

Just a few decades ago, when the word *modeling* suggested building a model airplane with glue, the idea of modeling as learning through observation was not well understood by educators. Today we know that one of the most important ways that children learn is by observing the patterns of behavior displayed by role models. Educators use the word *modeling* to refer to this learning process. *Role models* are individuals whose patterns of behavior are often observed, held in high regard, and used to guide the thoughts, feelings, and actions of others.

Children are often keen observers of how adults and other children behave and respond to one another. The early childhood education setting provides an observing child with many vivid examples of successful and unsuccessful behavior. Much of what occurs in the center or classroom is not designed to teach the observing child a lesson in how

to behave; nevertheless, children draw their own lessons from what they see and hear, and they often use this learning to guide their own behavior.

Among the most potent lessons children learn through their observations are the ways in which aggressive, assertive, and prosocial behaviors are used and responded to by children and adults. When children see their teachers scolding and yelling at children who misbehave, they are likely to try similar ways of relating to their peers. When children observe that aggressive behavior is often allowed to occur and to succeed, they are likely to increase their own level of aggression or to attempt aggression for the first time. On the other hand, when children observe that assertive and prosocial behaviors are used regularly and successfully and aggressive behavior is not, they are more likely to use these desirable behaviors in relating to their peers.

What research tells us

Research confirms that young children learn by observing others and clarifies the circumstances that affect their imitation of aggressive or prosocial behaviors.

Learning by observing others

Young children are avid people watchers, and they are constantly looking to others for examples of new and improved ways to deal with situations. One thing that children learn by observing is how people behave toward one another. Sometimes they learn entirely new behaviors, but more often they learn variations on patterns of behavior they already know, such as different ways to threaten or to ask politely for something from another child.

Children also observe how acceptable particular behaviors are (who uses them and under what circumstances), how others respond, and what effects the behaviors have. From these observations children develop their own expectations about what is likely to happen if they perform a given behavior. These expectations help to determine whether a child performs the behavior and under what circumstances.

Research indicates that children's later performance of observed behaviors depends on many factors, including (a) the personal characteristics of the role model, (b) whether the activity is within the child's present range of abilities, (c) whether the child's own situation is perceived to be similar to that of the role model (e.g., Rosekrans 1967), (d) what happens as a result of the role model's actions (e.g., Walters

& Parke 1964), and (e) whether the consequences are consistently applied (Rosekrans & Hartup 1967). Teachers are particularly potent models, because children generally imitate people they know and like and people who are powerful controllers of desired resources (Bandura 1973). Peers also have a major impact as models, as children tend to imitate people who perform activities within their own range of abilities and people whom they consider to be similar to themselves (Schunk 1987). The behavior of a peer model is particularly influential when it is seen as "successful" in gaining material objects, submission from other children, or attention from teachers or peers. Modeling effects also occur when children see adults interacting with other children. The attention, praise, or criticism the teacher gives another child teaches the observing children about what the teacher considers to be appropriate or desirable child behavior (Strain, Shores, & Kerr 1976; Kohler & Fowler 1985).

Learning from aggressive models

Most young children growing up in America today have abundant opportunities to observe aggressive models—in their homes, in television programs, in the community, and in the school or center. Children who witness a great deal of violence in their homes or communities are at increased risk for becoming involved with violence in other settings (see chapter 2). Children who view a great deal of violence in television programs and films are likely to initiate aggressive behavior in the

A child's aggressive behavior is most likely to be imitated when it is seen as "successful" in gaining material objects, submission from other children, or attention from teachers or peers.

early childhood program setting, particularly if they view television violence uncritically and regard it as realistic and relevant to their own lives (Singer & Singer 1981; Donnerstein, Slaby, & Eron 1994) (see chapter 13 for a discussion on strategies for helping children to become more critical as media viewers).

Thus, children often come to school prepared to apply what they have learned in other settings about the use and value of aggressive, submissive, or prosocial behaviors. The classroom also provides many opportunities for children to observe the real-life use and outcomes of

these types of behaviors. Besides observing the examples that teachers and peers provide, children experience violent or nonviolent models through books, videotapes, and other media. They encounter games, toys, and other play materials that are associated with role models who may be aggressive or prosocial (or, in some cases, a mix of both). Just as children often learn from the aggressive behavior of models, they can also learn the use and value of assertive and prosocial behaviors by observing role models who portray these characteristics. Among the role models that teachers might decide to include—and engage the children in discussing—are community helpers (e.g., the mail carrier, the bus driver, the school nurse), as well as various real-life or fictional role models known for their nonviolent, assertive, or prosocial behaviors (e.g., children's own parents and grandparents, Rosa Parks, Martin Luther King, Jr., The Reluctant Dragon, and Mister Rogers and his puppet characters).

Direct effects and modeling effects

Parents and teachers often think carefully about how to respond to a child, because they know it will have a direct effect on that child. Rarely, however, do they think about the indirect, modeling effect their responses will have on the child who is observing and listening to this interaction. Of course, in the classroom or center, most interactions occur in the presence of many pairs of observant eyes and attentive ears. Thus, teachers should be aware that each event will not only affect the children who are directly involved but also serve as a potential exemplar for the other children who observe the event. For example, if a teacher succeeds in controlling a misbehaving child by angrily raising her voice, she serves as a model for the use of verbal aggression that other children may observe and imitate.

In many early childhood settings, children frequently are able to get what they want from peers through using aggression. When a child gets what she wants by behaving aggressively, that child can be expected to

increase the use of aggression. In addition, many of the other children who observe this child's success through using aggression can be expected to try aggressive behaviors themselves.

The connection between direct effects and modeling effects is illustrated in a study in which children's behavior in preschool classrooms was observed at the beginning and end of the school year (Patterson, Littman, & Bricker 1967). About 80% of children's aggressive behaviors were directly rewarded by particular actions of the victims, such as giving up toys, crying, or withdrawing from the scene. These actions by the victims served to reward the aggressor, increasing the chances that the same aggressor would again attack the same victim in the near future. When the victim did not submit to (and thus reward) the aggressor but instead stood up to the aggressor firmly but nonviolently, the aggressor was likely to change both the type of aggression and the choice of victim (see chapter 10).

This study noted at the beginning of the program year that many of the children were passive victims who seldom initiated aggression. After observing the successful aggression of their peers, however, some of the victims began to counterattack. Initially passive children who succeeded in stopping the aggression with their counterattacks became increasingly aggressive themselves as the year progressed. By the end of the year, these children initiated their own aggressive attacks against new victims, and the level of aggression in the classroom increased dramatically. When other initially pas-

Teachers are most effective as models when they have a warm and nurturant relationship with the children.

Chapter 12—Providing Role Models

sive children attempted aggression but were unsuccessful in their first attacks, they did not increase their level of aggression over the course of the year. Thus, the modeling effect of observing one's peers successfully using aggression to get what they wanted seemed to stimulate many children to try aggression for the first time. Whether these children maintained, increased, or decreased their use of aggressive behavior once they had started, however, seemed to depend on its direct outcome for them.

Teaching guidelines

The classroom is not only a practice field upon which children learn directly by doing, it is also a theater where children learn by observing the performance of others. The knowledge that children inevitably learn a great deal by observing the behavior of others is useful in several different ways to reduce aggression in the classroom.

Reduce modeling of aggression

Reducing occurrences of children's aggression in the ways suggested in the previous chapters effectively lessens children's exposure to models of aggression in the classroom. Teachers can also consider how their own behavior looks to children and what steps they can take to avoid inadvertently modeling behaviors unworthy of imitation (e.g., using verbal rebukes, speaking in harsh tones, laying blame, threatening, rough handling, or even administering physical forms of punishment). Because teachers may find it difficult to examine their own habitual behaviors with an objective

view, they may find it helpful to observe one another in order to provide constructive and supportive criticisms and suggestions to each other.

Teachers can also work to ensure that children's aggression, when it does occur, is not successful in gaining, for the aggressor, material objects, peer submission, or excessive attention from teachers or peers. For example, teachers can direct their attention toward helping the victimized child respond to the aggressor in an assertive and effective way (see chapters 6 and 10). Children who observe that aggression is unsuccessful are likely to reject aggressive behavior as unworthy of performing themselves (Bandura 1973).

Teachers can ask parents to help support the school's efforts by reducing children's exposure to models of violence in television programming, films, and videotapes. When parents work to control the amount and content of their children's television viewing, their attempts are often effective (Stein & Friedrich 1972; Gadberry 1980). Teachers can also assist children in developing critical viewing skills to help them understand that violence on television is often presented in glorified and unrealistic ways and that a wide variety of alternatives are often available for resolving the presented conflicts effectively and nonviolently (see chapter 13).

Present effective models of prosocial, nonviolent behaviors

Teachers may need to review their own behavior to ensure that they present a variety of desirable examples to children. Teachers are most effective as models when they have a warm and nurturant relationship with the children. Helping children, listening to them, talking with them, and following their suggestions are some of the ways that teachers become important individuals in children's lives. Children are most heavily influenced by the words and behavioral examples of adults whom they trust and care about (Bandura 1973).

Actions speak louder than words, particularly for young children. Thus, teachers are effective models when they systematically and repeatedly demonstrate the behaviors that they want to encourage in children and, at the same time, explain or describe their behavior. Lectures alone are seldom effective with young children in producing the desired behaviors. In fact, if the lecture follows a child's aggression or other misbehavior, the child has gained the teacher's attention, and other children who see the incident learn that such misbehavior is a way to get attention. Older children are particularly likely to notice when teachers present either a hypocritical model (e.g., by saying one thing and doing another) or an inconsistent model (e.g., by responding differently and unpredictably each time). In these cases children are likely either to ignore the model's words, while following her actions, or else to reject both the words and actions of the model (e.g., Bryan & Walbeck 1970).

Teachers can introduce role models that exemplify a wide variety of nonviolent, assertive, and constructive ways to solve social problems. Prosocial role models can be presented to children during group times through stories, puppet plays, creative dramatics, or films and videos. For example, some children might hit another child or take a toy simply because they lack the particular social skills of how to enter a play group in an appropriate way. A teacher noticing this problem might model behavior for a group, using puppets and saying, "Our Lion looks sad. 'What's wrong, Lion? Oh, you don't have anyone to play with.' What could Lion do to find someone to play with?" The teacher could then lead a discussion about actions the lion could take and act them out or have the children take turns acting them out. As children observe the modeling of the puppets, they learn prosocial alternatives to aggression that enable them to achieve their goals successfully (Combs & Slaby 1977).

Although behavioral examples can be presented during special group-time activities, they may be particularly effective when used as an integral part of the daily activities. At these times children are often highly motivated to observe alternative ways of achieving their goals. Teachers can highlight noteworthy behavioral examples by describing their own actions and those of the children (e.g., "Mrs. Dennis and I are working together to prepare your snack" or "Felicia and Andy are taking turns using the typewriter").

Points to Remember

Review your own behavior patterns from the perspective of an observing child. Because teachers' behaviors have a modeling effect, as well as a direct effect, on children, it is doubly important for teachers to replace any inadvertent aggressive behaviors with behaviors worthy of emulation.

Become an effective model by developing a warm and nurturant relationship with the children. Teachers who have gained children's trust are the most effective models.

Reduce children's exposure to aggressive models by reducing the occurrence of aggression in the classroom. Decreasing the number of aggressive encounters will have an additional beneficial effect of reducing children's exposure to aggressive models.

When aggression occurs, help the victims prevent it from being successful for the aggressor. When children observe that teachers support the potential victim's right to stand up to the aggressor and to use assertive behavior to regain status or a lost object, they are likely to reject aggression as unworthy of their performing.

Model a wide variety of assertive and prosocial behaviors. The behavioral examples of teachers influence observing children.

Point out examples of nonviolence and effective behavior as they occur in the classroom or center. Besides rewarding those children involved in the interaction, this teacher attention may lead other children to further observe and learn from these children's modeling.

Introduce the children to other nonviolent and effective role models. The role models presented in stories, songs, videos, and other activities can affect children's subsequent behavior.

13

Controlling Media Effects

In the last few weeks, Jason has begun to destroy projects of other children when they are not looking. Each time he destroys something, he seems to take glee in doing it and makes an annoying, grunting laugh. One day Jason comes into the classroom proudly showing off a sweatshirt with a picture of TV characters Beavis and Butt-head. From what she has heard of this program, the teacher suspects a connection between these TV characters and Jason's recent behavior. **Is such a connection plausible? If so, what can the teacher do?**

From Saturday-morning cartoons to evening crime shows, television provides children with an extensive how-to course in aggression. Many young children are heavy and uncritical viewers of the violence depicted in television programs, films, and videotapes. We now know that the viewing of violence often leads to involvement with aggression in real life, particularly for young children (NIMH 1982; Liebert & Sprafkin 1988; Huston et al. 1992; Donnerstein, Slaby, & Eron 1994). Even though children are most likely to view television, film, and videotape violence outside the early childhood program setting, teachers can play an important role in helping to reduce the effects of media violence on young children.

Teachers can help young children begin to develop critical viewing skills appropriate for their developmental level. Learning to critically evaluate the ways in which media portrayals overrepresent, distort, and glorify violence can help young children begin to gain a realistic understanding of media violence and its connection to real life. Teachers can also support families in making sensible and constructive uses of the media, limiting children's exposure to violence, providing children with interesting alternatives to viewing violence, and preventing children from adopting an uncritical acceptance of violence as a solution to their own problems. Teachers, individually and collectively, can take steps to ensure that television broadcasters and cablecasters fulfill their legal and contractual responsibilities to children specifically in the area of violence-prevention education.

What research tells us

Research findings confirm that young children are often exposed to a great deal of media violence and that such exposure can have a variety of negative effects on the developing child. Although the young child is usually highly susceptible to these effects, teachers can counteract the negative effects of media violence in several different ways.

Gap between research and practice

The potential harmful effects of televised violence on children have been a continuous concern for more than four decades. Stimulated by the concern of parents, educators, and policymakers, researchers have extensively studied these effects and how to minimize or prevent them (Parke & Slaby 1983; Huston et al. 1992; Donnerstein, Slaby, & Eron 1994). Today, however, a major education gap exists between the large body of research evidence on media violence and what is known and applied by the general public, by educators, and by many other professionals.

Television has become a major source of our knowledge and concern about social issues; this medium often plays an important role in closing gaps between what scientists know and what the general public knows and applies by presenting significant evidence along with applications. On the issue of television violence, however, broadcasters have generally acted in their own self-interest at the expense of the public interest they have pledged to serve—a condition for receiving their license to operate on publicly owned airwaves. The television industry has instead widened the education gap by actively ignoring, denying, attacking, and even misrepresenting the evidence on television-violence effects. As a consequence, parents, teachers, and the general public often don't know what to believe or do about the effects of television violence on children (Slaby 1994a).

Many professional organizations have attempted to close this gap by reviewing the evidence, taking public positions, and disseminating suggestions for action by policymakers, educators, and the general public. Professional organizations that are contributing to this effort include the American Academy of Pediatrics (AAP), the American Medical Association (AMA), the American Psychological Association (APA), the National Association for the Education of Young Children (NAEYC), and the National Congress of Parents and Teachers Association (National PTA). Nearly two decades ago, the National PTA elevated the issue of controlling the effects of television violence to its top priority. The National PTA leadership continues to address the seriousness of the problem, the strength of the research evidence, and the potential for teachers and parents to work together to contribute to a solution. Recently, the APA renewed its long-term efforts by documenting specific media-violence effects on children's behavior and by proposing remedies (Huston et al. 1992; APA 1993; Donnerstein, Slaby, & Eron 1994). NAEYC (1990) has specifically recognized the important role early childhood educators may play in helping to remedy the effects of television violence on young children.

A number of public interest organizations are actively involved in education efforts, including the Alliance Against Violent Entertainment, the Center for Media Education, the Center for Media Literacy, Mediascope, Mediawatch, the National Alliance for Nonviolent Programming, the National Coalition on Television Violence, and the National Foundation to Improve Television (see "Resources"). Nevertheless, a large education gap still exists.

Children's exposure to media violence

Although many children occasionally watch television before they are 2 years old, it is between the ages of 2 and 3 that most children develop a favorite television program and begin to acquire their habit of watching television (Anderson & Collins 1988). By 6 years of age, more than 90% of American children watch television on a routine basis. American children 2 through 5 years of age typically spend even more time watching television than children 6 to 17 years of age, presumably because going to school cuts into the viewing time of older children (Condry 1989). Much of the programming that children view usually contains violence, and children's programming has consistently been found to contain higher levels of violence than any other category of programming (*TV Guide* 1992).

American television often presents violence in unrealistic, glorified, and misleading ways. Fictional television programming often presents violence as prevalent, legitimate, justified, socially approved, rewarded,

effective, and "clean." Sometimes violence is also portrayed as heroic, manly, funny, exciting, even pleasurable (Slaby 1994a). Many nonfictional programs, such as the news, also distort the reality of real-life violence by selectively exaggerating and sensationalizing reports of violence (Johnson & Russell 1990). Young children have relatively little real-world experience to use as a basis for understanding and critically evaluating the many unrealistic ways in which television portrays violence.

Changes in technology and increased program access for children in the last decade have broadened children's access to televised violence. Beyond broadcast television, children may be exposed to violence through cable television (including music television, or MTV), satellite-transmitted television, films, videos, interactive video games, and on-line computer networks. Although a large and compelling body of research evidence on the effects of television violence gives us a great deal of guidance, we are only beginning to learn about the effects of children's exposure to violence in other forms of media beyond broadcast television.

Effects of media violence

Television violence affects the thoughts, feelings, and actions of many young viewers, although the extent and nature of the impact is variable. The effects seem to depend, to a large extent, on what the individual child brings to the viewing experience that allows him or her to understand and critically evaluate the unrealistic ways in which violence is typically portrayed. The research identifies several effects on children of their viewing violent or prosocial programming, as well as factors that influence the susceptibility of individual viewers to these effects.

Several major effects of viewing violence have been identified and documented (Comstock & Paik 1990; Donnerstein, Slaby, & Eron 1994).

1. The *aggressor effect* consists of increased mean-spiritedness, aggressive behavior, and even serious violence toward others. Children who are most susceptible to the aggressor effect are often those who identify most strongly with the aggressive characters and those who perceive the portrayed violence as realistic and relevant to their own lives. The aggressor effect can occur immediately during or after viewing, and it can also contribute to long-term consequences. Young children who watch violent programs (e.g., violent cartoons) are generally more likely than those who view prosocial programming (e.g., *Mister Rogers' Neighborhood*) to engage in aggressive behaviors in the classroom, such as pushing, shoving, and aggressive play that escalates into hurtful aggression (Friedrich & Stein 1973; Singer & Singer 1981). In addition, when individuals were studied over major portions of their lives—in some cases over a 22-year period—their viewing of large quantities of television violence during childhood was found to be one of the best predictors of their likelihood of engaging in serious acts of violence and criminal violent behavior as adults, even after controlling for the effects of major background factors (Huesmann et al. 1984). Thus, children's heavy and uncritical viewing of vio-

lence can contribute to the building of aggressive habits that, unless changed, may continue to affect their behavior for many years.

2. The *victim effect* refers to increased fearfulness, mistrust, and self-protective behavior toward others (Gerbner et al. 1978). Children who are most susceptible to the victim effect are often those who identify most strongly with the victims and who perceive the portrayed violence as realistic and relevant to their own lives. After viewing television violence, some young children have recurrent nightmares or daytime fears of being the victim of violence.

3. The *bystander effect* consists of increased callousness, desensitization, and behavioral indifference toward real-life violence among others. Particularly when violence is portrayed as commonplace, acceptable, and justifiable, the viewing of violence can undermine the viewer's feelings of concern, empathy, or sympathy toward victims of real-life violence. Children who view a great deal of violence show increasingly lower levels of physiological arousal to portrayals of violence (Osborn & Endsley 1971), and they become less likely to respond responsibly to real-life aggression. For example, elementary school-age children who had been shown a violent program were found to be less likely than children who had been shown a neutral program to intervene or call for adult help when younger children for whom they were "babysitting" began to fight (e.g., Thomas et al. 1977).

4. The *increased-appetite effect* means an increased desire to view more violence. When children repeatedly view

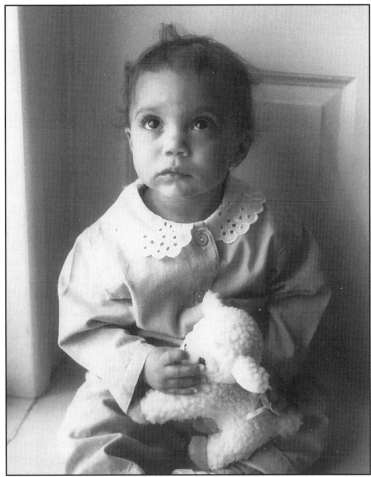

Between the ages of 2 and 3, many children develop a favorite television program and begin to acquire their habit of watching television.

and uncritically accept violence depicted in glorified, exciting, and heroic ways, they are likely to want to see more violence and initiate more aggressive games and weapon play. By choosing to watch more television violence, they expose themselves to violent programming that is likely to maintain and increase the other effects of viewing violence. By choosing to engage in aggressive games and weapon play, they expose themselves to a greater risk of becoming involved in aggressive encounters. When the

television industry argues that it is only giving viewers what they want, it fails to own up to the fact that viewers' appetites derive not from any pre-existing need to view violence but, rather, from the cultivation of an appetite for violence through television's own unrealistic and glorified portrayals of violence.

Despite repeated claims of "catharsis" effects of viewing violence on television made by the top executives of the broadcast industry during the 1960s, '70s, and part of the '80s, virtually no evidence exists that watching aggression enables children to release "pent-up" hostility, anger, or rage that otherwise might result in aggressive behavior. Instead, viewing violence generally increases children's knowledge of how to perform aggressive acts and decreases their inhibitions against behaving aggressively themselves (Parke & Slaby 1983; Huston et al. 1992).

Effects of prosocial media programs

The act of watching television is not what leads to the negative effects described earlier; it is watching *violence* on television that increases the likelihood of these outcomes. Viewing prosocial programming, such as *Sesame Street* and *Mister Rogers' Neighborhood,* on the other hand, tends to increase children's prosocial behavior and reduce their aggressive behavior (Liebert & Sprafkin 1988). Viewing programs that stress themes of positive and socially valued interaction among people can increase a wide range of prosocial behaviors, including helping, sharing, cooperating, playing imaginatively, and showing empathy (Slaby & Quarfoth 1980). These prosocial behaviors offer children alternatives to aggression.

Several effects of viewing prosocial programming have been identified (Slaby & Quarfoth 1980).

• The *prosocial effect* consists of increased helpful and constructive behaviors toward others. When children view programming that portrays individuals helping each other, they have an opportunity to learn how to engage in these behaviors and what the beneficial consequences may be for themselves and others.

• The *aggression-reduction effect* consists of reducing aggressive and hurtful behaviors toward others. When children view prosocial programming, they are less likely to engage in aggressive behavior, presumably because they have learned alternative behaviors (Friedrich & Stein 1973; Hearold 1979; Comstock & Paik 1990). To date, little has been done to develop and test the potential effects of television programming specifically designed to show children the many alternative ways of preventing aggression and responding to conflict nonviolently and effectively.

Children's susceptibility to media effects

Having amply demonstrated the existence of these effects, investigators have generally shifted their focus to tougher questions: Which individual children will be most likely to show each of these effects? Toward whom and under what circumstances will children most often show these effects? Which forms of media presentation are most likely to produce the effects and to what extent? Several general principles emerge from the research literature.

For several reasons young children are generally more susceptible than older children or adults to the effects of media violence. First, as discussed above, young children are often heavy viewers of media violence. Second, young children are often uncritical viewers of media violence because they have relatively little experience by which to critically evaluate its real-world significance. They often fail to distinguish adequately between portrayals of fantasy and reality. For example, in one study, the majority of kindergarten children failed to differentiate fully between human characters and cartoon characters, instead considering cartoon characters to be "alive" and "able to walk and talk by themselves" (Quarfoth 1979). Finally, young children are also quite likely to identify themselves with characters portrayed as powerful and effective, such as superheroes, who often solve their problems by using violence. Children's programming has presented many such characters (e.g., Ninja Turtles, Power Rangers, Hulk Hogan, the Incredible Hulk, He-Man, She-Ra, Beavis and Butt-head, Batman, Spiderman).

Boys and girls appear to be equally susceptible to media-violence effects, but effects may differ greatly because media experiences differ markedly for boys and girls. Male and female characters are commonly portrayed very differently in the media, and children tend to identify with the character of the same sex as themselves (Hendrix & Slaby 1991). During early childhood, boys and girls develop an understanding that gender is an identifiable, stable, and consistent social category that has important implications for themselves as well as for everyone else in our society (Slaby 1990). As children develop an understanding of the gender concept, usually between 2 and 5 years of age, they become highly motivated to learn both what it means to be a male or a female and how to apply it to their own lives. As children develop this gender concept, they increasingly seek out programming and imitate role models that provide them with clear examples of "appropriate" behavior for their own sex (Slaby & Frey 1975; Ruble, Balaban, & Cooper 1981; Luecke-Aleksa et al. 1995).

In seeking out television programming with strong male characters, boys often find male role models whose power comes from their superior strength and aggressive behavior (e.g., Popeye). Girls often find female role models who are victimized by aggression and rescued by male characters (e.g., Olive Oyl), or else female role models who show strength through their magical powers (e.g., She-Ra). Thus, boys and girls often have very different media experiences due to the programs they choose and the characters with whom they identify themselves. Even when boys and girls view the same program, boys may show an aggressor effect because of their identification with an aggressive male character, and girls may show a victim effect because of their identification with a victimized female character (Hendrix & Slaby 1991).

Minority and nonminority children appear to be equally susceptible to effects of media violence, but the effects may differ greatly because media experiences differ for minority and nonminority children. African American children have commonly been found to watch more television than European American children. In much of television programming, minority characters are either nonexistent or presented within a negative context. When African American, Hispanic, Asian, or Native American characters appear, television often stereotypes them as either dangerous perpetrators or victims of violence. Thus, when minority children identify with media characters of similar ethnicity, as they begin to do during early childhood (Triviz 1987), a different set of media-violence portrayals is likely to influence them than one that influences nonminority children.

Teaching guidelines

Both parents and teachers often have major concerns over children's exposure to violence in the media, and the evidence provides good reason for concern. Many parents, however, put no restrictions on either the amount or the content of the programs their children view. For their part, teachers rarely apply their advice, support, or teaching efforts to this problem. Teachers can play an effective role in helping to control media violence effects through (a) direct interaction with children in the classroom or center, (b) the alliances they develop with the children's families, and (c) their professional advocacy in favor of more developmentally and educationally appropriate nonviolent programming for young children (NAEYC 1990; Singer & Singer 1981).

Teach children to be critical viewers of media violence

Dealing with media violence is an important part of addressing children's concerns about real-life violence (see chapter 2). Parents and teachers can directly influence children's understanding and use of aggression through discussions about the violence and the alternatives to violence depicted in the programs children view. Teachers need to become aware

of the programs being viewed by children that they teach, of children's emerging television viewing habits, and of what children think about the characters and the problem-solving behaviors depicted in these programs. To become critical viewers, young children need to understand how and why media violence is exaggerated and glamorized and is unrealistic and unacceptable to perform in real life. Children often are less susceptible to the effects of media violence when they have a degree of critical understanding that media violence is an unrealistic and inappropriate guide to their own behavior (Eron 1986).

Because young children have relatively little real-world experience by which to evaluate the relation of media violence to real life, they stand to benefit greatly from discussing these connections with adults. Important topics for discussion include the unrealistic ways that violence is presented in the media, the inappropriateness of using media portrayals of violence to provide solutions to problems in real life, and the appropriateness of using effective and nonviolent solutions to real-life problems.

Young children also often fail to make connections between a violent act, the motives that precede it, and the consequences that follow it, particularly when there is a time lapse in between (Collins 1973; Collins, Berndt, & Hess 1974). Explanatory comments and questions at key points during the program can help young children understand these connections and think about alternatives. For example, a teacher might say, "He wants to stop that man from doing bad things, but the only way he knows how to do that is to fight him. I'll bet you can think

The effects of violence are reduced when adults view programs together with children, showing disapproval of the violence and suggesting nonviolent alternatives.

of other ways that he could stop him without fighting." Adults can also guide children in forming their own evaluations and critical judgments about the violent and prosocial behaviors they view by asking, "Do you think it's a good idea to hurt/help people like that in real life?"

Teachers can address these issues with children when themes of television violence appear in their play. Teachers can suggest alternative themes, provide alternative play equipment, or encourage children to explore creative and imaginative ways of converting aggressive characters and themes of conflict and power into helpful play characters and themes. If aggressive and destructive themes

persist as a regular part of children's play, teachers should inform parents and support them in their efforts to monitor children's viewing habits.

Many preschool and kindergarten programs have videotape recorders and monitors available for use in the classroom, thus permitting teachers to co-view and discuss television programming with children. Ideal times for making comments, asking questions, and answering questions often occur while co-viewing programs with children, holding the videotape on pause, or immediately after viewing. The effects of viewing violence are reduced when adults view programs together with children, while making disapproving comments about the violence or suggesting nonviolent alternatives, such as, "That wasn't a good thing to do. He could have gotten what he needed without hurting that man" (Hicks 1968; Grusec 1973; Collins, Sobol, & Westby 1981).

Support parents in helping their children make constructive use of the media

The amount and the specific content of the programming that children view make a critical difference in the likely effects of television viewing. Thus, young children need viewing limits. Although parental restrictions on viewing can be effective (e.g., Gadberry 1980), particularly for young children, all children ultimately need to learn how to regulate their own viewing. Parents usually appreciate any help, advice, and cooperation they can get from teachers to prepare their children to regulate their television viewing habits. Teachers, working in concert with families, can provide children with fundamental guidance in how to select programs that are both enjoyable and nonviolent. This guidance may help children take the first steps toward learning how to regulate their own media diet.

Several guides have been designed to help adults teach children to use television sensibly (e.g., Jurs 1992; Chen 1994). These materials may be useful in building an alliance between families and teachers on their common interest in dealing successfully with media effects on children. With guidance and initial incentives from families and teachers, even young children can be taught to select their favorite prosocial programs, turn the television set off after viewing those programs, and substitute interesting prosocial programs for violent ones. Use of a videocassette recorder to record favorite, high-quality programs makes it easier to offer children a prosocial substitute for violence, particularly because young children are often interested in viewing good programs over and over.

Besides recording programs from television, parents and teachers may obtain from video rental stores or from the publishers many delightful and educational videos developed particularly for preschool-age children. Several guides to quality children's videos are available (see "Resources"). For example, in its *Kids First!* directory, the Coalition for Quality Children's Video presents hundreds of videos for young children up to age 18, complete with descriptions, age recommendations, prices, information on where to find the titles, and tips for parents. The videos have been evaluated by a broad jury of children and adult professionals. A second example is *Children's Video Report,* developed by a former teacher specifically to provide parents and teachers with up-to-date reviews of available materials for preschool and elementary school children. The videos reviewed provide a wide variety of stories that can be used by preschool and kindergarten teachers as springboards for effective role modeling, discussion, and role playing of positive and nonviolent ways of solving problems. The teacher's use of verbal labeling, rehearsals, role-playing activities, and related play materials (e.g., hand puppets) can enhance preschool children's learn-

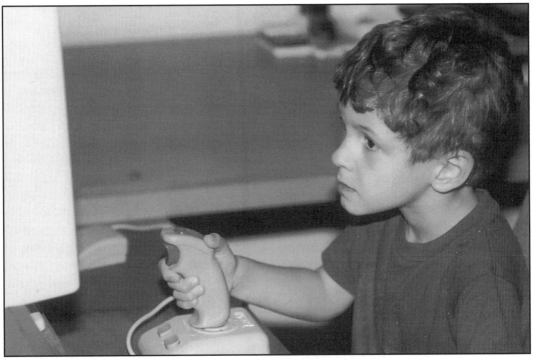

When children view violent television programs and play violent video games, they do not "get it out of their system," as some people argue; rather, they develop an increased appetite for more violence.

ing and performance of television content (Friedrich & Stein 1975; Singer & Singer 1981).

Hold the media responsible for helping to serve children and prevent violence

In addition to helping children and their parents cope with the problems of viewing the violence that the media present, teachers can act individually and collectively to create change in television, video, and film industries. For decades these industries have contributed not only to the problems of aggression in youth but also to the media's failure to use its potential in fostering a solution. Several recent developments, however, make clear the media industries' responsibility for action (Huston, Watkins, & Kunkel 1989).

The Children's Television Act of 1990 requires television broadcasters, as a condition for license renewal, to serve the "educational and informational needs of children" through both programming and nonbroadcast outreach efforts that "enhance the educational and informational value of such programming." Television cablecasters are often specifically obliged by their contractual agreements with municipalities to provide community access to programs and to serve the needs of children. These legal and contractual responsibilities can serve as important tools to empower educators and families to effect change in the nature of television programming designed for children.

Teachers can play an important role in encouraging the media industries to take responsible action. They can contact and work with their local broadcast stations, cable companies, and video distributors to win their support in providing more educational and informational programming to help prevent violence and aggression. Many creative, entertaining, nonviolent television programs and videos have been produced, but they are often not presented on television or made available in video stores unless parents and teachers directly request them. As educators of young children, teachers can guide the media in understanding how children learn, what kinds of media presentations would be useful at home and in the classroom, and what children need to learn to help counter the effects of media violence.

Teachers can amplify their individual contributions to counteracting the effects of media violence by working together with such professional organizations as the American Association of Pediatrics, the American Psychological Association, the National Association for the Education of Young Children, and the National Congress of Parents and Teachers Association. In addition, teachers may want to support and work with public interest organizations that are generating remedies to the effects of media violence (see "Resources").

Points to Remember

Discuss with children why media violence is unreal and inappropriate for their use. Because children are inexperienced in evaluating the unrealistic, glorified, and inappropriate ways in which the media portray violence, teachers need to help them understand that these portrayals do not apply to real-life interactions, including those in the classroom or center.

Help children begin to develop critical viewing skills for evaluating media violence. Teachers have opportunities to help children begin to critically evaluate media violence when themes of television violence appear in children's play and when teachers co-view and discuss video materials with children.

Develop an alliance with children's families to help control media-violence effects. The topic of how media influence children's behavior at home and in the classroom presents an important opportunity for teachers to develop connections with the children's families.

Reduce children's viewing of violence. Because children's viewing of violence can contribute to their involvement with violence in several ways, teachers can discuss with parents various ways to reduce children's viewing of violence.

Increase children's viewing of prosocial programming. Children's viewing of prosocial programs can increase constructive behavior and reduce aggressive behavior. Thus, teachers can present and discuss prosocial programs in the classroom and provide families with suggestions for effective ways of viewing such programs at home.

Hold media producers and distributors accountable for reducing violent programming and presenting alternative programming that helps to prevent aggression and violence. Early childhood educators can influence the media, ensuring that television broadcasters, cablecasters, and video distributors extend their responsibilities to children to the topic of violence prevention.

14

Getting Started

Violence in America can seem like an overwhelming problem, particularly when we see how it touches our children's lives. We all know that many factors contribute to violence: experiencing child abuse, witnessing violence at home or in the community, viewing media violence, involvement with alcohol and other drugs, widespread availability of guns, socioeconomic inequalities and discrimination, and a general acceptance of violent problem-solving behavior in our society. The causes and the effects of violence, some of which have been discussed in this book, are so complex and so disturbing that we may have an urge to give up and decide that someone else "out there" will have to cope with this problem.

Unfortunately, we cannot avoid violence. It touches us all. Whether we read about it, see it on television, attempt to comfort victims or their friends and relatives, or experience it ourselves, violence intrudes into our lives. We must all take individual and collective responsibility for reversing the tide of violence threatening our communities and our children's safety and well-being. Violence will only be meaningfully reduced when we each make a personal choice to take action against it in whatever way we can. It is possible for each of us to make a difference within our own spheres of influence.

The *NAEYC Position Statement on Violence in the Lives of Children* (1993) calls upon the early childhood community to act—to support violence-prevention efforts and promote children's resilience to violence. The statement proposes that "the early childhood profession has an important role to play in breaking the cycle of violence in the lives of children" through (1) professional preparation, development, and support; (2) early childhood programs and curricula; and (3) partnerships with parents. The materials presented in this book can be useful in all three of these areas in which NAEYC recommends action.

Professional preparation, development, and support

As early childhood professionals prepare to work with young children and their families on articulated issues of violence prevention, they need an opportunity to confront their own feelings, beliefs, and reactions to violence. This book offers a source of information and a guide for professional development, as adults work to support one another in confronting violent behavior in the classroom or center and the effects upon children of violence in the community.

Taking in at one reading all the issues and suggestions addressed in this book would be arduous. One approach to using the book as a staff-development resource is to form staff discussion groups that meet on a regular basis. Group members might begin by discussing their reactions to the issues of violence presented in the first two chapters and discussing, to the extent each person is comfortable, their individual experiences and emotional reactions to violence, as well as their ideas about how to prevent violence. Next, staff can discuss the *example and question* presented at the beginning of each chapter. They can talk about their experiences in similar situations and what attempts worked or failed. They can then read through the chapter and discuss their own reactions to *what research tells us* and the *teaching guidelines*. Staff can ask themselves questions: What techniques have we already tried? What seems challenging and why? What specific techniques might we be willing to use in our classrooms tomorrow? As staff then try out a new approach or strategy, integrate it into their ongoing program, and try to make it work for them, they will need support from each other and from their director or education coordinator. Teachers may want to post or circulate *points to remember* and use them as brief reminders of each chapter's recommendations. Ongoing discussion groups can provide this support, as well as additional resources, as staff members problem solve with each other.

Finally, staff can use this book as a reference when discussing approaches to working with individual children who pose challenging behaviors. Each time a problem emerges that involves violence, it will be helpful to consider the environment, the materials, the planned activities, the teacher and peer responses, the skills that are taught, and the role models that are present in the classroom. A teaching and behavior-change plan might then be designed specifically to work with each of the challenging children in the classroom.

Early childhood programs and curriculum

This book suggests many teaching techniques and curriculum strategies that can be used in early childhood programs to reduce violence, promote positive social interactions, and help develop the resiliency of children. Although these suggestions derive from research evidence supporting their effectiveness, not all of the techniques will work well in every situation or with every child. Each teacher's own experience and personal judgment are required to determine what approach

© Nancy P. Alexander

to use in a given situation, how to adapt it to best fit the needs and interests of a particular child or class, and when to modify the approach as circumstances change. This volume provides neither a cookbook nor a specific curriculum. Rather, we present some effective approaches that teachers can infuse into the activities and atmosphere of the classroom or center and incorporate into their own teaching strategies and styles. In some cases we provide a framework for understanding a problem and a starting point from which the teacher might choose to explore additional, listed resources.

Teachers can choose to become working partners with the research community, applying research findings and extending the experimental process into the classroom on a daily basis. Thoughtful teachers constantly analyze situations, try different approaches, observe the results, and modify their methods in accordance with new information. The information presented here can be used systematically to enhance classroom applications and "experiments."

As an initial step, we suggest that teachers (or those preparing to become teachers) discuss the real-life problems of violence faced by teachers and children and the strategies for addressing issues of violence in the classroom (presented in chapters 1 and 2). Today, all teachers need to be familiar with the procedures for responding to suspected abuse or traumatic exposure to violence, which are described in chapter 2.

Second, teachers should take the time to analyze their classroom environment, materials, and planned activities in relation to the suggestions presented in chapters 3, 4, and 5. If aggression tends to break out in certain areas of the room or at certain times of the day, the environment or the program schedule might be contributing to this aggression. The teacher could try some new room arrangements, add or change some materials, reorganize the schedule, and observe what happens. It will be important to keep careful records of children's behavior before and after the changes in order to determine whether the changes have made a difference.

Third, thinking about children's social environment is important. What are the typical ways that teachers and peers respond when conflict or aggression occurs? This analysis will require teachers to engage in some self-examination (or observation of each other) to identify their usual responses and to consider what effect these responses may have on aggression and victimization in the classroom. Following this reflection, teachers may want to plan how they could change their patterns of response in order to better serve the needs of children who are aggressive or victimized (discussed in chapter 6).

Fourth, teachers need to think about the children as individuals.

• Are there children who display more severe or frequent aggressive behaviors?

• Are there children who seem to act as magnets for aggression—children who are frequently victimized by others?

• Are there certain children who often seem to be standing by when aggression occurs, contributing to the escalation of conflict among others?

• Are there children who seem to be one step ahead of the others in coming up with creative and effective ways to resolve conflict nonviolently?

Teachers will want to take some time to observe children in each of these situations, note where and when the aggression occurs, and look at what happens just before the aggression and then just after the aggressive incident.

• Was there a discernible trigger for the aggression?

• Did the aggressor receive attention from adults or other children for the aggressive behavior?

• Did the victim respond in helpless, nonassertive ways?

If children are clearly in need of extra help, individualized plans can be developed for this purpose (described in chapter 7).

As a fifth step, teachers need to decide which specific social skills would make the greatest difference in preparing individual children and the group as a whole to deal with the kinds of conflicts and aggressions they face.

• Do children lack skills, primarily in problem solving, sharing, assertiveness, or perspective taking?

• Do children become extremely emotional, need assistance in calming themselves, or seem to have only one way of responding to conflict?

• Do children have difficulty in sharing resources?

• Do children share voluntarily but get taken advantage of because they don't know how to say, "No"?

• Do children seem to be oblivious to how others may feel?

Observations about the skills children seem to need most can guide the teacher's choice of which social skills to address first, from among those described in chapters 8, 9, 10, and 11.

Finally, teachers will find it useful to observe children in their fantasy play. They can notice which children serve as role models for others and which characters the children identify with and imitate. Do they seem preoccupied with violent themes and violent characters from television, films, or videogames? Chapters 12 and 13 provide guidelines for examining modeling effects in the classroom and for effective consultation with parents about media violence and how to control its effects.

These examples on using assorted chapters of the book may be helpful for various needs and situations. Of course, real-problem situations and children who are aggressive do not generally fall into neat categories that lend themselves to clear-cut solutions found exclusively in one chapter or another. The approaches presented in the different chapters of the book complement and strengthen each other. Application of various strategies in combination with each other, rather than in isolation, will be most effective. We recommend that teachers review the book in its entirety first before returning to those sections that they find most relevant to their particular needs.

Whatever approaches a teacher chooses will probably *not* have an immediate effect on behavior. The unfortunate truth is that because children's behavior has been learned over a period of years, it is not likely to change overnight. The problem behavior may get worse, for a brief time, before it gets better, as the child initially reacts to changed adult responses. The techniques outlined in this book are designed to increase children's social skills and to reduce their tendency to act aggressively, over time. To be effective, however, these techniques require patience and consistent use by everyone in the classroom and over a period of time (several weeks at a minimum). Sometimes the changes in behavior will begin slowly, so slowly that staff may not notice that things are improving and may impatiently give up and stop using the technique. This is why consistent observation is so useful. For example, by counting a child's aggressive actions on a daily basis, teachers can see if small improvements are being made. Even though the child may occasionally still hit or kick other children, if the frequency has been reduced, then the techniques are apparently working and should be continued.

The approaches discussed here are not designed only for serious problem situations. Rather, they can enhance the learning experience of all children. Respecting diversity, taking the points of view of other individuals, standing up for one's own rights nonviolently, learning to participate cooperatively in group interactions—these are all appropriate skills for young children to develop. Teachers can use the ideas presented in this book to enrich their existing programs by creating an overall teaching strategy designed to build positive social skills that enhance children's ability to get along with others and feel good about themselves, without perpetrating violence or being victimized by it.

Partnerships with parents

As their child's first and most influential teachers, parents shape children's attitudes about violence. Yet many of today's families feel so stressed by external conditions that they need support, encouragement, and sound information to enhance their parenting efforts. Some families are striving to help their children cope with the emotional stress of violence in the community and in the media. Some families are struggling so hard for basic survival that they may lack time to provide children with the nurturance they need. In some cases violence has invaded family life to the extent that children themselves are victims.

Early childhood staff can use the information in this book to work as partners with families in promoting the development of positive social behavior and discouraging aggression. Teachers need to inform parents about the profound effect that violence has on children's lives. As teaching staff discuss with parents the steps they are taking in the classroom or center to reduce violence, they can ask for parents' cooperation in using some of the same techniques at home. Strongly discouraging the use of physical punishment at home and assisting the family to find appropriate disciplinary alternatives are important. Working with parents on methods for controlling the effects of media violence is also helpful, because parents have more control over television viewing than do school or center staff.

Some parents may be concerned that teachers' efforts to reduce aggression could result in their children being weak or ineffectual. Teachers can gain the support of parents by appealing to the universal desire of all to protect their children. Parents are eager to learn how to help children avoid violence and remain safe and, at the same time, empower them to stand up for themselves. Teachers can demonstrate specific violence-prevention strategies and explain how these help. Teaching children nonviolent ways of succeeding in the classroom can have long-term effects on preventing their involvement with violence in other settings. Once teachers and parents have established a working partnership on violence prevention within the early childhood setting, they can work together in reducing violence in the community at large and creating a safer place for children to grow up and to thrive. Collaborations outside the classroom might include calling upon television station managers to remedy the problem of televised violence, working for community gun control and safety efforts, or disseminating information about community resources that support families in their personal violence-prevention efforts.

Taking charge

The enormous problem of violence in our society can leave individuals feeling powerless. To keep from getting caught up in this inertia, teachers can take charge of the issue of violence as it relates to the early childhood setting. By clearly articulating violence issues that can be addressed by early childhood educators, staff will increasingly see ways in which their efforts make a difference. There is no one way to begin this process. Each early childhood program has its own resources and faces unique challenges. Every early childhood setting can be effective to the extent that staff clearly define the challenges and make positive, creative use of existing resources.

Violence-prevention efforts are currently taking place on many fronts. As early childhood staff take responsibility for their part of the effort, they will need to make connections with other participants. One obvious connection is with staff of the elementary schools that children will attend next. As early childhood programs begin to implement specific approaches aimed at reducing violence, the director and teachers can discuss these attempts with other educators and ask for their support and ideas. In addition, early childhood staff can connect with parents, social service providers, and other early childhood programs in the community to create a strong network of support for themselves and for violence-prevention efforts.

* * *

In this book we have provided a starting point and resources for enhancing teachers' violence-reduction efforts in the classroom or center. However, these ideas are only words on a page. It will take the creative initiative of early childhood educators to make these words come to life. The reader has a choice: glance through this book and set it back on the shelf *or* take these suggestions, combine them with your own practical wisdom, and proceed with the business of making a positive difference in the lives of children and families.

References

Aboud, F. 1988. *Children and prejudice.* New York: Blackwell.

Adcock, D., & M. Segal. 1983. *Play together grow together: A cooperative curriculum for teachers of young children.* White Plains, NY: Mailman Family.

Ahammer, I.M., & J.P. Murray. 1979. Kindness in the kindergarten: The relative influence of role-playing and prosocial television in facilitating altruism. *International Journal of Behavioral Development* 2: 133-57.

Allen, K.E., K.D. Turner, & P.M. Everett. 1970. A behavior modification classroom for Head Start children with problem behaviors. *Exceptional Children* 37: 119-27.

Anderson, D.R., & P.A. Collins. 1988. *The influence on children's education: The effects of television on cognitive development.* Washington, DC: U.S. Department of Education.

APA (American Psychological Association). 1993. *Violence and youth: Psychology's response. Vol. I Summary report of the American Psychological Association Commission on Violence and Youth.* Washington, DC: APA.

Arezzo, D. 1978. Role-reversal in parent training: A cognitive-behavioral approach. Paper presented at the Fourth Annual Western Regional Conference, Humanistic Approaches to Behavior Modification, March, Las Vegas, Nevada.

Arezzo, D. 1991. Assertiveness training for young children. Paper presented at the 7th Annual Conference of Franciscan Children's Hospital and Rehabilitation Center: Children with Behavior and Learning Problems: Innovations in Therapy and Education, October, Boston, Massachusetts.

Arezzo, D. 1993. Beyond the sharing lecture: Assertiveness in action. *Parenting Around the Hub* (Spring/Summer): 53-54.

Azrin, N.H., & V.A. Besalel. 1980. *How to use overcorrection for misbehavior and errors.* Lawrence, KS: H & H Enterprises.

Bandura, A. 1973. *Aggression: A social learning analysis.* Englewood Cliffs, NJ: Prentice Hall.

Batchelow, J., & N. Wicks. 1985. *Study of children and youth as witness to homicide, City of Detroit.* Detroit: Family Bereavement Center, Frank Murphy Hall of Justice—Victim Services.

Beland, K. 1986. *Talking about touching: Personal safety for preschoolers and kindergartners.* Seattle, WA: Committee for Children.

Bell, C.C., & E.J. Jenkins. 1991. Traumatic stress and children. *Journal of Health Care for the Poor and Underserved* 2 (1): 175-85.

Bell, C.C., & E.J. Jenkins. 1993. Community violence and children on Chicago's south-side. *Psychiatry* 56: 46-54.

Berkowitz, L. 1993. *Aggression: Its causes, consequences, and control.* New York: McGraw-Hill.

Blau, B., & J. Rafferty. 1970. Changes in friendship status as a function of reinforcement. *Child Development* 41: 115-21.

Borke, H. 1971. Interpersonal perception of young children: Egocentrism or empathy? *Developmental Psychology* 5: 263-69.

Bronfenbrenner, U. 1970. *Two worlds of childhood.* New York: Russell Sage Foundation.

Bronson, W.C. 1975. Developments in behavior with age-mates during the second year of life. In *Friendship and peer relations,* eds. M. Lewis & L.A. Rosenblum. New York: Wiley.

Brophy, J.E. 1981. Teacher praise: A functional analysis. *Review of Educational Research* 51 (1): 5-32.

Brownell, C.A., & M.S. Carriger. 1990. Changes in cooperation and self-other differentiation during the second year. *Child Development* 61: 1164-74.

Bryan, J.H. 1975. Children's cooperative and helping behavior. In *Review of child development research,* vol. 5, 127-82. Chicago: University of Chicago Press.

Bryan, J.H., & N.B. Walbeck. 1970. The impact of words and deeds concerning altruism upon children. *Child Development* 41: 747-57.

Cameron, J., & W.D. Pierce. 1994. Reinforcement, reward, and intrinsic motivation: A meta-analysis. *Review of Educational Research* 64 (3): 363-423.

Camp, B.W. 1977. Verbal mediation in young aggressive boys. *Journal of Abnormal Psychology* 86: 145-53.

Caney, S. 1972. *Toy book*. New York: Workman.

Caplan, M., J. Vespo, J. Pedersen, & D. Hay. 1991. Conflict and its resolution in small groups of one- and two-year olds. *Child Development* 62: 1513-24.

Carlsson-Paige, N., & D.E. Levin. 1987. *The war play dilemma: Balancing needs and values in the early childhood classroom*. New York: Teachers College Press.

Carlsson-Paige, N., & D.E. Levin. 1990. *Who's calling the shots? How to respond effectively to children's fascination with war play and war toys*. Philadelphia: New Society.

Carlsson-Paige, N., & D.E. Levin. 1991. The subversion of healthy development and play: Teachers' reactions to "The teenage mutant Ninja turtles." *Day Care and Early Education* 19 (2): 14-20.

Cartledge, G., & J.F. Milburn. 1980. *Teaching social skills to children*. New York: Pergamon.

Cautela, J.R., & J. Groden. 1978. *Relaxation: A comprehensive manual for adults, children and children with special needs*. Champaign, IL: Research Press.

CEASE (Concerned Educators Allied for a Safe Environment). 1993. *Violence as a product of injustice: CEASE's statement on violence*. Cambridge, MA: CEASE.

Ceci, S.J., & M. Bruck. 1993. Child witnesses: Translating research into policy. *Social Policy Report* 7 (3): 1-31.

Chapman, M., & C. Zahn-Waxler. 1982. Young children's compliance and non-compliance to parental discipline in a natural setting. *International Journal of Behavioral Development* 5: 81-94.

Charlesworth, R., & W. Hartup. 1967. Positive social reinforcement in the nursery school peer group. *Child Development* 38: 993-1002.

Chen, M. 1994. *The smart parent's guide to kid's TV*. San Francisco: KQED-TV.

Children's Defense Fund. 1992. *The state of America's children*. Washington, DC: Children's Defense Fund.

Children's Safety Network. 1994. *Firearm facts: Information on gun violence and its prevention*. Arlington, VA: National Center for Education in Maternal and Child Health.

Chittenden, G.E. 1942. An experimental study in measuring and modifying assertive behavior in young children. *Monographs of the Society for Research in Child Development* 7 (1, Serial No. 31).

Christy, P.R., D.M. Gelfand, & D.P. Hart-mann. 1971. Effects of competition-induced frustration on two classes of modeled behavior. *Developmental Psychology* 5: 104-11.

Coie, J.D., K.A. Dodge, & J. Kupersmidt. 1990. Peer group behavior and social status. In *Peer rejection in childhood,* eds. S.R. Asher & J.C. Coie. New York: Cambridge University Press.

Collins, W.A. 1973. Effect of temporal separation between motivation, aggression, and consequences: A developmental study. *Developmental Psychology* 8: 215-21.

Collins, W.A., T.V. Berndt, & V.L. Hess. 1974. Observational learning of motives and consequences for television aggression: A developmental study. *Child Development* 65: 799-802.

Collins, W.A., B.L. Sobol, & S. Westby. 1981. Effects of adult commentary on children's comprehension and inferences about a televised aggressive portrayal. *Child Development* 52: 158-63.

Combs, M.L., & D.A. Slaby. 1977. Social skills training with children. In *Advances in clinical child psychology* 1, 161-201. New York: Plenum.

Comstock, G., & H. Paik. 1990. The effects of television violence on aggressive behavior: A metanalysis. Unpublished report to the National Academy of Sciences Panel on the Understanding and Control of Violent Behavior, Washington, DC.

Condry, J. 1989. *The psychology of television*. Hillsdale, NJ: Lawrence Erlbaum.

Cooper, A., & J. LeBlanc. 1973. An experimental analysis of the effects of contingent related teacher attention and special activities for developing cooperative play. Paper presented at the Biennial Meeting of the Society for Research in Child Development, 29 March–1 April, Philadelphia, Pennsylvania.

CPI (Crisis Prevention Institute). 1994. *Managing the crisis moment* (catalog). Brookfield, WI: National Crisis Prevention Institute.

Crary, E. 1979. *Kids can cooperate: A practical guide to teaching problem solving*. Seattle, WA: Parenting Press, Inc.

Damon, W. 1983. *Social and personality development: Infancy through adolescence*. New York: Norton.

Davitz, J. 1952. The effects of previous training on post-frustration behavior. *Journal of Abnormal and Social Psychology* 47: 309-15.

Denham, S.A., & M.C. Almeida. 1987. Children's social problem-solving skills, behavioral adjustment, and interventions: A met-analysis evaluating theory and practice. *Journal of Applied Developmental Psychology* 8: 391-409.

Denham, S.A., M. McKinely, E.A. Couchard, & R. Holt. 1990. Emotional and behavioral predictors of preschool peer ratings. *Child Development* 61: 1145-52.

Derman-Sparks, L., & the A.B.C. Task Force. 1989. *Anti-bias curriculum: Tools for empowering young children.* Washington, DC: NAEYC.

DeRosier, M.E., A.H.N. Cillessen, J.D. Coie, & K.A. Dodge. 1994. Group social context and children's aggressive behavior. *Child Development* 65: 1068-69.

Dodge, K.A. 1986. A social information-processing model of social competence in children. In *Social-cognitive and social behavioral perspectives on problem solving: Minnesota symposia on child psychology,* vol. 18, ed. M. Perlmutter, 77-125. Hillsdale, NJ: Lawrence Erlbaum.

Dodge, K.A., J.D. Coie, G.S. Pettit, & J.M. Price. 1990. Peer status and aggression in boys' groups: Developmental and contextual analyses. *Child Development* 61: 1289-309.

Doescher, S., & A. Sugawara. 1986. *Prosocial activity guide.* (Available from Dr. Susan Doescher, Dept. of Human Development and Family Studies, Oregon State University, Corvallis, Oregon 97331).

Doland, D.M., & K. Adelberg. 1967. The learning of sharing behavior. *Child Development* 38: 695-700.

Dolins, J.C., & K.K. Christoffel. 1994. Reducing violent injuries: Priorities for pediatrician advocacy. *Pediatrics* 94 (supplement): 638-51.

Donnerstein, E., R.G. Slaby, & L. Eron. 1994. The mass media and youth aggression. In *Reason to hope: A psychosocial perspective on violence and youth,* eds. L.D. Eron, J.H. Gentry, & P. Schlegel. Washington, DC: American Psychological Association.

Dubrow, N.F., & J. Garbarino. 1989. Living in the war zone: Mothers and young children in a public housing development. *Journal of Child Welfare* 68: 3-20.

Eckerman, C., & H. Rheingold. 1974. Infants' exploratory responses to toys and people. *Developmental Psychology* 10: 255-64.

Eisenberg, A., & C. Garvey. 1981. Children's use of verbal strategies in resolving conflicts. *Discourse Processes* 4: 149-70.

Eisenberg, N., & P.H. Mussen. 1989. *The roots of prosocial behavior in children.* New York: Cambridge University Press.

Eisenberg, N., & J. Strayer. 1987. *Empathy and its development.* New York: Cambridge University Press.

Eisenberg, N., R. Fabes, P.A. Miller, R. Shell, C. Shea, & T.M. May-Plumlee. 1990. Preschoolers' vicarious emotional responding and their situational and dispositional prosocial behavior. *Merrill-Palmer Quarterly* 36 (4): 507-29.

Enright, R.D., & D.K. Lapsley. 1980. Social-role taking: A review of the constructs, measures, and measurement properties. *Review of Educational Research* 50 (4): 647-74.

Eron, L.D. 1986. Interventions to mitigate the psychological effects of media violence on aggressive behavior. *Journal of Social Issues* 42 (3): 155-69.

Eron, L.D., & R.G. Slaby. 1994. Introduction. In *Reason to hope: A psychosocial perspective on violence and youth,* eds. L.D. Eron, J.H. Gentry, & P. Schlegel. Washington, DC: American Psychological Association.

Fabes, R.A., & N. Eisenberg. 1992. Young children's coping with interpersonal anger. *Child Development* 63: 116-28.

Farrington, D.P. 1993. Childhood origins of teenage antisocial behavior and adult social dysfunction. *Journal of the Royal Society of Medicine* 86: 13-16.

Fassler, J., & M.G. Janis. 1983. Books, children, and peace. *Young Children* 38 (6): 21-30.

Feshbach, N.D. 1974. The relationship of child rearing factors to children's aggression, empathy, and related positive and negative social behaviors. In *Determinants and origins of aggressive behavior,* eds. W.W. Hartup & J. DeWit. The Hague: Mouton.

Feshbach, N.D. 1975. Empathy in children: Some theoretical and empirical considerations. *The Counseling Psychologist* 5: 25-30.

Feshbach, N.D., & S. Feshbach. 1969. The relationship between empathy and aggression in two age groups. *Developmental Psychology* 1: 102-07.

Feshbach, N.D., & S. Feshbach. 1982. Empathy training the regulation of aggression. Potentialities and limitations. *Academic Psychology Bulletin* 4: 399-413.

Feshbach, S. 1956. The catharsis hypothesis and some consequences of interaction with aggressive and neutral play objects. *Journal of Personality* 24: 449-61.

Field, T. 1991. Quality infant day-care and grade school behavior and performance. *Child Development* 62: 863-70.

Finkelhor, D., & J. Dziuba-Leatherman. 1994. Victimization of children. *American Psychologist* 49: 173-83.

References

Fluegelman, A. 1976. *The new games book.* Garden City, NY: Doubleday, Dolphin Books.

Fluegelman, A. 1981. *More new games.* Garden City, NY: Doubleday, Dolphin Books.

Friedrich, L.K., & A.H. Stein. 1973. Aggressive and prosocial television programs and the natural behavior of preschool children. *Monographs of the Society for Research in Child Development* 38 (4, Serial No. 151).

Friedrich, L., & A.H. Stein. 1975. Prosocial television and young children: The effects of verbal labeling and role playing on learning and behavior. *Child Development* 46: 27-38.

Furby, L. 1978. Sharing: Decisions and moral judgments about letting others use one's possessions. *Psychological Reports* 43: 595-609.

Gadberry, S. 1980. Effects of restricting first graders' TV viewing on leisure time use, IQ change, and cognitive style. *Journal of Applied Developmental Psychology* 1: 161-76.

Galinsky, E., & J. David. 1988. *The preschool years: Family strategies that work—from experts and parents.* New York: Ballantine.

Garbarino, J., K. Kostelny, & N. Dubrow. 1991. *No place to be a child: Growing up in a war zone.* New York: Lexington.

Garvey, C. 1984. *Children's talk.* Cambridge, MA: Harvard University Press.

George, C., & M. Main. 1979. Social interactions of young abused children: Approach, avoidance, and aggression. *Child Development* 50: 306-18.

Gerbner, G., L. Gross, M. Jackson-Beeck, S. Jeffries-Fox, & N. Signorielli. 1978. Cultural indicators: Violence profile No. 9. *Journal of Communication* 28 (3): 176-207.

Ginsburg, H.J. 1975. Variations of aggressive interaction among male elementary school children as a function of spatial density. Paper presented at the Biennial Meeting of the Society for Research in Child Development, 10-13 April, Denver, Colorado.

Goffin, S.G. 1987. Cooperative behaviors: They need our support. *Young Children* 42 (2): 75-81.

Goldstein, A.P. 1994. *The ecology of aggression.* New York: Plenum.

Gottman, J., J. Gonso, & B. Rasmussen. 1975. Social interaction, social competence and friendship in children. *Child Development* 46: 709-18.

Greenburg, P. 1988. Ideas that work with young children. Avoiding "me against you" discipline. *Young Children* 44 (1): 24-29.

Greven, P. 1990. *Spare the child: The religious roots of punishment and the psychological impact of physical abuse.* New York: Knopf.

Grusec, J.E. 1973. Effects of co-observer evaluations on imitation: A developmental study. *Developmental Psychology* 8: 141.

Guerra, N.G., & R.G. Slaby. 1989. Evaluative factors in social problem solving skills by aggressive boys. *Journal of Abnormal Child Psychology* 17: 277-89.

Guerra, N.G., & R.G. Slaby. 1990. Cognitive mediators of aggression in adolescent offenders: 2. Intervention. *Developmental Psychology* 26: 269-77.

Gump, P.V. 1975. Ecological psychology and children. In *Review of child development research,* vol. 5, ed. E.M. Hetherington, 75-126. Chicago: University of Chicago Press.

Hart, B.A., N.J. Reynolds, D.M. Baer, E.R. Brawley, & F.R. Harris. 1968. Effect of contingent and noncontingent social reinforcement on the cooperative play of a preschool child. *Journal of Applied Behavior Analysis* 1: 73-76.

Hartup, W.W. 1983. Peer relations. In *Handbook of child psychology. Vol. 4: Socialization, personality, and social development,* series ed. P.H. Mussen, vol. ed. E. Hetherington, 4th ed., 103-96. New York: Wiley.

Hartup, W.W., J. Glazer, & R. Charlesworth. 1967. Peer reinforcement and sociometric status. *Child Development* 39: 1017-24.

Hartup, W.W., B. Laursen, M. Stewart, & A. Eastenson. 1988. Conflict and friendship relations of young children. *Child Development* 59: 1590-600.

Hawkins, D.F. 1993. Inequality, culture, and interpersonal violence. *Health Affairs* 12: 80-95.

Hawkins, J.D., E. Von Cleve, & R.F. Catalano. 1991. Reducing early childhood aggression. *Journal of the American Academy of Child and Adolescent Psychiatry* 30 (2): 208-17.

Hay, D.F., & H.S. Ross. 1982. The social nature of early conflict. *Child Development* 53: 105-13.

Hazen, N., B. Black, & F. Fleming-Johnson. 1984. Social acceptance: Strategies children use and how teachers can help children learn them. *Young Children* 39 (6): 26-36.

Hearold, S.L. 1979. Metanalysis of the effects of television on social behavior. Ph.D. diss., University of Colorado.

Heber, R.F., & M.E. Heber. 1957. The effect of group failure and success on social status. *Journal of Educational Psychology* 48: 129-34.

Hendrix, K., & R.G. Slaby. 1991. Cognitive mediation of television violence effects in adolescents. Paper presented at the biennial meeting of the Society for Research in Child Development, 18-20 April, Seattle, Washington.

Hicks, D.L. 1968. Effects of co-observer's sanctions and adult presence on imitative aggression. *Child Development* 39: 303-09.

Hitz, R., & A. Driscoll. 1988. Praise or encouragement? New insights into praise: Implications for early childhood teachers. *Young Children* 43 (5): 6–13.

Hobbs, S.A., & R. Forehand. 1977. Effects of differential release from timeout on children's deviant behavior. *Journal of Behavior Therapy and Experimental Psychiatry* 6: 256–57.

Hoffman, S., & B. Wundram. 1984. Sharing is . . . : Views from three-year-olds and thoughts for teachers. *Childhood Education* 60 (March/April): 261–65.

Hopkins, B.L., & T.C. Mawhinney. 1992. *Pay for performance: History, controversy, and evidence.* New York: Haworth.

Howe, N., L. Moller, B. Chambers, & H. Petrakos. 1993. The ecology of dramatic play centers and children's social and cognitive play. *Early Childhood Research Quarterly* 9: 235–51.

Huesmann, L.R., L.D. Eron, M.M. Lefkowitz, & L.O. Walder. 1984. The stability of aggression over time and generations. *Developmental Psychology* 20: 1120–34.

Huston, A.C., B. Watkins, & D. Kunkel. 1989. Public policy and children's television. *American Psychologist* 44: 424–33.

Huston, A.C., E. Donnerstein, H. Fairchild, N.D. Feshbach, P. Katz, J.P. Murray, E.A. Rubinstein, B.L. Wilcox, & D. Auckerman. 1992. *Big world, small screen: The role of television in American society.* Lincoln, NE: University of Nebraska Press.

Huston-Stein, A.C., L. Friedrich-Cofer, & E.J. Susman. 1977. The relationship of classroom structure to social behavior, imaginative play, and self-regulation of economically disadvantaged children. *Child Development* 48: 908–16.

Iannotti, R.J. 1978. Effect of role-taking experiences on role taking, empathy, altruism, and aggression. *Developmental Psychology* 14: 119–24.

Iannotti, R.J. 1985. Naturalistic and structures assessments of prosocial behavior in preschool children: The influence of empathy and perspective taking. *Developmental Psychology* 21: 46–55.

Johnson, R.N., & G. Russell. 1990. A comparison of violence and conflict presented on Canadian and American commercial TV news broadcasts: CTV and CBS evening news. Paper presented at the IX Biennial World Meeting of the International Society for Research on Aggression, 13 June, Banff, Canada.

Jurs, A. 1992. *Becoming unglued: A guide to help children develop positive TV habits.* San Marcos, CA: Robert Erdmann.

Katz, L.G., & S.C. Chard. 1989. *Engaging children's minds: The project approach.* Norwood, NJ: Ablex.

Kazdin, A.E. 1975. *Behavior modification in applied settings.* Homewood, IL: Dorsey.

Kellerman, A.I., & D.T. Reay. 1986. Protection or peril? An analysis of firearms-related deaths in the home. *New England Journal of Medicine* 314: 1557–60.

Kohlberg, L. 1976. Moral stages and moralization: The cognitive-developmental approach. In *Moral development: Theory, research, and social issues,* ed. T. Lickona. New York: Holt, Rinehart & Winston.

Kohler, F.W., & S.A. Fowler. 1985. Training prosocial behaviors in young children: An analysis of reciprocity with untrained peers. *Journal of Applied Behavior Analysis* 18: 187–200.

Koralek, D. 1992. *Caregivers of young children: Preventing and responding to child maltreatment.* Washington, DC: National Center on Child Abuse and Neglect, U.S. Department of Health and Human Resources.

Kotlowitz, A. 1987. Day to day violence takes a terrible toll on inner-city youth. *Wall Street Journal,* 13 June, 1.

Krasnor, L.R., & K. Rubin. 1983. Preschool social problem solving: Attempts and outcomes in naturalistic interaction. *Child Development* 54: 1545–58.

Kreidler, W.J. 1984. *Creative conflict resolution: More than 200 activities for keeping peace in the classroom K-6.* Glenview, IL: Scott, Foresman.

Krogh, S., & L. Lamme. 1983. Learning to share: How literature can help. *Childhood Education* 59 (3): 18–92.

Krudek, L.A. 1978. Perspective taking as the cognitive basis of children's moral development: A review of the literature. *Merrill-Palmer Quarterly* 24: 3–28.

Laursen, B., & W.W. Hartup. 1989. The dynamics of preschool children's conflicts. *Merrill-Palmer Quarterly* 35 (3): 28–97.

Lee, L.C. 1975. Toward a cognitive theory of interpersonal development: Importance of peers. In *Friendship and peer relations,* eds. M. Lewis & L.A. Rosenblum. New York: Wiley.

Leonard, G. 1973. Winning isn't everything—it's nothing. *Intellectual Digest* 4 (October): 45–47.

LeVine, R.A. 1991. Influences of culture and schooling on mothers' models of infant care: A comparative perspective. Paper presented at the 59th biennial meeting of the Society for Research in Child Development, 18–20 April, Seattle, Washington.

Liebert, R.M., & J. Sprafkin. 1988. *The early window: Effects of television on children and youth.* 3rd ed. New York: Pergamon.

Loo, C.M. 1972. Effects of spatial density on social behavior of children. *Journal of Applied Social Psychology* 2: 372.

Luecke-Aleksa, D.M., D.R. Anderson, P.A. Collins, & K.L. Schmitt. 1995. Gender constancy and television viewing. *Developmental Psychology* 31 (5): 773-80.

MacDonough, T.S., & R. Forehand. 1973. Response-contingent time out: Important parameters in behavior modification with children. *Journal of Behavior Therapy and Experimental Psychiatry* 4: 231-36.

Mallick, S.K., & B.R. McCandless. 1966. A study of the catharsis of aggression. *Journal of Personality and Social Psychology* 4: 591-96.

Martinez, P., & J.E. Richters. 1993. The NIMH community violence project: II. Children's distress symptoms associated with violence exposure. *Psychiatry* 56 (1): 22-35.

McCord, J. 1983. A forty year perspective on effects of child abuse and neglect. *Child Abuse and Neglect* 7: 265-70.

McGinnis, E., & A.P. Goldstein. 1990. *Skill-streaming in early childhood: Teaching prosocial skills to the preschool and kindergarten child.* Champaign, IL: Research Press.

McGrew, W.C. 1972. Aspects of social development in nursery school children, with emphasis on introduction to the group. In *Ethnological studies of child behavior,* ed. N.B. Hones, 129-56. New York: Cambridge University Press.

Merriam Webster's Collegiate Dictionary. 1993. 10th ed. Springfield, MA: Merriam-Webster, Inc.

Messner, S.G. 1990. Income inequality and murder rates: Some cross-national findings. *Comparative Social Research* 3: 185-98.

Mischel, W., & H.N. Mischel. 1976. A cognitive social-learning approach to morality and self regulation. In *Moral development and behavior,* ed. T. Lickona. New York: Holt, Rinehart & Winston.

Mize, J., & G.W. Ladd. 1990. A cognitive-social learning approach to social skill training with low-status preschool children. *Developmental Psychology* 26 (3): 388-97.

Mood, D.W., J.E. Johnson, & C.U. Shantz. 1978. Social comprehension and affect matching in young children. *Merrill-Palmer Quarterly* 24: 63-66.

Moore, B., & K. Beland. 1991. *Preschoolers & kindergartners learn empathy, impulse control and how to manage their anger. Evaluation of "Second step, preschool-kindergarten: A violence-prevention curriculum kit."* Seattle, WA: Committee for Children.

Moore, B.S., B. Underwood, & D.L. Rosenhan. 1973. Affect and altruism. *Developmental Psychology* 8: 99-104.

Mueller, E., & T.A. Lucas. 1975. A developmental analysis of peer interaction among toddlers. In *Friendship and peer relations,* eds. M. Lewis & L.A. Rosenblum. New York: Wiley.

Myhre, S.M. 1993. Enhancing your dramatic-play area through the use of prop boxes. *Young Children* 48 (5): 6-11.

NAEYC (National Association for the Education of Young Children). 1990. NAEYC position statement on media violence in children's lives. *Young Children* 45 (5): 18-21.

NAEYC. 1993. NAEYC's position statement on violence in the lives of children. *Young Children* 48 (6): 80-84.

NIMH (National Institute of Mental Health). 1982. *Television and behavior. Ten years of scientific progress and implications for the eighties: I. Summary report.* Washington, DC: U.S. Department of Health and Human Services.

O'Leary, K.D., & S.G. O'Leary. 1972. *Classroom management: The successful use of behavior modification.* New York: Pergamon.

Olweus, D. 1979. Stability of aggressive reaction patterns in males: A review. *Psychological Bulletin* 86: 852-75.

Olweus, D. 1993a. *Bullying at school: What we know and what we can do.* Cambridge, MA: Blackwell.

Olweus, D. 1993b. Victimization by peers: Antecedents and long-term outcomes. In *Social withdrawal, inhibition, and shyness in childhood,* eds. K.H. Rubin & J.B. Asendorf, 315-41. Hillsdale, NJ: Lawrence Erlbaum.

Orlick, T. 1978. *Cooperative sports and games book: Challenge without competition.* New York: Pantheon.

Orlick, T. 1982. *The second cooperative sports and games book.* New York: Pantheon.

Osborn, D.K., & R.C. Endsley. 1971. Emotional reactions of young children to TV violence. *Child Development* 42: 321-31.

Parke, R.D., & R.G. Slaby. 1983. The development of aggression. In *Handbook of child psychology, Vol. 4: Socialization, personality, and social development.* 4th ed., series ed. H. Mussen, vol. ed. E. Hetherington, 547-641. New York: Wiley.

Parry, A. 1993. Children surviving in a violent world—"Choosing non-violence." *Young Children* 48 (6): 13-15.

Parry, A., K. Walker, & C. Heim. 1990. *Choosing non-violence: The Rainbow House handbook to a violence-free future.* Chicago, IL: Rainbow House.

Parten, M.B. 1933. Social play among preschool children. *Journal of Abnormal and Social Psychology* 28: 136-47.

Patterson, G.R. 1982. *Coercive family process.* Eugene, OR: Castalia.

Patterson, G.R., & G.D. White. 1970. It's a small world: The application of time-out from reinforcement. In *Learning foundations of behavior therapy,* eds. F.H. Kanfer & J. S. Phillips. New York: Wiley.

Patterson, G.R., R.A. Littman, & W. Bricker. 1967. Assertive behavior in children: A step toward a theory of aggression. *Monographs of the Society for Research in Child Development* 32 (5, Serial No. 113).

Pepler, D., & R.G. Slaby. 1994. Theoretical and developmental perspectives on youth and violence. In *Reason to hope: A psychosocial perspective on violence and youth,* eds. L.D. Eron, J.H. Gentry, & P. Schlegel, 22–58. Washington, DC: American Psychological Association.

Perry, D.G., & L.C. Perry. 1974. Denial of suffering in the victim as a stimulus to violence in aggressive boys. *Child Development* 45: 55–62.

Perry, D.G., & L.C. Perry. 1976. A note on the effects of prior anger arousal and winning or losing a competition on aggressive behavior in boys. *Journal of Child Psychology and Psychiatry* 17: 145–49.

Perry, D.G., S.L. Kusel, & L.C. Perry. 1988. Victims of peer aggression. *Developmental Psychology* 24 (6): 807–14.

Perry, D.G., L.C. Perry, & P. Rasmussen. 1986. Cognitive social learning mediators of aggression. *Child Development* 57: 700–11.

Piaget, J. 1932. *The moral judgment of the child.* London: Routledge & Kegan Paul.

Pinkston, E.M, N.M. Reese, J.J. LeBlanc, & D.M. Baer. 1973. Independent control of a preschool child's aggression and peer interaction by contingent teacher attention. *Journal of Applied Behavior Analysis* 6: 115–24.

Quarfoth, J.M. 1979. Children's understanding of the nature of television characters. *Journal of Communication* 29: 210–18.

Quay, L.C., J.H. Weaver, & J.H. Neel. 1986. The effects of play materials on positive and negative social behaviors in preschool boys and girls. *Child Study Journal* 16 (1): 67–76.

Ramsey, P.G. 1980. Solving the dilemma of sharing. *Day Care and Early Education,* 8 (4): 6–10.

Ramsey, P.G. 1987. *Teaching and learning in a diverse world.* New York: Teachers College Press.

Rardin, D.R., & C.E. Moan. 1971. Peer interaction and cognitive development. *Child Development* 42: 1685–99.

Rathjen, D., A. Hiniker, & E. Rathjen. 1976. Incorporation of behavioral techniques in a game format to teach children social skills. Paper presented at the tenth annual convention of the Association for Advancement of Behavior Therapy, New York.

Richters, J.E., & P. Martinez. 1993. The NIMH community violence project: I. Children as victims of and witnesses to violence. *Psychiatry* 56: 7–21.

Risley, T.R., & D.M. Baer 1973. Operant behavior modification: The deliberate development of behavior. In *Review of child development research,* vol. 3., eds. B.M. Caldwell & H.M. Ricciuti, 283–329, Chicago: University of Chicago Press.

Rocha, R.F., & R.W. Rogers. 1976. Ares and Babbitt in the classroom: Effects of competition and reward on children's aggression. *Journal of Personality and Social Psychology* 33: 588–93.

Roedell, W.C. 1992. Personal observation. Seattle, WA.

Roedell, W.C., R.G. Slaby, & H.B. Robinson. 1976. *Social development in young children: A report for teachers.* Washington, DC: National Institute of Education, U.S. Department of Health, Education, and Welfare.

Roedell, W.C., R.G. Slaby, & H.B. Robinson. 1977. *Social development in young children.* Monterey, CA: Brooks/Cole.

Rosekrans, M.A. 1967. Imitation in children as a function of perceived similarity to a social model and vicarious reinforcement. *Journal of Personality and Social Psychology* 7: 307–15.

Rosekrans, M.A., & W.W. Hartup. 1967. Imitative influences of consistent and inconsistent response consequences to a model on aggressive behavior in children. *Journal of Personality and Social Psychology* 7: 429–34.

Rosenhan, D.L. 1972. Prosocial behavior of children. In *The young child: Reviews of research, vol. 2,* ed. W.W. Hartup, 340–59. Washington, DC: NAEYC.

Rosenhan, D.L., & G.M. White. 1967. Observation and rehearsal as determinants of prosocial behavior. *Journal of Personality and Social Psychology* 5: 424–31.

Ross, H., C. Tesla, B. Kenyon, & S. Lollis. 1990. Maternal intervention in toddler peer conflict: The socialization of principles of justice. *Developmental Psychology* 26: 994–1003.

Rubin, K.H. 1977. The social and cognitive value of preschool toys and activities. *Canadian Journal of Behavioral Sciences* 9: 382–85.

Rubin, K.H., & B. Everett. 1982. Social perspective-taking in young children. In *The young child: Reviews of research, vol. 3,* eds. S.G. Moore & C.R. Cooper, 97–113. Washington, DC: NAEYC.

Rubin, K.H., & L.R. Krasnor. 1986. Social-cognitive and social behavioral perspectives on problem solving. In *Cognitive perspectives on children's social and behavioral development: Minnesota symposia on child psychology,* vol. 18, ed. M. Perlmutter, 1–68. Hillsdale, NJ: Lawrence Erlbaum.

References

Ruble, D., T. Balaban, & J. Cooper. 1981. Gender constancy and the effect of televised toy commercials. *Child Development* 52: 667-73.

Salyer, D.M. 1994. Noise or communication? Talking, writing, and togetherness in one first grade class. *Young Children* 49 (4): 42-47.

Schunk, D.G. 1987. Peer models and children's behavioral change. *Review of Educational Research* 57: 149-74.

Schwartz, B. 1990. The creation and destruction of value. *American Psychologist* 45: 7-15.

Schwartz, D., K.A. Dodge, & J.D. Coie. 1994. The emergence of chronic peer victimization in boys' play groups. *Child Development* 64: 1755-72.

Shantz, C.U., & D.W. Shantz. 1985. Conflict between children: Social-cognitive and sociometric correlates. In *Peer conflict and psychological growth: New directions for child development,* ed. M.W. Berkowitz, 3-21. San Francisco: Jossey-Bass.

Shantz, D.W., & D.A. Voydanoff. 1973. Situational effects on retaliatory aggression at three age levels. *Child Development* 44: 149-53.

Shapiro, S. 1975. Some classroom ABC's: Research takes a closer look. *Elementary School Journal* 75: 436-41.

Sharp, K.C. 1981. Impact of interpersonal problem-solving training on preschoolers' social competency. *Journal of Applied Developmental Psychology* 2: 129-43.

Sharp, K.C. 1983. Quantity or quality of strategies: Which indicates competency in social problem-solving? Paper presented at the 55th biennial meeting of the Society for Research in Child Development, 21-24 April, Detroit, Michigan.

Sherif, M., O.J. Harvey, B.J. White, W.R. Hood, & C.W. Sherif. 1961. *Intergroup conflict and cooperation: The Robber's Cave experiment.* Norman, OK: University of Oklahoma Press.

Shure, M.B. 1992. *I can problem solve: An interpersonal cognitive problem-solving program: Preschool.* Champaign, IL: Research Press.

Shure, M., & G. Spivack. 1982. Interpersonal problem-solving in young children: A cognitive approach to prevention. *American Journal of Community Psychology* 10: 341-56.

Shure, M., & G. Spivack. 1988. Interpersonal cognitive problem solving. In *14 ounces of prevention: A casebook for practitioners,* eds. R.G. Price, E.L. Cowen, R.P. Lorion, & J. Ramos-McKay, 69-82. Washington, DC: American Psychological Association.

Siegel, A.E., & L.G. Kohn. 1959. Permissiveness, permission, and aggression: The effects of adult presence or absence on aggression in children's play. *Child Development* 36: 131-41.

Singer, J.L., & D.G. Singer. 1981. *Television, imagination, and aggression: A study of preschoolers.* Hillsdale, NJ: Lawrence Erlbaum.

Slaby, R.G. 1974. Verbal regulation of aggression and altruism. In *Determinants and origins of aggressive behavior,* eds. J. DeWit & W.W. Hartup, 206-16. The Hague: Mouton.

Slaby, R.G. 1990. The gender concept development legacy. In *New directions for child development: The legacy of Lawrence Kohlberg,* ed. D. Schrader, 21-29. San Francisco: Jossey-Bass.

Slaby, R.G. 1994a. Combating television violence. *The Chronicle of Higher Education* 40 (18): B1-2.

Slaby, R.G., 1994b. Personal observation. Arlington Children's Center, Arlington, MA.

Slaby, R.G., & C.G. Crowley. 1977. Modification of cooperation and aggression through teacher attention to children's speech. *Journal of Experimental Child Psychology* 23: 442-58.

Slaby, R.G., & K.S. Frey. 1975. Development of gender constancy and selective attention to same-sex models. *Child Development* 46: 849-56.

Slaby, R.G., & N.G. Guerra. 1988. Cognitive mediators of aggression in adolescent offenders: 1. Assessment. *Developmental Psychology* 24: 580-88.

Slaby, R.G., & G.R. Quarfoth. 1980. Effects of television on the developing child. In *Advances in behavioral pediatrics,* ed. B.W. Camp, 225-66. Greenwich, CT: Johnson Associates.

Slaby, R.G., & W.C. Roedell. 1982. Development and regulation of aggression in young children. In *Psychological development in the elementary years,* ed. J. Worell, 97-149. New York: Academic.

Slaby, R.G., & P. Stringham. 1994. Prevention of peer and community violence: The pediatrician's role. *Pediatrics* 94 (4): 608-16.

Slaby, R.G., R. Wilson-Brewer, & K. Dash. 1994. *Aggressors, victims, & bystanders: Thinking and acting to prevent violence (Curriculum for grades 6-9).* Newton, MA: Education Development Center.

Slaby, R.G., R. Wilson-Brewer, E. DeVos. 1994. *Aggressors, victims, and bystanders: An assessment-based middle school violence prevention curriculum.* Final report of Grant #R49/CCR103559 from the Centers for Disease Control and Prevention, Atlanta, GA. National Technical Information Service, 5285 Port Royal Rd., Springfield, VA 22161.

Smith, P.K. 1974. Social and situational determinants of fear in the playgroup. In *The origin of fear: The origins of behavior,* eds. M. Lewis & L. Rosenblum, 107-29. New York: Wiley.

Sobel, J. 1983. *Everybody wins: Noncompetitive games for young children.* New York: Walker.

Spivack, G., & M.B. Shure. 1974. *Social adjustment of young children*. San Francisco: Jossey-Bass.

Spivack, G., & M.B. Shure. 1982. Interpersonal cognitive problem solving and clinical theory. In *Advance in child clinical psychology: Vol. 5*, eds. B. Lahey & A.E. Kazdin, 323–72. New York: Plenum.

Staub, E. 1971. The use of role playing and induction in children's learning of helping and sharing behavior. *Child Development* 42: 805–16.

Staub, E. 1974. Helping a distressed person: Social, personality and stimulus determinants. In *Advances in experimental social psychology*, ed. L. Berkowitz, 293–341. New York: Academic.

Staub, E. 1989. *The roots of evil: The origins of genocide and other group violence*. New York: Cambridge University Press.

Staub, E., & L. Sherk. 1970. Need for approval, children's sharing behavior, and reciprocity in sharing. *Child Development* 41: 243–52.

Stein, A.H., & L.K. Freidrich. 1972. Television content and young children's behavior. In *Television and social behavior, Vol. 2: Television and social learning*, eds. J.P. Murray, E.A. Rubinstein, & G.A. Comstock, 203–317. Washington, DC: U.S. Government Printing Office.

Stocking, S.H., D. Arezzo, & S. Leavitt. 1979. *Helping kids make friends*. Allen, TX: Argus Communications.

Strain, P., R. Shores, & M. Kerr. 1976. An experimental analysis of spillover effects on the social interaction of behaviorally handicapped preschool children. *Journal of Applied Behavior Analysis* 9: 31–40.

Straus, M.A. 1991. Discipline and deviance: Physical punishment of children and violence and other crime in adulthood. *Social Problems* 38: 101–23.

Straus, M.A. 1995a. *Beating the devil out of them: Corporal punishment in American families*. New York: Lexington Books.

Straus, M.A. 1995b. Corporal punishment of children, adult depression, and suicide ideation. In *Coercion and punishment in long term perspective*, ed. J. McCord, 59–77. New York: Cambridge University Press.

Strayer, J. 1980. A naturalistic study of empathic behaviors and their relation to affective states and perspective-taking skills in preschool children. *Child Development* 51: 815–22.

Sutherland, S. 1993. Impoverished minds. *Nature* 364: 767.

Thomas, M.H., R.W. Horton, E.C. Lippincott, & R.S. Drabman. 1977. Desensitization to portrayals of real-life aggression as a function of exposure to television violence. *Journal of Personality and Social Psychology* 35: 450–58.

Tower, C.C. 1992. *The role of educators in the prevention and treatment of child abuse and neglect*. Washington, DC: National Center on Child Abuse and Neglect.

Triviz, R.M. 1987. Gender's salience over ethnicity in first grader's identifications. Ed.D. diss., Harvard University, Cambridge, Massachusetts.

Turner, C.W., & D. Goldsmith. 1976. Effects of toy guns and airplanes on children's antisocial free play behavior. *Journal of Experimental Child Psychology* 21: 303–15.

TV Guide. 1992. Is TV violence battering our kids? New study, new answers. *TV Guide*, 22 August, 8–23.

Wallach, L.B. 1993. Helping children cope with violence. *Young Children* 48 (4): 4–11.

Walters, R.H., & R.D. Parke. 1964. Influence of response consequences to a social model on resistance to deviation. *Journal of Experimental Child Psychology* 1: 269–80.

Weinstein, M., & J. Goodman. 1990. *Playfair*. San Luis Obispo, CA: Impact.

Whiteside, M.F., F. Busch, & T. Horner. 1976. From egocentric to cooperative play in young children. *Journal of the American Academy of Child Psychiatry* 15: 294–313.

Widom, C.S. 1989. The cycle of violence. *Science* 244: 160–66.

Willer, B., S.L. Hofferth, E.E. Kisker, P. Divine-Hawkins, E. Farquhar, & F.B. Glantz. 1991. *The demand and supply of child care in 1990*. Washington, DC: NAEYC.

Yarrow, M.R., P. Scott, & C.Z. Waxler. 1973. Learning concern for others. *Developmental Psychology* 8: 240–60.

Yoshikawa, H. 1994. Prevention as cumulative protection: Effects of early family support and education on chronic delinquency and its risks. *Psychological Bulletin* 115 (1): 28–54.

Zahavi, S., & S.R. Asher. 1978. The effect of verbal instructions on preschool children's aggressive behavior. *Journal of School Psychology* 16: 146–53.

Resources

As early childhood educators plan the steps they will take toward preventing violence, they may find a variety of resources to be useful: curriculum and activity resources, books and materials for adults, reports and surveys, organizations and community resources, and books and materials for children.

Curriculum and activity resources

Camp, B.W., & M.A.S. Bash. 1981. *Think aloud: Increasing social and cognitive skills–A problem-solving program for children* (small group program). Research Press, 2612 North Mattis Ave., Champaign, IL 61821; 217-352-3273. A detailed, research-based program for teaching children to use language as a thinking tool to talk themselves through the process of solving problems. Designed for use with small groups of 6- to 8-year-olds who need extra help in controlling aggressiveness or other behavior problems.

Cautela, J.R., & J. Groden. 1978. *Relaxation: A comprehensive manual for adults, children and children with special needs*. Champaign, IL: Research Press. Provides a variety of methods designed to teach relaxation to children.

Committee for Children. 1991. *Second step: A violence prevention curriculum* (preschool–kindergarten). Committee for Children, 172 20th Ave., Seattle, WA 98122; 800-634-4449. A broad-based curriculum for dealing with violence through empathy training, impulse control, and anger management. Materials include photograph cards that present a situation for discussion, puppets and scripts to use in role modeling, structured skill-building activities, an evaluation kit, take-home letters, activities for parents, an annotated list of children's books, songs, and a Spanish supplement to the manual. (Additional versions of this curriculum are available for grades one to five and grades six to eight.) An evaluation by the authors indicates that participation in the program has resulted in higher violence-prevention knowledge and skills.

Crary, E. 1979. *Kids can cooperate: A practical guide to teaching problem solving*. Parenting Press, Inc., 7750 31st Ave., NE, Seattle, WA 98115. A useful set of exercises offers parents help in developing problem-solving skills in preschool and elementary school children. Some exercises may be appropriate for the early childhood classroom or center, as well as for fostering connections between teachers and parents.

Derman-Sparks, L., & the A.B.C. Task Force. 1989. *The anti-bias curriculum: Tools for empowering young children*. Washington, DC: NAEYC. A comprehensive guide to understanding how societal bias against groups of individuals can influence and hurt young children. Presents strategies for actively counteracting these effects, celebrating diversity, and teaching children to stand up for what's right.

Dewing, M. 1992. *Beyond TV: Activities for using video with children*. ABC-CLIO, Inc., 130 Cremona Drive, P.O. Box 1911, Santa Barbara, CA 93116-1911. Guide written by a former teacher providing hundreds of suggestions for using video as a tool for constructive, innovative learning, including a list of recommended videos and their distributors.

Glass, D.L., & B.A. O'Neill. 1994. *Kelso's choice: Conflict management for children*. Rhinestone

Press, P.O. Box 30, Winchester, OR 97495; 503-672-3826. This curriculum is designed to teach children a wide variety of social skills including how to wait and cool off, share and take turns, talk it out, walk away, ignore provocation, tell others to stop, apologize, and make a deal.

Harvard Pilgrim Health Care Foundation. 1995. *Violence prevention kit.* 185 Dartmouth St., Boston, MA 02116; 617-859-5030. Joint project with Harvard health care professionals and WBZ-TV/Radio. The kit contains a videotape with eight vignettes portraying nonviolent solutions to various dilemmas in which violence could play a part, two brochures on "bully-proofing" your child and using time-out, and a handbook "Domestic Violence: The Facts." Appropriate for health professionals, educators, and parents—vignettes for ages 8 and up and brochures for parents of children of all ages.

Jackson, N.F., D.A. Jackson, & C. Monroe. 1983. *Getting along with others: Teaching social effectiveness to children.* Champaign, IL: Research Press. A systematic curricular intervention for teaching social skills to elementary school children, including group activities, teacher scripts, role plays, and home assignments. Some activities are appropriate for kindergarten and first-grade children.

Kreidler, W.J. 1984. *Creative conflict resolution: More than 200 activities for keeping peace in the classroom K-6.* Scott, Foresman, & Co., 1900 E. Lake Ave., Glenview, IL 60025; 708-729-3000. Offers many activities for children from kindergarten through sixth grade that are designed to enhance their skills in resolving conflict creatively and nonviolently. The activities include ways to help children deal with anger, frustration, and aggression.

Levin, D. 1994. *Teaching young children in violent times: Building a peaceable classroom.* Educators for Social Responsibility, 23 Garden St., Cambridge, MA 02138; 617-492-1764. A practical and informative guide to violence prevention and conflict resolution for teachers of children in preschool to grade three.

McGinnis, E., & A.P. Goldstein. 1990. *Skillstreaming in early childhood: Teaching prosocial skills to the preschool and kindergarten child.* Champaign, IL: Research Press. Designed for children who have problems with aggression or who lack prosocial skills, this curriculum focuses on the development of six skill groups: beginning social skills, school-related skills, friendship-making skills, dealing with feelings, alternatives to aggression, and dealing with stress. The alternatives-to-aggression skill group includes dealing with teasing, handling feeling mad, deciding if it's fair, solving a problem, and accepting consequences. Systematic procedures for developing prosocial skills and managing behavior problems are provided and accompanied by progress charts, measurement instruments, and child skill checklists for teacher, parent, and child.

Parry, A., K. Walker, & C. Heim. 1990. *Choosing non-violence: The Rainbow House handbook to a violence-free future.* Rainbow House, P.O. Box 29019, Chicago, IL 60629; 312-521-5501. Delineates an approach to directly teach young children about violence and nonviolent alternatives—in their homes, schools, and neighborhoods and in their own behavior. Includes a set of creative classroom and community activities and an extensive list of resources. Originating from Rainbow House's abuse-prevention mini-course, this curriculum was designed as part of a training program for Head Start and Title 20 teachers, with more than 250 Head Start and child care teachers having completed the course in Chicago.

Shure, M.B. 1992. *I can problem solve: An interpersonal cognitive problem-solving program for children* (preschool). Champaign, IL: Research Press. This curriculum offers preschool teachers 59 lessons of 20 minutes each that are designed to foster pre-problem-solving skills (learning a problem-solving vocabulary, identifying one's own and others' feelings, and considering others' points of view), followed by problem-solving skills (thinking of more than one solution, considering consequences, and deciding which solution to choose). Developed and tested over a 20-year period, the curriculum demonstrates that these skills are teachable and that children's learning of them is related to their rated and observed behavioral adjustment. Specific effects on children's aggressive behavior are less clear. The strongest effects of training are found for younger children, for more experienced investigators, and for longer intervention.

Sobel, J. 1983. *Everybody wins: Noncompetitive games for young children.* Walker & Co., 720 Fifth Ave., New York, NY 10019; 800-289-2553. Describes of a wide variety of cooperative games that encourage full participation by all children, creativity, and striving for a common goal rather than emphasizing winning or losing.

Wichert, S. 1989. *Keeping the peace: Practicing cooperation and conflict resolution with preschoolers.* New Society Publishers, 4527

Springfield Ave., Philadelphia, PA 19143; 215-382-6543. A handbook for parents, child care providers, and teachers, designed to bolster children's self-esteem and encourage creative, cooperative interactions among children ages 2 to 6.

Books and materials for adults

APA (American Psychological Association). 1992. *What makes kids care? Teaching gentleness in a violent world* (brochure). APA, 750 First St., NW, Washington, DC 20002; 202-336-6046.

Baker, B.L., A.J. Brightman, L.J. Heifetz, & D.M. Murphy. 1976. *Behavior problems: Steps to independence—A skills training series for children with special needs.* Research Press, 2612 North Mattis Ave., Champaign, IL 61821; 217-352-3273. A step-wise plan for parents and teachers for systematically changing a wide variety of children's behavior problems.

Blechman, E.A. 1985. *Solving child behavior problems at home and at school.* Champaign, IL: Research Press. A comprehensive manual that focuses on communication, responsibility, and emotions, as well as behavior change.

Caney, S. 1972. *Toy book.* Workman Publishing Co., 708 Broadway, New York, NY 10003; 800-722-7202. Instructions for helping children to create engaging toys and games from everyday materials.

Carlsson-Paige, N., & D.E. Levin. 1987. *The war play dilemma: Balancing needs and values in the early childhood classroom.* Teachers College Press/Columbia University, P.O. Box 20, Williston, VT 05495-0020; 800-575-6566. An analysis of the ways in which the mass-marketing of violence undermines children's play and social development.

Chen, M. 1994. *The smart parent's guide to kid's TV.* San Francisco: KQED-TV. Contact *Focus Magazine*, KQED-TV, 2601 Mariposa St., San Francisco, CA 94110; 415-864-2000. A guide presenting many different ways for adults to help children use television constructively.

Children's Safety Network. 1994. *Firearm facts: Information on gun violence and its prevention.* Arlington, VA: National Center for Education in Maternal and Child Health. Available from the National Maternal and Child Health Clearinghouse, 8201 Greensboro Dr., Suite 600, McLean, VA 22102; 703-524-7802. A set of fact sheets useful for firearm safety education.

Clark, L. 1985. *SOS! Help for parents.* Parents Press, P.O. Box 2180, Bowling Green, KY 42102-2180. A popular and practical guide for handling the common, everyday behavior problems parents face with their children.

Galinsky, E., & J. David. 1988. *The preschool years: Family strategies that work—From experts and parents.* New York: Ballantine. A comprehensive and useful guide for parents and early childhood educators, presenting practical solutions for the everyday problems of raising children ages 2 to 5.

Gelles, R.J., & M.A. Straus. 1988. *Intimate violence: The causes and consequences of abuse in the American family.* New York: Simon & Schuster. Based on a national survey of violence within the American family, this book presents a full picture of the problem and its effects on children.

Head Start Bureau. 1994. *Responding to children under stress: A skill-based training guide for classroom teams.* Government Printing Office Publication No. 515-032/03010. Washington, DC: U.S. Department of Health and Human Services, Administration on Children and Families. Designed for use in Head Start, but an excellent staff development resource for any early childhood program.

Jurs, A. 1992. *Becoming unglued: A guide to help children develop positive TV habits.* Robert Erdmann Publishing, 810 W. Los Vallecitos Blvd., #210, San Marcos, CA 92069. Designed for families who want to enjoy the best of TV, develop TV decisionmaking skills, question what they see on TV, and find ways to become unglued from TV.

Olweus, D. 1993. *Bullying at school: What we know and what we can do.* Blackwell Publishers, 3 Cambridge Center, Cambridge, MA 02142; 800-445-6638. A clear and practical account of bully–victim problems in schools and effective ways of counteracting and preventing such problems, based on the author's extensive research over the last several decades.

Patterson, GR. 1976. *Living with children: New methods for parents and teachers.* Rev. ed. Champaign, IL: Research Press. A widely used manual presented in the form of a programmed text that guides parents and teachers through self-check learning steps on how to deal effectively with children. Use of this book has been shown to produce improved parenting effectiveness.

Stocking, S.H., D. Arezzo, & S. Leavitt. 1979. *Helping kids make friends.* Allen, TX: Argus Communications. Now available from Tabor Publishing, 200 East Bethany Dr., Allen, TX 75002; 800-822-6701. A guide to understanding children's social development and to encouraging skills related to friendship, including a section on how to respond to behavior problems.

Reports and surveys

APA (American Psychological Association). 1993. *Violence and youth: Psychology's response–Vol. 1: Summary Report of the American Psychological Association Commission on Violence and Youth.* APA, 750 First Ave., SE, Washington, DC 20002-4242; 202-336-6046. A broad and readable summary of the evidence on the problem and the potential remedies for youth violence. This report is available free, and it is currently being rewritten specifically for use by parents.

Aspen Institute. 1994. *Children and violence.* The Aspen Institute, Wye Center, P.O. Box 222, Queenstown, MD 21658; 410-827-7168. Report of a conference on violence in the lives of children sponsored by the Aspen Institute, involving 16 members of Congress and leading scholars and practitioners in the field.

Casey Journalism Center for Children and Families. 1994. *Covering violence: A report on a conference on violence and the young.* University of Maryland, College of Journalism, College Park, MD 20742-7111; 301-405-2482. A summary of a conference for journalists and others on the roots and impact of violence in the lives of children and the news coverage of such issues.

Center for School Counseling Practitioners. 1993. *Coping with violence in the schools: A report of the 1993 summer conference.* Harvard University Graduate School of Education, Appian Way, Cambridge, MA 02138; 617-496-4570. Proceedings of a five-day symposium attended by school counselors, social workers, nurses, school principals, administrators, and superintendents.

Earls, F.J., R.G. Slaby, A. Spirito, L.E. Saltzman, T.N. Thornton, A. Berman, L. Davidson, J. Fagan, A. Goodman, D. Hawkins, F.F. Kraus, C. Loftin, E. Moscicki, P. Muehrer, P. O'Carroll, H. Sudak, C. Visher, C.S. Widom, G. Wintemute, & K. Baer. 1992. Prevention of violence and injuries due to violence. In *Injury control: Position papers from the third national injury control conference–Setting the national agenda for injury control in the 1990s.* Centers for Disease Control and Prevention, U.S. Department of Health and Human Services, Atlanta, GA; 404-488-4646. A national agenda for preventing violence in America by addressing the problems of both interpersonal and self-directed violence, the solutions, and the strategies for implementing the solutions.

Eron, L.D., J. Gentry, & P. Schlegel, eds. 1994. *Reason to hope: A psychosocial perspective on violence and youth.* Washington, DC: American Psychological Association. Presents 19 research-based chapters addressing the etiology of violence, the experience of violence for ethnic groups and vulnerable populations, societal influences on youth violence, preventative and rehabilitative interventions, and recommendations. Proceeding from the empirically based conviction that violence is learned and, therefore, can be unlearned or that conditions can be changed so that it is not learned in the first place.

Goodwillie, S., ed. 1994. *The Children's Express national hearings on violence in the child's life at home, at school and on the streets.* Children's Express Foundation, 1440 New York Ave., NW, Suite 510, Washington, DC 20005; 202-737-7377. Proceedings of the foundation's series of hearings on Capitol Hill, with 56 expert witnesses and children and teens who are experiencing violence.

Huston, A.C., E. Donnerstein, H. Fairchild, N.D. Feshbach, P. Katz, J.P. Murray, E.A. Rubinstein, B.L. Wilcox, & D. Auckerman. 1992. *Big world, small screen: The role of television in American society.* Lincoln, NE: University of Nebraska Press. Based on the work of the American Psychological Association Task Force on Television and Society, this book presents evidence of children's uses of television and other media, the constructive and destructive effects of such use, and the potential remedies to the effects of media violence.

Illinois Council for the Prevention of Violence. 1994. *Peacing it together: A violence prevention resource for Illinois schools.* Illinois Council for the Prevention of Violence, 220 S. State St., Suite 1215, Chicago, IL 60604; 312-986-9200. Presents 27 violence-prevention programs that the council has distributed to schools across Illinois.

Koralek, D. 1992. *Caregivers of young children: Preventing and responding to child maltreatment.* Stock #20-10017. Single copies, bound or unbound, free from the National Clearinghouse on Child Abuse and Neglect, 3998 Fair Ridge Dr., Suite 350, Fairfax, VA 22033; 800-FYI-3366. A user manual detailing the roles and responsibilities of early childhood education professionals in recognizing, reporting, treating, and preventing child abuse and neglect, including ways to support parents and to care for maltreated children.

The Metropolitan Life Survey of the American Teacher. 1994. *Violence in America's public schools: The family perspective*. Louis Harris and Associates, Inc., 111 Fifth Ave., New York, NY 10003; 212-539-9600. Part of a series of surveys that focus on the experiences and opinions of American teachers, students, and parents on such topics as communication between adults and students, violence-related stress, and violence-prevention efforts.

NASBE (National Association of State Boards of Education). 1994. *Schools without fear: Study group on violence and its impact on schools and learning*. NASBE Publications, 1012 Cameron St., Alexandria VA 22314; 800-220-5183. Presents recommendations for stemming the violence in America's schools through statewide violence-prevention plans, including long-term strategies focusing on school climate and culture, instruction in conflict resolution and ethics, peer mediation, and mentoring and counseling. Exemplary programs are profiled.

National Center for Injury Prevention and Control. 1993. *The prevention of youth violence: A framework for community action*. Centers for Disease Control and Prevention, 4770 Buford Highway, NE, Mailstop F36, Atlanta, GA 30341; 404-488-4646. Provides a framework and set of resources for generating and advancing community initiatives to prevent youth violence.

NSBA (National School Boards Association). 1994. *Violence in the schools: How America's school boards are safeguarding our children*. NSBA, P.O. Box 630422, Baltimore, MD 21263-0422; 703-838-6722. Describes conflict resolution and other violence-prevention efforts by schools.

Osofsky, J.D., & E. Fenichel, eds. 1994. *Caring for infants and toddlers in violent environments: Hurting, healing, and hope*. Zero to Three Study Group on Violence, Zero to Three/National Center for Clinical Infant Programs, 2000 14th St. North, Suite 380, Arlington, VA 22201-2500; 703-528-4300. A variety of essays and reviews, as well as a call for violence prevention and intervention on behalf of very young children.

Reiss, A.J., Jr., & J.A. Roth, eds. 1993. *Understanding and preventing violence*. National Research Council, National Academy Press, 2101 Constitution Ave., NW, Washington, DC 20418. An interdisciplinary approach to understanding and preventing interpersonal violence in America—based on biological, psychological, situational, and social processes.

Thirteen/WNET. 1994. *Community resource guide: Act against violence—Join the new peace movement*. WNET Educational Resource Center, P.O. Box 245, Little Falls, NJ 07424-0245; 212-560-6661. Brief articles and a directory of violence-prevention organizations, initiatives, and resources distributed in connection with the public television's National Campaign to Reduce Youth Violence, involving television programming and community outreach activities.

Tower, C.C. 1992. *The role of educators in the prevention and treatment of child abuse and neglect*. Publication No. ACF 92-30172. Washington, DC: National Center on Child Abuse and Neglect, U.S. Department of Health and Human Services. A user manual detailing the teacher's role in the identification, treatment, and prevention of child abuse and neglect. Might be used to complement the training of educators on how they can intervene.

U.S. Department of Education. 1993. *Reaching the goals: Goal 6—Safe, disciplined, and drug free schools*. Stock #065-000-00555-7. U.S. Government Printing Office, Superintendent of Documents, P.O. Box 371954, Pittsburgh, PA 15250-7954; 202-512-1800. Overview of research and action strategies for safe, disciplined, and drug-free schools.

Organizations and community resources

American Academy of Pediatrics, 141 Northwest Point Blvd, P.O. Box 927, Elk Grove Village, IL 60009-0927.

Center for Media Education, 1511 K St., NW, Suite 518, Washington, DC 20005; 202-628-2620.

Center for the Study & Prevention of Violence, University of Colorado at Boulder, Institute of Behavioral Science, Campus Box 442, Boulder CO 80309-0442; 303-492-1032.

Children's Defense Fund, 25 E St., NW, Washington, DC 20001; 202-628-8787. Conducts Cease Fire!, a public education campaign, to educate parents and others about the impact of violence on children and to present facts about gun-related injuries in order to dispel myths about guns and warn people of the special risks that guns pose to children.

Children's Video Report, 370 Court St., Suite 76, Brooklyn, NY 11231; 718-935-0600. A periodical that provides reviews of available video materials for preschool and elementary school children, rating the age appropriateness, production quality, and audience appeal of available videos. May be used to promote violence-prevention curriculum goals.

Coalition for Quality Children's Video, 535 Cordova Rd., Suite 456, Sante Fe, NM 87501; 505-989-8076. Publishes *Kids First*, a directory of quality videos for children up to age 18, with descriptions, age recommendations, pricing information, and tips for parents and children.

Concerned Educators Allied for a Safe Environment (CEASE), 17 Gerry St., Cambridge, MA 02138; 617-864-0999. Develops peace-education materials; conducts petition campaigns on such issues as child care, the military budget, and war toys; and works for the re-regulation of the amount of violence and commercialism on children's TV programming.

Education Development Center, Inc. (EDC), 55 Chapel St., Newton, MA 02160; 800-225-4274. Dedicated to promoting human development through education. EDC's Center for Violence Prevention and Control applies an interdisciplinary approach and a life-cycle perspective to the prevention and control of violence through a wide range of initiatives that integrate the perspectives of public health, criminal justice, education, and behavioral science.

Educators for Social Responsibility, 23 Garden St., Cambridge, MA 02160; 617-492-1764. Dedicated to children's ethical and social development. Its primary objective is to help children develop a commitment to the well-being of others and make a positive difference in the world.

Family Information Services, 12565 Jefferson St., NE, Suite 102, Minneapolis, MN 55434; 800-852-8112. Provides innovative services for professionals serving parents and families, including audiotaped interviews and resource materials on violence prevention.

Mediascope, 12711 Ventura Blvd., Suite 250, Studio City, CA 91604; 818-508-2080. A nonprofit organization founded in 1992 to promote constructive depictions of health and social issues in film, television, music, and interactive games.

National Alliance for Nonviolent Programming, 1846 Banking St., Greensboro, NC 27408; 910-370-0401. A national network of women's organizations that addresses the issue of entertainment violence and media violence as children's health issues, including the American Medical Women's Association and the Association of Junior Leagues International among the eight member organizations.

National Crime Prevention Council, 1700 K St., NW, Washington, DC 20006-3817; 202-466-6272. Works toward enabling people to prevent crime and build safer, more caring communities. Provides publications, training, demonstration programs, and comprehensive planning efforts.

National Foundation to Improve Television, 60 State St., Boston, MA 02109; 617-523-6353. This organization has developed a number of initiatives designed to reduce the effects of dramatized television violence on children. In addition, the foundation is active in a number of projects to use television as a tool to prevent violence.

The National Parent Teachers Association, 330 N. Wabash Ave., Suite 2100, Chicago, IL 60611-3690. Deals with a variety of education and societal issues affecting children's education; develops information, programs, and projects encouraging parents to participate in their children's education.

National School Safety Center, 4165 Thousand Oaks Blvd., Suite 290, Westlake Village, CA 91362; 805-373-9977. Focuses on solutions to problems that disrupt the educational process, including crime, violence, and drugs. Provides technical assistance in improving student discipline, attendance, achievement, and the school climate.

Books and materials for children

Aliki. 1963. *The story of Johnny Appleseed.* Englewood Cliffs, NJ: Prentice-Hall. A brave and gentle man comes to life in this story.

Bunting, E. 1994. *Smoky night.* Orlando, FL: Harcourt Brace Jovanovich. A young boy worries about his lost cat after looting and rioting disrupt his neighborhood.

Caseley, J. 1989. *Ada potato.* New York: Greenwillow. Ada finds a way of confronting a gang of boys and discouraging them from teasing her about her violin playing.

Chapman, C. 1981. *Herbie's troubles.* New York: Dutton. Herbie's attitude toward school quickly changes the day he meets a bullying classmate, Jimmy John.

Clifton, L. 1988. *Everett Anderson's goodbye.* New York: Henry Holt & Co. An African American boy comes to terms with the death of his father.

Cohn, J. 1994. *Why did it happen? Helping children cope in a violent world.* New York: Morrow. When a neighborhood grocer is robbed and injured, a young boy confronts his fears. Author and psychotherapist Janice Cohn prefaces this book with a note to parents discussing the issue of children and violence.

Davis, D. 1985. *Something is wrong at my house: A book about parents' fighting.* Parenting Press, P.O. Box 75267, Seattle, WA 98125; 206-364-2900. Based on a true story of a boy living in a violent household. Encourages children from violent and nonviolent homes to acknowledge and express common feelings of anger, fear, and loneliness, and offers ways to cope with violence witnessed in the home.

De Lynam, A. G. 1988. *It's mine.* New York: Dial Books for Young Readers. Two young children discover that although it's difficult to share a favorite toy, it can be more fun to play with it together.

de Paola, T. 1981. *Now one foot, now the other.* New York: G.P. Putnam's Sons. A small boy lovingly teaches his grandfather to walk, following a stroke.

Durrell, A., & J. Bierhorst, eds. 1993. *The big book for peace.* New York: Dutton Children's Books. Stories, poems, and pictures by some famous artists and writers make up this collection.

Fitzhugh, L., & S. Scoppottone. 1969. *Bang, bang, you're dead.* New York: HarperCollins. Children's outside play leads to violence when play fighting gets out of hand.

Garbarino, J. 1993. *Let's talk about living in a world with violence: An activity book for school-age children.* Erikson Institute, 420 N. Wabash Ave., Chicago, IL 60611; 312-755-2244. An activity workbook that combines reading, writing, drawing, and discussion to help children express their thoughts and feelings about violence.

Hill, E.S. 1967. *Evan's corner.* New York: Holt, Rinehart & Winston. Needing a place to call his own, Evan is thrilled when his mother points out that their crowded apartment has eight corners, one for each family member.

Jones, R. 1991. *Matthew and Tilly.* New York: Dutton Children's Books. Like all good friends, Matthew and Tilly have an occasional tiff, but their friendship prevails despite their differences.

Kasza, K. 1993. *The rat and the tiger.* New York: G. P. Putnam's Sons. In his friendship with Rat, Tiger takes advantage and plays the bully because of his greater size, but one day Rat stands up for his rights.

Leaf, M. 1938. *The story of Ferdinand.* New York: Viking. A dreamy, poetic bull likes to sit quietly and smell the flowers.

Lucas, E. 1991. *Peace on the playground.* New York: Franklin Watts. The concept of nonviolent resolution of conflicts is introduced, with practical tips, hands-on activities, and appropriate role models for guidance and inspiration.

Scholes, K. 1990. *Peace begins with you.* San Francisco: Sierra Club Books/Boston: Little, Brown. In simple terms, the author explains the concept of peace, why conflicts occur, how they can be resolved in positive ways, and how to protect peace.

Seuss, Dr. 1984. *The butter battle book.* New York: Random. An imaginative storyteller recites the events that could lead to war between the Wooks and the Zooks.

Singer, I.B. 1973. *Why Noah chose the dove.* New York: Farrar, Straus & Giroux. After the animals vie with one another for a place on the Ark, Noah picks the bird of peace to be his messenger.

Young, E. 1979. *The lion and the mouse: An Aesop's fable.* Garden City, NY: Doubleday. The tiny mouse helps the mighty lion when he becomes ensnared by hunters.

Zolotow, C. 1969. *The hating book.* New York: Harper & Row. A little girl knew her friend hated her, but she didn't know why—until she finally got up the courage to ask why they were being so mean to each other.